unfairness 불공평
citizen 시민
die 죽다

Unit 08 분위기·심경 파악하기

Reading 20

season 계절
no more 더 이상 ~이 아니다
biting 살을 에는 듯한
melt 녹다
flower bud 꽃봉오리
be about to 막 ~하려고 하다
bloom 꽃이 피다
suddenly 갑자기
humming 콧노래, 흥얼거림
no longer 더 이상 ~이 아니다
Grouchy 만화 '개구쟁이 스머프'의 투덜이 스머프
complain 불평하다
dull 지루한, 단조로운
boring 재미없는, 따분한
cheerful 쾌활한, 명랑한
lively 활기찬
romantic 낭만적인
moving 감동적인
lonely 외로운
gloomy 우울한
tense 긴장되는
frightening 무시무시한

Reading 21

starve 굶다
luckily 운 좋게도
hunt 사냥하다
catch 잡다
squirrel 다람쥐
gather 모으다
wood 나무, 장작
build a fire 불을 지피다
roast 굽다
take place 일어나다
silently 조용히
joy 즐거움, 기쁨
voice 목소리
need to ~할 필요가 있다
last 지속되다, 오래가다
quick 빠른, 빨리
turn over 뒤집다
juice 즙, 육즙

drip 떨어지다
sizzle 지글지글 끓다
air 공기, 대기
delicious 맛있는
smell 냄새

Reading 22

mall 쇼핑몰, 가게
present 선물
pretty 매우, 꽤
be sure that ~을 확신하다
thrilled 매우 신이 난, 흥분한
soon 곧
cool 멋진
hand 건네다
flip through 휙휙 넘기다, 훑어보다
inside 안에, 속에

Unit 09 글의 순서 파악하기

Reading 23

benefit 이득, 이점
interestingly 흥미롭게도
reduce 감소시키다
lower 낮추다
blood pressure 혈압
heart rate 심장 박동 수
tension 긴장, 긴장감
anywhere 어디서나
cost 비용이 들다
step away from ~에서 멀어지다, 발을 떼다
find 알아내다
effective 효과적인
go for a walk 산책하다

Reading 24

see a doctor 진료를 받다
crazy 미친, 제정신이 아닌
shocked 충격을 받은
cheap 가격이 싼
later 후에, 나중에
visit 방문하다, 방문
disappear 사라지다
once a week 1주일에 1번씩

Reading 25

major 주요한, 중요한
correct 정확한, 올바른
proper 적절한, 알맞은

weight 무게
be made of ~로 만들어지다
steel 철
foam rubber 발포 고무
characteristic 특징
certain 특정한
amount 양
bounce 튕기다, 튕김
solid 단단한, 순수한(다른 물질이 섞이지 않은)
bouncy 튕기는, 튀어오르는
clay 점토, 흙

Unit 10 주어진 문장 넣기

Reading 26

be famous for ~로 유명하다
be careful 조심하다
spit 침을 뱉다, 침
protect A from B B로부터 A를 보호하다
danger 위험
include 포함하다
peaceful 평화로운

Reading 27

suggest 제안하다
imagine 상상하다
desert 사람이 살지 않는, 사막
survive 생존하다
even 심지어
tip (실용적인) 조언
stream 개울, 시내
disease 질병
rainwater 빗물
drinkable 마실 수 있는
keep in mind 명심하다

Reading 28

term 기간
calm down 진정시키다
focus 초점
something else 다른 것
bored 지루한

Unit 11 무관한 문장 찾기

Reading 29

department store 백화점
marketing 마케팅

Words Preview

skill 기술
decorate 꾸미다, 장식하다
hang 걸다
advertisement 광고
look around 둘러보다
get attention 주의를 끌다

Reading 30

wake up 깨우다
awake 깨어 있는
react 반응하다
headache 두통
medicine 약
take the place of ～을 대신하다
increase 늘리다, 증가시키다
fully 완전히
make up for 보충하다, 보상하다

Unit 12 빈칸 완성하기 1 (단어)

Reading 31

trash 쓰레기
throw away 버리다
harm 해치다
field 분야
fancy 근사한
product 물건
creative 창의적인, 창조적인
waterproof 방수의
cloth 천
safety belt 안전벨트
tons of 아주 많은, 몇 톤의
eco-friendly 친환경적인
trend 추세, 동향
not only A but also B A뿐만 아니라 B도
unique 독특한

Reading 32

press 누르다
key (피아노) 건반
piece 작품, 곡
artist 연주자
remove 제거하다
performance 공연
composer 작곡가
make an impact on ～에 영향을 주다
control 제어하다, 통제하다
real-life 실제의, 현실의
noise 소음

Unit 13 빈칸 완성하기 2 (표현·문장)

Reading 33

content 내용, 콘텐츠
familiar 익숙한
information 정보
rise 출현, 상승
turn away from ～을 외면하다
decrease 감소시키다, 줄이다
attention 집중
serious 심각한
goldfish 금붕어

Reading 34

package (껌 등의) 통
gum 껌
reality 현실
misunderstand 오해하다

Unit 14 밑줄 친 부분 파악하기

Reading 35

traffic light 신호등
go wrong 잘못되다
law 법, 법칙
negatively 부정적으로
selective 선택적인
memory 기억
remain 남다, 남아 있다
positive 긍정적인
cross 건너다
repeat 반복하다

Reading 36

body language 몸짓 언어
approach 접근
social 사회적인
crossed 교차한
memorize 암기하다, 기억하다
signal 신호
complicated 복잡한
robotic 로봇 같은
confusing 혼란스러운
naturally 자연스럽게
expert 전문가
total 합계, 전체

Unit 15 장문 독해하기

Reading 37

related (～에) 관련된

manual 설명서
explanation 설명
visual 시각의
diagram 도표
role-play 역할극
ineffectively 비효율적으로, 헛되게 (↔ effectively 효율적으로)

Reading 38

security 보안
follow 따르다, (법을) 준수하다
law 법
hack 해킹을 하다
steal 훔치다
data 자료, 정보
solve 해결하다
attack 공격하다 (↔ protect 보호하다)
since ～ 때문에
play a role 역할을 하다
personal 개인적인

Unit 16 복합 문단 독해하기

Reading 39

thick 울창한, 빽빽한
huge 거대한
tiny 아주 작은
look down on ～을 무시하다
be proud of ～을 자랑스러워하다
show off 뽐내다
crawl 기다
continue 계속하다
against ～에 대응하여
shout 소리 지르다, 소리치다
pain 고통
apologize 사과하다
spray 뿌리다
stupid 어리석은, 바보 같은
lesson 교훈

Reading 40

bunch 송이
excited 기쁜, 흥분한
by oneself 혼자서
impressed 감명받은
politely 정중하게
pleased 기쁜
close 가까운
whatever 무엇이든
sour 시큼한, 신

Words Preview

Unit 01 주제 파악하기

Reading 01

warm-blooded 온혈의
freezing 너무 추운, 영하의
Arctic 북극 (지방)
temperature 온도, 기온
thanks to ～ 덕분에
clear 투명한
colorless 무색의
empty 비어 있는
be filled with ～로 가득 차다
trap 가두다
come off 떨어지다
stop A from B A가 B하는 것을 막다
underneath ～의 밑(아래/안)에
soak up 빨아들이다, 흡수하다
thick 두꺼운, 울창한
layer (하나의 표면이나 여러 표면 사이를 덮고 있는) 층
body fat 체지방

Reading 02

national park 국립공원
type 형(태), 유형, 종류
activity 활동
waterfall 폭포
trail 등산로
kind 종류, 친절한
such as 예를 들어, ～와 같은
jaguar 재규어, 아메리카 표범
go -ing ～하러 가다
around 둘레에, 주위에
rainforest (열대) 우림
below (위치가 ～보다) 아래에
on top of ～의 위에
remember 기억하다, 명심하다
raincoat 비옷

Reading 03

view 관점, 보다
please (남을) 즐겁게 하다, 기쁘게 하다
famous 유명한
work 작품
abstract 추상적인
shape 모양, 형태
notice 알아차리다
object 물체, 사물, 대상
unique 독특한, 특별한
whole 완전한, 전체의

Unit 02 제목 파악하기

Reading 04

ancient 고대의
Egyptian 이집트 사람, 이집트의
magical 마법의
creature 생물, 동물
bring 가져오다
honor 경의를 표하다
jewelry 보석, 보석류
high-quality 고품질의, 고급의
owner 주인, 소유주
shave 면도하다, 깎다
eyebrow 눈썹
protect 보호하다

Reading 05

enough 충분한
astronaut 우주비행사
space 우주, 공간
prepare 준비하다
meal 한 끼, 식사
dried 건조된
common 흔한
canned 통조림으로 된
spacecraft 우주선
store 저장하다
refrigerator 냉장고
packet 팩, 통
storage 저장
liquid 액체
ordinary 보통의, 평범한
float away 떠가다
available 이용할 수 있는
various 다양한

Reading 06

failure 실패, 실패자
think of ～을 생각해보다, ～을 고려하다
record 기록
probably 아마
for example 예를 들어
grand slam 그랜드 슬램(골프나 테니스에서 한 해에 4대 메이저 대회에서 모두 우승하는 것)
actually 실제로, 정말로
tournament (골프·스쿼시·테니스 등의) 토너먼트
in other words 다시 말해서
two-thirds 3분의 2($\frac{2}{3}$)

champion 챔피언, 선수권 대회 우승자
be afraid of ～을 두려워하다
pass a test 시험을 통과하다
perfect 완벽한
accept ～을 받아들이다

Unit 03 목적·주장 파악하기

Reading 07

wonderful 멋진
favor 부탁, 청
throw 던지다
waste 쓰레기, 낭비
trash 쓰레기
in place (제자리에) 있는
harmful 해로운
mistake 착각하다, 오해하다
swallow 삼키다
cooperation 협조

Reading 08

right away 즉시, 바로
terrible 끔찍한
misspelling 철자 오류
error 오류, 잘못
fact 사실
matter 문제가 되다
fix 고치다, 수정하다
mistake 실수, 오류, 잘못
difference 차이
hurry 서두르다
forget 잊다
assignment 과제

Unit 04 요지 파악하기

Reading 09

tutor 개인 교사
tutee 개인 지도 받는 학생
project 프로젝트
peer 또래 친구
be good at ～을 잘하다
volunteer 자원하다
be poor at ～을 못하다
at first 처음에는
spend 소비하다, 보내다
waste 낭비
material 자료
clearly 분명하게

Words Preview

grade 등급, 성적
realize 깨닫다

Reading 10

nature 자연
special 특별한, 특수한
keep (~하게) 유지하다
surface 표면
push away 밀어내다
dust 먼지
lotus 연꽃 식물
leaf 잎
muddy 진흙의
pond 연못
microscope 현미경
tiny 매우 작은
bump 돌기, 혹
keep off 차단하다

Reading 11

gesture 몸동작, 몸짓 언어
communication 의사소통
daily 일상의
abroad 해외로
culture 문화
thumb 엄지손가락
popular 인기 있는
beloved 사랑하는
agreement 동의
insult 모욕
Thailand 태국
rudeness 무례(함)
Australia 호주
avoid 피하다

Reading 12

nervous 불안한, 초조한
annoyed 짜증 나는, 화나는
experience 경험하다
score 점수
overcome 극복하다
relaxed 편안한
save 절약하다, 아껴 쓰다
focus on ~에 집중하다
urgent 시급한
time-saving 시간을 절약해 주는
delivery 배달
instead of ~ 대신에
eat out 외식하다

cook (one's) meal 요리해 먹다

Reading 13

share 공유, 몫, 공유하다, 나누다
toilet paper 화장지, 휴지
fair 공정한, 공평한
upset 화난
note 쪽지, 메모
shared 공유의
item 물건
change 변화, 변하다, 변화시키다
behavior 행동, 태도

Reading 14

turn lights off 불을 끄다
globe 지구, 세계
celebrate 기념하다
take action 행동을 하다
symbolic 상징적인
symbol 상징
unity 화합, 통합
collective 집단의
join 참가하다
neighbor 이웃

Reading 15

name 이름 짓다
contest 대회
create 만들다, 창조하다
alone 혼자서
in groups 여럿이, 단체로
take part in ~에 참가하다
participate 참가하다
gift 선물, 상품
winner 수상자, 우승자
submit 제출하다
post 게시하다, 올리다
meaning 의미
through ~을 통하여
prize 상, 상품
1st place 1등, 1위
announcement 발표

Reading 16

health care 의료 서비스
among ~ 중(사이)에
least 가장 적은
between ~ 사이에
highest 가장 높은

the same 똑같은

Reading 17

history 역사
publisher 출판업자
author 작가
inventor 발명가
scientist 과학자
formal 정식의, 정규의
education 교육
mostly 주로, 대부분(의)
self-taught 독학의, 혼자 공부하는
age 나이, 연령
newspaper 신문, 신문사
own 자신의, 독자적인
pen name 필명
married 결혼한, 기혼의

Reading 18

shark 상어
shallow 얕은
sharp 날카로운
teeth tooth(이빨)의 복수형
while 반면에, ~하면서
bite 물다
chew 씹다
grab 잡다, 움켜쥐다
seal 물개
prey 먹이, 사냥감
eyesight 시력
night vision 야간 시력
bottom 아래
hide 숨다, 감추다
threat 위협(받는 상황(존재)), 위험

Reading 19

be born 태어나다
slave 노예
turn down 거부하다
black 흑인
design 디자인
drawing 그림, 데생
university 대학교
master's degree 석사 학위
fine art 미술
throughout one's life 일생 동안
create 창조하다
injustice 부당함

Reading ∞ master 중등
수능
plus
내신
Level 1

WRITERS

오은빈 류애현 이지현 진성인 김민주 김수현 이윤희 하주영

STAFF

발행인 정선욱
퍼블리싱 총괄 남형주
기획 · 개발 김태원 박하영
디자인 김정인 차혜린
유통 · 마케팅 서준성 김지희
제작 김한길 김경수

Reading master 중등 Level 1 202306 제2판 1쇄 202507 제2판 5쇄

펴낸곳 이투스에듀(주) 서울시 서초구 남부순환로 2547
고객센터 1599-3225
등록번호 제2007-000035호
ISBN 979-11-389-1410-9 [53740]

기본 독해부터 수능 독해까지 한번에 완성

Reading master 중등
수능+내신

"한 권의 독해서로 독해 기본기도 쌓고,
수능식 영어 지문 독해까지 할 수는 없을까?"

Reading master 중등은 이와 같은 고민으로 태어났습니다.

수능 경향을 담되,
어휘 및 문장 구조는 중등 수준에 맞는 지문으로 구성하였습니다.

Level별로 단어 수와 렉사일 지수로 중등 난이도를 적용하며
수능 영어식 지문과 문제로 구성하여
Reading master 중등 한 권으로
'영어 독해'를 완성하도록 담아냈습니다.

Level 1	Level 2	Level 3
Words: 120-140 Lexile: 500-700	Words: 140-150 Lexile: 700-900	Words: 150-160 Lexile: 800-1000

* LEXILE® measures(렉사일 지수)는 MetaMetrics® 라는 미국 교육연구소에서 개발한 가장 공신력 있는 읽기 지수입니다.

How to Study

독해의 기본을 위한
Reading Key

수능 유형의 대표 문제 + 내신형 문제로
독해 실력 완성

- ❶ 도식화로 확인하고 간략한 설명으로 이해하는 독해 비법

- ❷ 각 레벨 수준에 맞게 응용된 교육청·평가원 모의평가 및 수능 기출 문제로 핵심 독해 스킬 습득

- ❸ 독해 지문 속 어휘 실력 강화

- ❶ 수능 유형의 대표 문제 제시

- ❷ 원어민의 지문 음원 QR 코드 제시

- ❸ 어떤 부분에 지문 이해의 중점을 두어야 하는지 Mini Quiz를 통해 가이드

- ❹ 문제 해결을 위한 다양한 독해 전략과 Reading 비법을 제공

- ❺ 독해 유형별 지문에 적용되는 Reading Skill 연습으로 글의 구조 분석

Workbook으로
내신 대비 및 직독직해 연습

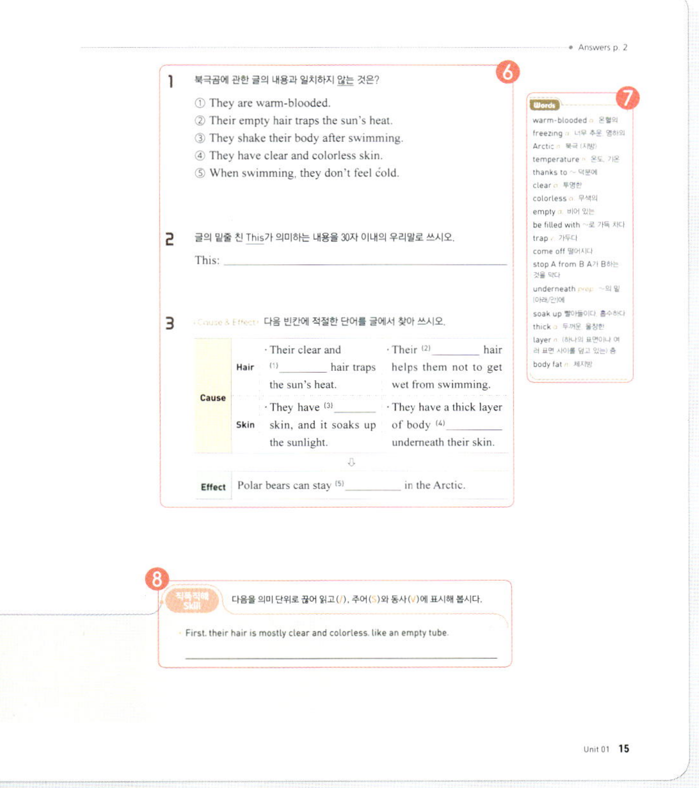

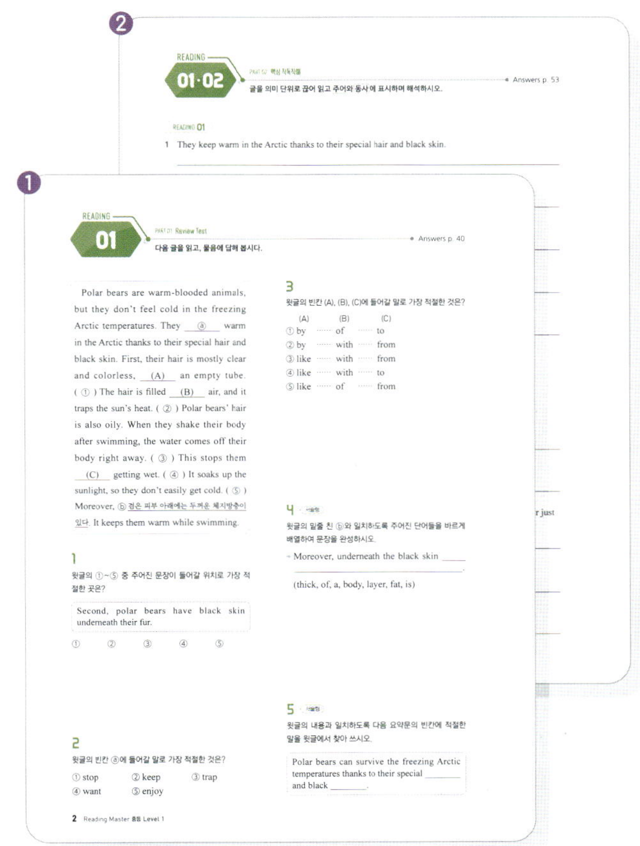

❻ 지문의 완벽한 이해를 돕는 다양한 독해 내신 문제 및 지문 구조화 연습

❼ 독해 지문 속 어휘 실력 강화

❽ 의미 단위 끊어 읽기 방식의 직독직해와 주어와 동사 찾기를 통해 정확한 문장 해석 연습

❶ Review Test 지문별 내신 문제 및 서술형 문제 완벽 대비

❷ 핵심 직독직해 지문별 주요 문장의 직독직해 및 주어와 동사 찾기를 통해 정확한 문장 해석과 독해 속도를 높이는 연습

Contents

중심 내용 파악하기

영어 지문 구조 이해하기

A 시험에 자주 나오는 지문 구조 1

주제문 | 예시 또는 부연 설명

전달하고자 하는 내용의 핵심적인 부분을 가장 먼저 제시한 후에 그에 대한 예시나 부연 설명을 구체적으로 제시하는 구조의 영어 지문이 모평·수능·내신 등의 시험에 자주 출제된다.

기출 예제

Noise in the classroom has negative effects on children's schoolwork. **[주제문]** In some studies, children could communicate better in quieter classrooms, and their test results improved. **[예시 1]** Research with elementary and high school students has similar findings. On reading and math tests, students in noisy classrooms did worse than students in a quieter environment. **[예시 2]**

주제문	교실 __________은/는 학생들의 학업 성적에 __________ 영향을 미친다.
예시	예시 1: 더 조용한 교실에서 아이들이 더 잘 의사소통하고 성적이 __________ 예시 2: __________ 교실에 있는 학생들이 더 __________ 환경에 있는 학생들보다 성적이 낮음

Words negative *a.* 부정적인　　effect *n.* 영향　　study *n.* 연구　　communicate *v.* 의사소통하다　　improve *v.* 개선되다, 나아지다
research *n.* 연구　　finding *n.* (조사) 결과

예시 또는 소재 소개	주제문

주제와 관련 있는 소재를 소개하거나 사례를 먼저 제시한 후에 글쓴이가 전달하고자 하는 주제를 마지막에 결론처럼 제시하는 구조의 영어 지문이 모평·수능·내신 등의 시험에 자주 출제된다.

기출 예제

Imagine *Superman* without Kryptonite. How about the Harry Potter series without
예시 1   예시 2
Voldemort? The movies would be boring and predictable. Too much harmony makes a dull
story. Conflict is necessary for a good story. No conflict, no story.
주제문

예시	Kryptonite가 없는 '슈퍼맨' & Voldemort가 없는 해리 포터 시리즈 → __________ 예측 가능할 것이다.
주제문	__________ 은/는 좋은 __________ 의 필수 요소이다.

Words   imagine *v.* 상상하다   How about ~? ~는 어때?   predictable *a.* 예측할 수 있는   harmony *n.* 조화
           dull *a.* 따분한, 재미없는   conflict *n.* 갈등

C 시험에 자주 나오는 지문 구조 3

일반적인 이야기   반론(주제문)

일반적인 상식 또는 당연하게 생각되는 사실로 글을 시작한 후, '그렇지만 더 중요한 것이 있다'는 반론을 통해 글을 읽는 사람들의 주의를 집중시키는 구조의 영어 지문이 모평·수능·내신 등의 시험에 자주 출제된다.

기출 예제

It is easy to judge people on their actions. People usually say that we should place more value on actions than words. But you should give someone a second chance before you define them. Some of them can be your best friends. So don't judge people hastily.

일반적인 이야기	보통 말보다는 행동에 더 많은 가치를 두라고 하므로, __________에 근거해 사람들을 판단하기 쉽다.
반론(주제문)	사람들을 성급하게 __________해서는 안 된다.

Words   judge *v.* 판단하다   value *n.* 가치   define *v.* 정의하다   hastily *ad.* 성급하게

| 주제문 | 예시나 근거 | 주제문 |

처음 글을 시작할 때 주제를 언급하고 나서 소재를 소개하거나, 사례를 제시한 후에 마지막에 글쓴이가 말하고자 하는 주제를 결론처럼 제시하는 구조의 글이다.
cf 주제문이 명확하게 드러나지 않지만 주제를 단락 내용 전체에 포함하고 있는 경우도 있으니 이 점에도 유의한다.

기출 예제

You can buy the conditions for happiness, but you can't buy happiness. It's like playing
〈주제문〉
tennis. You can buy the ball and the racket at a store, but you can't buy the joy of playing. To
〈예시 1〉
experience the joy of tennis, you have to learn to play and train yourself. Happiness is also
〈예시 2〉
like that. You have to build up happiness; you cannot buy it at a store.
〈주제문〉

주제문	행복을 위한 ___________은/는 살 수 있지만, 행복은 살 수 없다.
예시	예시 1: 테니스공과 라켓은 가게에서 살 수 있지만, ___________은/는 살 수 없다. 예시 2: 테니스의 즐거움을 경험하려면 치는 법을 _________ 스스로 _________ 한다.
주제문	행복은 _________ 한다. 그것을 가게에서 살 수 없다.

Words   condition *n.* 조건   experience *v.* 경험하다   train *v.* 훈련하다, 연마하다   yourself *n.* 너 자신   build up 키우다

READING 01

다음 글의 주제로 가장 적절한 것은?

Polar bears are warm-blooded animals, but they don't feel cold in the freezing Arctic temperatures. They keep warm in the Arctic thanks to their special hair and black skin. First, their hair is mostly clear and colorless, like an empty tube. The hair is filled with air, and it traps the sun's heat. Polar bears' hair is also oily. When they shake their body after swimming, the water comes off their body right away. <u>This</u> stops them from getting wet. Second, polar bears have black skin underneath their fur. It soaks up the sunlight, so they don't easily get cold. Moreover, underneath the black skin is a thick layer of body fat. It keeps them warm while swimming.

① animals in the Arctic
② polar bears in danger
③ temperatures of the Arctic
④ how polar bears swim in water
⑤ the way polar bears stay warm

Mini Quiz

글을 읽으면서 주제문을 찾아 밑줄을 그어 봅시다.

Reading 비법

단락의 첫 문장이나 두 번째 문장이 주제문인 경우가 많다. 또한, first, second, next, finally 등의 연결어 다음에서 글의 주제문을 뒷받침하는 세부 내용을 찾을 수 있다.

Reading Skill

주제문과 근거 문장을 찾아 다음 표를 완성해 봅시다.

주제문	• __________은/는 영하의 기온에도 __________을/를 __________ 않는다.
근거문	• __________은/는 __________와/과 __________ 덕분에 북극에서 __________ 하게 __________ 수 있다.

1 북극곰에 관한 글의 내용과 일치하지 <u>않는</u> 것은?

① They are warm-blooded.
② Their empty hair traps the sun's heat.
③ They shake their body after swimming.
④ They have clear and colorless skin.
⑤ When swimming, they don't feel cold.

2 글의 밑줄 친 <u>This</u>가 의미하는 내용을 30자 이내의 우리말로 쓰시오.

This: ___________________________________

3 ꤖ Cause & Effect ꤖ 다음 빈칸에 적절한 단어를 글에서 찾아 쓰시오.

Cause	Hair	·Their clear and (1)________ hair traps the sun's heat.	·Their (2)________ hair helps them not to get wet from swimming.
	Skin	·They have (3)________ skin, and it soaks up the sunlight.	·They have a thick layer of body (4)________ underneath their skin.

⇩

Effect	Polar bears can stay (5)________ in the Arctic.

Words

warm-blooded *a.* 온혈의
freezing *a.* 너무 추운, 영하의
Arctic *n.* 북극 (지방)
temperature *n.* 온도, 기온
thanks to ~ 덕분에
clear *a.* 투명한
colorless *a.* 무색의
empty *a.* 비어 있는
be filled with ~로 가득 차다
trap *v.* 가두다
come off 떨어지다
stop A from B A가 B하는 것을 막다
underneath *prep.* ~의 밑 (아래/안)에
soak up 빨아들이다, 흡수하다
thick *a.* 두꺼운, 울창한
layer *n.* (하나의 표면이나 여러 표면 사이를 덮고 있는) 층
body fat *n.* 체지방

직독직해 Skill 다음을 의미 단위로 끊어 읽고(/), 주어(S)와 동사(V)에 표시해 봅시다.

· First, their hair is mostly clear and colorless, like an empty tube.

____

READING 02

다음 글의 주제로 가장 적절한 것은?

Iguazú National Park is a very big national park in Argentina. You can enjoy many types of activities ⓐ<u>there</u>. First, you can see the Iguazú Falls. ⓑ<u>They</u>'re the world's biggest waterfalls with about 275 different waterfalls. You can experience the highest point, the Devil's Throat, by taking a boat tour, helicopter ride, or just by walking on the trails. You can also see wild animals in the park. There are many kinds of animals such as jaguars, fish, turtles, and monkeys. Last, you can go hiking to different places. You can hike around the rainforest, below the falls, and even on top of the falls. Just remember to bring your raincoat, or you may get wet.

① the size of the Iguazú Falls
② national parks in Argentina
③ hiking courses of the Iguazú Falls
④ the location of Iguazú National Park
⑤ activities to do in Iguazú National Park

Mini Quiz

글을 읽으면서 주제문과 주제를 뒷받침하는 문장 3개를 찾아 밑줄을 그어 봅시다.

Reading 비법

첫 문장이 주제문인 경우도 있지만, 일반적인 정보나 배경지식을 전달하는 문장이 첫 문장으로 제시되는 경우도 많다.

Reading Skill 주제문과 근거 문장을 찾아 다음 표를 완성해 봅시다.

주제문	• ____________에서 ________한 ________을/를 즐길 수 있다.
근거문	1. ____________을/를 볼 수 있다. 2. ____________을/를 볼 수 있다. 3. ________, ________, ________에서 하이킹을 할 수 있다.

1 글을 읽고 답할 수 <u>없는</u> 질문은?

① Where is Iguazú National Park?
② How high are the Iguazú Falls?
③ What is the highest point of the Iguazú Falls?
④ How can you get to the Devil's Throat?
⑤ Why do you need a raincoat when you visit Iguazú National Park?

2 밑줄 친 ⓐ와 ⓑ가 가리키는 것을 글에서 찾아 각각 쓰시오.

ⓐ: _______________________

ⓑ: _______________________

3 ⏐ Making a Guide Book ⏐ 다음 빈칸에 적절한 단어를 글에서 찾아 쓰시오.

Guide Book of Iguazú National Park

1. Come and see the world's (1)______________ waterfalls, the Iguazú Falls.
2. See many kinds of (2)______________ such as jaguars, fish, turtles, and monkeys.
3. Visit different (3)______________ courses around the rainforest and below and on top of the falls.

직독직해 Skill 다음을 의미 단위로 끊어 읽고(/), 주어(S)와 동사(V)에 표시해 봅시다.

· There are many kinds of animals such as jaguars, fish, turtles, and monkeys.

____

Words

national park *n.* 국립공원
type *n.* 형(태), 유형, 종류
activity *n.* 활동
waterfall *n.* 폭포
trail *n.* 등산로
kind *n.* 종류 *a.* 친절한
such as 예를 들어, ~와 같은
jaguar *n.* 재규어, 아메리카 표범
go -ing ~하러 가다
around *prep.* 둘레에, 주위에
rainforest *n.* (열대) 우림
below *prep.* (위치가 ~보다) 아래에
on top of ~의 위에
remember *v.* 기억하다, 명심하다
raincoat *n.* 비옷

READING 03

다음 글의 주제로 가장 적절한 것은?　　기출 응용

Sometimes a different view pleases us. For example, Pablo Picasso, a famous artist, tried to see the world differently. In his famous work *Three Musicians*, he painted three music players. But he did not draw three people. Instead, he used abstract shapes. When you first see this work, you may not notice the players. Nothing makes sense to you. But when you keep looking at the painting, you can see them in it! It's like a puzzle. Picasso's work shows a special way of painting. His work used shapes, objects, and colors so differently from the real world. His paintings look very unique. To understand the work, you should view things completely differently. This can be a whole new joy. It is the joy of viewing the world differently.

① the life of Pablo Picasso
② the benefits of living with art
③ different ways of using colors
④ the pleasure of seeing differently
⑤ the importance of sharing different views

Mini Quiz

글을 읽으면서 주제문을 찾아 밑줄을 그어 봅시다.

Reading 비법

예시를 나타내는 for example 이나 for instance 앞에 주제가 제시되는 경우가 많다.

Reading Skill　　주제문과 근거 문장을 찾아 다음 표를 완성해 봅시다.

주제문	• 때때로 __________ 관점은 우리를 __________ 한다.
근거문	• 작가: __________ • 작품명: __________ • 특징: __________ 을/를 그리기 위해 __________ 을/를 사용했다.

1 *Three Musicians*에 관한 글의 내용을 바르게 이해하지 <u>못한</u> 학생은?

① 민지: 추상적인 형태를 사용했군.
② 소라: 전혀 새로운 관점의 작품이군.
③ 민수: 처음 봤을 땐 무엇을 그렸는지 알아차리기 쉽지 않겠군.
④ 유빈: 형태나 색깔을 매우 다르게 사용했군.
⑤ 하늘: 실제 세상의 모습과 비슷하게 그렸군.

Words

view *n.* 관점 *v.* 보다
please *v.* (남을) 즐겁게 하다,
기쁘게 하다
famous *a.* 유명한
work *n.* 작품
abstract *a.* 추상적인
shape *n.* 모양, 형태
notice *v.* 알아차리다
object *n.* 물체, 사물, 대상
unique *a.* 독특한, 특별한
whole *a.* 완전한, 전체의

2 다음 밑줄 친 단어의 의미를 글에서 찾아 한 단어로 쓰시오.

You cannot <u>amuse</u> everyone around you.

3 | Summary | 다음 빈칸에 공통으로 들어갈 적절한 단어를 글에서 찾아 쓰시오.

> With Pablo Picasso's work, you can discover the joy of seeing the world ___________. When we view things ___________, we can experience a whole new joy just like Picasso.

직독직해 Skill 다음을 의미 단위로 끊어 읽고(/), 주어(S)와 동사(V)에 표시해 봅시다.

· To understand the work. you should view things completely differently.

READING 04

다음 글의 제목으로 가장 적절한 것은?

For ancient Egyptians, cats were the most special animal. <u>They</u> first kept cats as pets. Egyptians believed cats were magical creatures. They thought that cats brought good luck. To honor the cats, rich families put jewelry on them. They also gave high-quality food to the cats. Cats were an important part of ancient Egyptian life. When cats died, their owners would shave their eyebrows. They showed their sadness until their eyebrows grew back. The ancient Egyptians protected cats even by law. When a human killed a cat, he or she was killed, too. Cats were clearly more than just pets to them.

① The Need for Animal Protection Laws
② The Special Function of Eyebrows
③ Cats' Importance to Ancient Egyptians
④ Favorite Animals in Different Countries
⑤ Differences between Cats and Dogs

Mini Quiz

글을 읽으면서 반복되는 중심 소재를 찾아 밑줄을 그어 봅시다.

Reading 비법

They와 같은 대명사가 지칭하는 것이 무엇인지 잘 파악하며 글을 읽어야 한다.

Reading Skill

주제문과 근거 문장을 찾아 다음 표를 완성해 봅시다.

주제문	• __________은/는 __________에게 가장 __________한 동물이었다.
근거문	• __________에게 __________을/를 걸어 주거나 __________을/를 주었다. • __________이/가 죽으면 __________을/를 밀었다.

1 글의 내용과 일치하지 <u>않는</u> 것은?

① Cats were special pets to ancient Egyptians.
② Some cats wore jewelry in ancient Egypt.
③ Ancient Egyptians shaved their eyebrows to play with cats.
④ Ancient Egyptians had laws for cats.
⑤ Cats were not just animals for ancient Egyptians.

2 밑줄 친 <u>They</u>가 가리키는 것을 글에서 찾아 두 단어로 쓰시오.

They: ________________ ________________

3 | Summary | 다음 빈칸에 적절한 단어를 글에서 찾아 쓰시오. (단, 주어진 철자로 시작할 것)

> Cats were (1)i____________ for ancient Egyptians. Ancient Egyptians thought that cats were (2)m____________ creatures. Cats in ancient Egypt even had (3) j____________ and high-quality food. People took great care of cats.

Words

ancient *a.* 고대의
Egyptian *n.* 이집트 사람 *a.* 이집트의
magical *a.* 마법의
creature *n.* 생물, 동물
bring *v.* 가져오다
honor *v.* 경의를 표하다
jewelry *n.* 보석, 보석류
high-quality *a.* 고품질의, 고급의
owner *n.* 주인, 소유주
shave *v.* 면도하다, 깎다
eyebrow *n.* 눈썹
protect *v.* 보호하다

직독직해 Skill 다음을 의미 단위로 끊어 읽고(/), 주어(S)와 동사(V)에 표시해 봅시다.

· They showed their sadness until their eyebrows grew back.

____

READING 05

다음 글의 제목으로 가장 적절한 것은?

When you go camping, you make sure to bring enough food. Astronauts do the same thing when they go to space. They prepare food. Like on Earth, astronauts eat three meals a day. There are many different foods for astronauts in space. Dried food is very common. There are canned potatoes and meats. A spacecraft can ⁵ store some fresh fruit and vegetables. There is also an oven in a spacecraft and it can make food warm. But there is no refrigerator. So all the food comes in packets for easy storage. Salt comes as liquid. Ordinary salt would simply float away. Sauces like ketchup, mustard, and mayonnaise are also available in tubes. With these various space foods, astronauts can stay healthy in space. ¹⁰

① Various Kinds of Salt
② Space Food for Astronauts
③ What You Need for Camping
④ How to Become an Astronaut
⑤ Foods from Different Cultures

Mini Quiz
글을 읽으면서 주제문을 찾아 밑줄을 그어 봅시다.

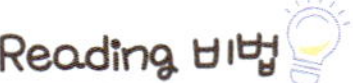

Reading 비법
주제문은 일반적인 내용으로 제시되고 그 뒤에 구체적인 내용을 담은 예시가 온다.

Reading Skill — 주제문과 근거 문장을 찾아 다음 표를 완성해 봅시다.

주제문	• __________을/를 위한 다양한 __________이/가 있다.
근거문	• __________ 음식과 감자와 __________ 통조림이 있으며, 신선한 __________와/과 __________을/를 보관할 수도 있다. • __________은/는 __________ 형태이고, __________은/는 __________에 넣어져 있다.

1 우주비행사에 관한 글의 내용을 바르게 이해하지 <u>못한</u> 학생은?

① 현지: 그들도 하루에 세 끼를 먹는구나.
② 세호: 그들도 다양한 종류의 음식을 먹는구나.
③ 동혁: 그들은 냉장고가 없어서 불편하겠네.
④ 승현: 그들은 소금이 필요하지 않겠네.
⑤ 서윤: 그들도 케첩이나 마요네즈와 같은 소스를 먹을 수 있구나.

2 글의 내용과 일치하도록 다음 질문에 영어로 답하시오.

> Q: Why does food in space come in packets for easy storage?
> A: ____

3 |Summary| 다음 빈칸에 적절한 단어를 |보기|에서 골라 쓰시오.

보기

| dried | tubes | canned | liquid |

Astronauts can eat many different foods in space. All food is packaged for easy storage. Although there are some fresh foods available, other foods can be (1) ___________ or (2) ___________ . Sauces come out of (3) ___________ .

직독직해 Skill 다음을 의미 단위로 끊어 읽고(/), 주어(S)와 동사(V)에 표시해 봅시다.

· With these various space foods, astronauts can stay healthy in space.

____

Words

enough *a.* 충분한
astronaut *n.* 우주비행사
space *n.* 우주, 공간
prepare *v.* 준비하다
meal *n.* 한 끼, 식사
dried *a.* 건조된
common *a.* 흔한
canned *a.* 통조림으로 된
spacecraft *n.* 우주선
store *v.* 저장하다
refrigerator *n.* 냉장고
packet *n.* 팩, 통
storage *n.* 저장
liquid *n.* 액체
ordinary *a.* 보통의, 평범한
float away 떠가다
available *a.* 이용할 수 있는
various *a.* 다양한

READING 06

다음 글의 제목으로 가장 적절한 것은? 기출 응용

Do you know anybody with no failure at all? Or can you think of anyone in sports history with a record of only wins? Probably not. Roger Federer, for example, is the world's greatest tennis player with twenty Grand Slam titles. But he actually played in more than sixty Grand Slam tournaments. In other words, he lost in more than two-thirds of the tournaments. He lost many more tournaments than he won. Still, we think of him as a champion, not as a failure. Failure makes success. So don't be afraid of failure. Losing a game or not passing a test is okay. No one is perfect. Try to accept your failure and move on from it.

① Be Perfect
② Create Your Own Game
③ Winning Is the Most Important
④ Success Doesn't Come Without Failure
⑤ Set Your Goals and Practice for the Game

Mini Quiz

글을 읽으면서 반복되는 핵심어 두 개를 찾아 밑줄을 그어 봅시다.

Reading 비법

글에 반복적으로 나오는 핵심 소재와 핵심 어구를 찾으면 글쓴이가 말하고자 하는 주제를 파악할 수 있다.

Reading Skill 주제문과 예시 문장을 찾아 다음 표를 완성해 봅시다.

주제문	⦁ __________은/는 __________을/를 만든다.
예시	⦁ Roger Federer는 __________에서 __________ 횟수보다 __________ 횟수가 훨씬 더 많다.

1 Roger Federer에 관한 글의 내용과 일치하지 <u>않는</u> 것은?

① He is a very good tennis player.
② He has a record of only wins.
③ He won twenty Grand Slam titles.
④ He played in more than sixty Grand Slam tournaments.
⑤ People think of him as a success, not a failure.

2 다음 대화의 빈칸에 적절한 단어를 글에서 찾아 쓰시오.

Ann: I couldn't pass the English exam yesterday.
Jiho: Don't worry too much. Failure is a stepping stone to
___________.

* stepping stone: 디딤돌

3 | Summary | 다음 빈칸에 적절한 단어를 글에서 찾아 쓰시오.

Writer's Suggestion

People learn from their (1)___________, and it leads to
success. It is more important than (2)___________ a
game. So don't fear your (3)___________.

다음을 의미 단위로 끊어 읽고(/), 주어(S)와 동사(V)에 표시해 봅시다.

· Losing a game or not passing a test is okay.

failure *n.* 실패, 실패자
think of ~을 생각해보다, ~을 고려하다
record *n.* 기록
probably *ad.* 아마
for example 예를 들어
grand slam 그랜드 슬램(골프나 테니스에서 한 해에 4대 메이저 대회에서 모두 우승하는 것)
actually *ad.* 실제로, 정말로
tournament *n.* (골프·스쿼시·테니스 등의) 토너먼트
in other words 다시 말해서
two-thirds 3분의 2($\frac{2}{3}$)
champion *n.* 챔피언, 선수권 대회 우승자
be afraid of ~을 두려워하다
pass a test 시험을 통과하다
perfect *a.* 완벽한
accept *v.* ~을 받아들이다

다음 글의 목적으로 가장 적절한 것은?

Dear Mr. Kang,

  I am a tour guide at Fun & Joy Zoo. Thank you for visiting our zoo for your field trip! I hope you will have a wonderful day here. I would like to ask you a favor. Before your visit, please advise your students not to throw waste in the zoo. Trash cans are in place all around the zoo. Plastic bags and other trash can be very harmful to our animals. Like small children, animals love to test things with their mouths. They may mistake this trash for food and swallow it. <u>It</u> can make them very sick. So, for the health of our lovely animals, students should not throw waste in the zoo. I thank you for your cooperation.

Sincerely,

Danna Smith

① 다양한 동물원 투어 코스를 소개하려고
② 학생들에게 쓰레기 분리수거의 필요성을 교육하려고
③ 현장 체험을 통해 동물원 투어가 얼마나 흥미로운지 홍보하려고
④ 학생들이 동물원에 쓰레기를 버리지 않도록 지도해 줄 것을 부탁하려고
⑤ 플라스틱 사용의 증가로 인한 환경 오염의 심각성을 학생들에게 알리려고

글을 읽으면서 필자가 글을 쓴 목적이 드러난 문장을 찾아 밑줄을 그어 봅시다.

Reading 비법

ask ~ a favor는 '~에게 부탁하다'라는 의미로, 요청이나 요구의 내용이 이어진다.

Reading Skill 주제문과 근거 문장을 찾아 다음 표를 완성해 봅시다.

주제문	• 학생들은 __________에 __________을/를 __________(하)면 안 된다.
근거문	• __________은/는 __________을/를 __________(해)서 __________ 수 있다.

1 글을 읽고 답할 수 <u>없는</u> 질문은?

① Who wrote this mail?
② What is Danna Smith's job?
③ To whom will the writer send this mail?
④ Where will Mr. Kang and his students go for the field trip?
⑤ What are the students' favorite activities at the zoo?

Words

wonderful *a.* 멋진
favor *n.* 부탁, 청
throw *v.* 던지다
waste *n.* 쓰레기, 낭비
trash *n.* 쓰레기
in place (제자리에) 있는
harmful *a.* 해로운
mistake *v.* 착각하다, 오해하다
swallow *v.* 삼키다
cooperation *n.* 협조

2 글의 밑줄 친 It이 가리키는 것을 10자 이내의 우리말로 다음 빈칸에 쓰시오.

<u>It</u> can make them very sick.

→ _______________________

3 ǀ Cause & Effect ǀ 다음 빈칸에 적절한 단어를 ǀ보기ǀ에서 골라 쓰시오.

ǀ 보기 ǀ

| eat | harmful | sick | trash |

Cause	Effect
(1) ___________ can be (2) ___________ in the zoo.	Animals in the zoo may (3) ___________ the waste, and they can become (4) ___________.

직독직해 Skill 다음을 의미 단위로 끊어 읽고(/), 주어(S)와 동사(V)에 표시해 봅시다.

· For the health of our lovely animals, students should not throw waste in the zoo.

READING 08

다음 글에서 필자가 주장하는 바로 가장 적절한 것은? 기출 응용

Don't click the Send button right away when you send emails. Nothing terrible will happen before you click the Send button. There can be misspellings or errors of fact in your writing. However, it doesn't matter if you don't click the Send button. Why? You can take some time to fix mistakes. And nobody will ⁵ be able to know the difference. So, never hurry to click the Send button. Looking again and fixing should come first; sending should come later. If you see any mistakes after sending an email, it can be a big problem. So, don't forget to read your writing carefully before you click the Send button. The same goes for sending school assignments or business letters by email. ¹⁰

① 과제의 제출 기한을 반드시 지켜야 한다.
② 글을 쓸 때에는 맞춤법을 잘 지켜야 한다.
③ 중요한 이메일은 출력하여 보관해야 한다.
④ 이메일을 보내기 전에 주의 깊게 검토해야 한다.
⑤ 컴퓨터에 보관된 자료는 주기적으로 정리해야 한다.

Mini Quiz

글을 읽으면서 필자의 주장이 가장 잘 드러난 문장을 찾아 밑줄을 그어 봅시다.

Reading 비법

필자가 자신의 주장을 강조하고자 할 때, 명령문이나 should, must, don't forget to ~ 등의 표현을 자주 사용하는 것에 유의한다.

Reading Skill 주제문과 근거 문장을 찾아 다음 표를 완성해 봅시다.

주제문	• __________ __________을/를 __________(하)기 __________에 __________을/를 __________ __________ 한다.
근거문	• 이메일을 보낸 후에 __________을/를 __________하면 큰 __________이/가 될 수 있다.

1 밑줄 친 <u>any mistakes</u>의 구체적인 예로 글에서 언급된 것을 <u>모두</u> 고르면?

① 주소 오류　　② 잘못된 철자　　③ 잘못된 존칭어 사용

④ 사실의 오류　　⑤ 비속어 사용

Words

right away 즉시, 바로
terrible *a.* 끔찍한
misspelling *n.* 철자 오류
error *n.* 오류, 잘못
fact *n.* 사실
matter *v.* 문제가 되다
fix *v.* 고치다, 수정하다
mistake *n.* 실수, 오류, 잘못
difference *n.* 차이
hurry *v.* 서두르다
forget *v.* 잊다
assignment *n.* 과제

2 글의 내용과 일치하도록 다음 빈칸에 적절한 단어를 주어진 철자로 시작하여 쓰시오.

Q: What should I remember before sending an email?

A: You should read your writing carefully because you can't f______________ your mistakes a______________ you click the Send button.

3 |Process| 글의 내용과 일치하도록 제시된 문장을 바르게 배열하시오.

[　] → [　] → (D) → [　]

(A) Click the Send button.
(B) Write your email.
(C) Read your writing carefully.
(D) Correct any mistakes in your writing.

직독직해 Skill　다음을 의미 단위로 끊어 읽고(/), 주어(S)와 동사(V)에 표시해 봅시다.

· Nothing terrible will happen before you click the Send button.

READING 09

다음 글의 요지로 가장 적절한 것은?

We started a new tutor-tutee project in science class last month. It was a kind of peer teaching. My science teacher said, "This project will be helpful for the tutees. It will also be good for the tutors!" I liked science best. I was good at science, so I volunteered as a student teacher. I taught my friend. He was poor at science. At first, I thought I was spending too much time with the tutee. I also thought it was a waste of time. But later, I found out I was wrong. As a tutor, I began to understand the material better and more clearly. I also got a better grade on the final exam thanks to the project. I realized that I could learn more by teaching others.

① Time is money.
② Teaching is learning twice.
③ One is never too old to learn.
④ The first step is always the hardest.
⑤ A friend in need is a friend indeed.

Mini Quiz

글을 읽으면서 글의 핵심 내용이 잘 드러난 문장을 찾아 밑줄을 그어 봅시다.

Reading 비법

글의 중간에서 But으로 시작되는 문장은 앞의 내용과는 대비되는 내용이 될 것임을 알 수 있다.

Reading Skill

글의 중심 내용에 맞게 다음 표를 완성해 봅시다.

상황	• __________ 시간에 나는 _______________을/를 자원했다.
Tutor-tutee에 대한 나의 생각	• 생각 1: __________라고 생각했다. ↓ • 생각 2: 자료를 더 __________하게 __________ 시작했다.
결론	• __________을/를 __________ 것은 더 많이 __________ 수 있는 것임을 깨달았다.

1 글을 읽고 답할 수 있는 질문은?

① How can students save time?
② When did peer teaching finish?
③ What was the benefit of peer teaching?
④ What is the best way to make new friends?
⑤ Why were some students poor or good at science?

Words

tutor *n.* 개인 교사
tutee *n.* 개인 지도 받는 학생
project *n.* 프로젝트
peer *n.* 또래 친구
be good at ~을 잘하다
volunteer *v.* 자원하다
be poor at ~을 못하다
at first 처음에는
spend *v.* 소비하다, 보내다
waste *n.* 낭비
material *n.* 자료
clearly *ad.* 분명하게
grade *n.* 등급, 성적
realize *v.* 깨닫다

2 다음 대화의 빈칸에 적절한 말을 |보기|에서 골라 쓰시오.

┤ 보기 ├

at first　　hate　　helped　　learning　　teaching

A: How was the new project in science class?
B: It was really good. In fact, I didn't like it ___________ .
　　However, it ___________ me in the end.
A: How come?
B: I could learn more by ___________ others.

3 | Summary Map | 다음 빈칸에 적절한 단어를 글에서 찾아 쓰시오. (단, 필요시 형태를 바꿔 쓸 것)

Bad Point about Tutor-Tutee		Good Point about Tutor-Tutee
"I (1)___________ too much (2)___________ ."	**vs.**	"I begin to (3)___________ the material better and more (4)___________ ."

직독직해 Skill　다음을 의미 단위로 끊어 읽고(/), 주어(S)와 동사(V)에 표시해 봅시다.

• I realized that I could learn more by teaching others.

READING 10

다음 글의 요지로 가장 적절한 것은?

Nature is a source of discovery. Observing nature can make human life better. It means that our life can be easier and more comfortable. For example, special paint can keep your house clean. The rough surface of the paint pushes away dust. After using this paint, you can wash the outside of your house less often. This discovery came from looking at lotus leaves. As people know, lotus lives in muddy ponds. However, its leaves always look clean. Why is this possible? Look at a lotus leaf under a microscope. Then you can know the answer. There are many tiny bumps on it. They look like small nails and make the surface rough. So it can keep dust off. Always try to observe nature closely!

* observe: 관찰하다

① 연꽃은 진흙 연못에 살지만 깨끗하다.
② 집의 외벽은 자주 청소해 줄 필요가 있다.
③ 페인트의 발명은 건축 발전에 큰 기여를 했다.
④ 현미경이 없었다면 현재의 과학 발전도 없었을 것이다.
⑤ 자연은 발견의 원천이므로 자연을 면밀히 관찰해야 한다.

Mini Quiz

글을 읽으면서 글의 주제가 잘 드러난 문장을 찾아 밑줄을 그어 봅시다.

Reading 비법

구체적인 예를 들어 설명할 때는 for example, for instance 등을 사용하며, 이러한 표현 뒤에 이어지는 내용을 보면 주제를 추측하는 데 도움이 된다.

Reading Skill 주제문과 근거 문장을 찾아 다음 표를 완성해 봅시다.

주제문	• __________은/는 __________의 원천이므로 __________을/를 면밀히 __________해라.
근거문	• 연꽃잎의 __________ __________은/는 __________을/를 __________하게 한다. ↓ 활용 • 특수한 __________은/는 __________을/를 __________하게 한다.

1 글에서 사용된 다음 단어의 우리말 뜻이 <u>잘못</u> 연결된 것은?

① source : 원천　　　② discovery : 발견(물)

③ rough : 거친　　　④ nail : 손톱

⑤ surface : 표면

2 글의 내용과 일치하도록 틀린 부분을 찾아 바르게 고쳐 쓰시오.

> Like a lotus leaf, the soft surface of the special paint pushes away dust.

____________ → ____________

3 |Summary| 다음 빈칸에 적절한 단어를 글에서 찾아 쓰시오.

> Nature is a source of (1)__________ for human life. For example, the (2)__________ surface of a lotus leaf keeps (3)__________ off. Humans discovered this by observing a lotus leaf and applied it to special (4)__________.

직독직해 Skill 다음을 의미 단위로 끊어 읽고(/), 주어(S)와 동사(V)에 표시해 봅시다.

· For example, special paint can keep your house clean.

____

Words

nature *n.* 자연
special *a.* 특별한, 특수한
keep *v.* ~하게 유지하다
surface *n.* 표면
push away 밀어내다
dust *n.* 먼지
lotus *n.* 연꽃 식물
leaf *n.* 잎
muddy *a.* 진흙의
pond *n.* 연못
microscope *n.* 현미경
tiny *a.* 매우 작은
bump *n.* 돌기, 혹
keep off 차단하다

READING 11

다음 글의 내용을 한 문장으로 요약하고자 한다. 빈칸 (A), (B)에 들어갈 말로 가장 적절한 것은?

We communicate with others through language. But we use hand gestures for communication, too. We often use them in daily life. We can also use them when we travel abroad. However, not all hand gestures have the same meaning in every culture! Therefore, we should be careful about when and how we use them. The <u>thumbs up</u> is a good example. This gesture is very popular and well known. People often use it all over the world. It is a beloved emoji, too. It usually means agreement or "okay" in many countries like Korea and Japan. However, it may be an insult in Thailand. And it may mean "no" or show rudeness in Australia. Gestures such as a thumbs up have different meanings in many cultures or countries. So, to avoid misunderstandings, be careful how you use them!

The _____(A)_____ meanings of hand gestures in different cultures may lead to _____(B)_____.

	(A)		(B)		(A)		(B)
①	universal	……	agreement	②	various	……	agreement
③	different	……	disagreement	④	various	……	misunderstandings
⑤	same	……	misunderstandings				

Mini Quiz

글을 읽으면서 반복되는 중심 소재를 찾아 밑줄을 그어 봅시다.

Reading 비법

요약문을 먼저 읽으면 보다 쉽고 빠르게 글의 주제를 파악할 수 있다.

Reading Skill 주제문과 근거 문장을 찾아 다음 표를 완성해 봅시다.

주제문	• __________은/는 나라마다 __________이/가 __________.
근거문	1. 한국과 일본 등의 많은 나라: __________, __________ 2. 태국: __________ 3. 호주: __________, __________

1 밑줄 친 thumbs up의 의미로 글에서 언급되지 <u>않은</u> 것을 <u>모두</u> 고르면?

① 동의　　　② 승낙　　　③ 미안함　　　④ 무례함　　　⑤ 사과

2 다음 빈칸에 적절한 한 단어를 글에서 찾아 쓰시오.

> A(n) ___________ means a digital image. It is used to express an emotion or idea in an electronic communication such as an email or text message.

3 ｜Summary｜ 다음 빈칸에 적절한 단어를 글에서 찾아 쓰시오.

> People use (1)___________ gestures for (2)___________ in daily life. People can also use them when they travel abroad. One hand gesture doesn't have the (3)___________ meaning in every culture! For this reason, people should be (4)___________ when they use them.

직독직해 Skill　다음을 의미 단위로 끊어 읽고(/), 주어(S)와 동사(V)에 표시해 봅시다.

· Not all hand gestures have the same meaning in every culture!

____

Words

gesture *n.* 몸동작, 몸짓 언어
communication *n.* 의사소통
daily *a.* 일상의
abroad *ad.* 해외로
culture *n.* 문화
thumb *n.* 엄지손가락
popular *a.* 인기 있는
beloved *a.* 사랑하는
agreement *n.* 동의
insult *n.* 모욕
Thailand *n.* 태국
rudeness *n.* 무례(함)
Australia *n.* 호주
avoid *v.* 피하다

READING **12**

다음 글의 내용을 한 문장으로 요약하고자 한다. 빈칸 (A), (B)에 들어갈 말로 가장 적절한 것은?

Do you often feel that there is not enough time? It is the feeling of having too much to do when you do not have enough time. It is _time famine_. It makes you feel nervous. It makes you annoyed, too. You may experience this when you study for exams. One study shows that time famine can make students feel more stressed than when they get a low score. But do not worry. There is a way to overcome this. You can feel more relaxed by saving time. To save time, make a to-do list. It helps you to focus on the more urgent things. Also, use time-saving services. For instance, you can use a food delivery service instead of eating out or cooking meals.

* famine: 기근, 굶주림

> Saving _____ (A) _____ can help you _____ (B) _____ time famine.

	(A)		(B)		(A)		(B)
①	money	……	avoid	②	energy	……	encourage
③	time	……	avoid	④	money	……	overcome
⑤	time	……	encourage				

Mini Quiz

글을 읽으면서 문제 해결 방법이 가장 잘 드러난 문장을 모두 찾아 밑줄을 그어 봅시다.

Reading 비법

단락글에서 앞의 내용에 추가적인 내용을 덧붙일 때 Also를 종종 사용한다.

Reading Skill 글의 중심 내용에 맞게 다음 표를 완성해 봅시다.

의미 정의	______ ______ : ______ ______은/는 많은데 ______ ______이/가 ______고 느끼는 것
대응 방안	1. ______ ______ ______ 만들기 2. ______ ______ ______ 이용하기 → ______을/를 ______하기

1 밑줄 친 부분에 대해 바르게 이해하지 <u>못한</u> 학생은?

① 진희: 짜증 나고 긴장돼.
② 민수: 나는 시간이 충분하지 않다고 느껴.
③ 소라: 나는 주어진 시간에 비해 할 일이 너무 많다고 느껴.
④ 시진: 시험 못 봤을 때보다 더 스트레스 받아.
⑤ 태원: 나는 더 긴급한 일에 집중할 수 있어.

2 글의 내용과 일치하도록 빈칸에 적절한 단어를 글에서 찾아 쓰시오.

Making a(n) ___________ ___________ helps you to ___________ on the more important things.

3 | Problem & Solution | 다음 빈칸에 적절한 단어를 |보기|에서 골라 쓰시오.

| 보기 |

| waste | use | upset | create | save |

Problem	You feel (1)___________ because of time famine.
Solution	(2)___________ your time.
Examples of Solution	- to (3)___________ a to-do list - to (4)___________ time-saving services

직독직해 Skill 다음을 의미 단위로 끊어 읽고(/), 주어(S)와 동사(V)에 표시해 봅시다.

· It helps you to focus on the more urgent things.

____

Words

nervous *a.* 불안한, 초조한
annoyed *a.* 짜증 나는, 화나는
experience *v.* 경험하다
score *n.* 점수
overcome *v.* 극복하다
relaxed *a.* 편안한
save *v.* 절약하다, 아껴쓰다
focus on ~에 집중하다
urgent *a.* 시급한
time-saving 시간을 절약해 주는
delivery *n.* 배달
instead of ~ 대신에
eat out 외식하다
cook (one's) meal 요리해 먹다

13

READING

다음 글의 내용을 한 문장으로 요약하고자 한다. 빈칸 (A), (B)에 들어갈 말로 가장 적절한 것은?

기출 응용

Rhonda was living in a share house. When the cleaners came on weekends, they left some toilet paper in the two bathrooms. However, all the toilet paper was gone by Monday. The toilet paper was for everyone, but some took more than their fair share. She felt upset about the matter. So, she decided to put a note in one ⁵ of the bathrooms. It said, "Do not take all the toilet paper, please. It is a shared item. It is for everyone." Then there was a surprising change. She was glad to see that one roll came back in a few hours and another the next day. However, in the other bathroom with no note, no toilet paper came back until the cleaners brought more. ¹⁰

> Rhonda's small _____(A)_____ made a _____(B)_____ in people's behavior.

	(A)		(B)			(A)		(B)
①	note	······	problem		②	money	······	problem
③	action	······	change		④	note	······	plan
⑤	money	······	change					

Mini Quiz

글을 읽으면서 상반된 상황이 일어날 것임을 나타내는 연결어를 찾아 밑줄을 그어 봅시다.

Reading 비법

요약문을 먼저 읽고 난 후, 글을 읽으면서 요약문의 빈칸에 들어갈 내용과 관련 있는 단어를 빈칸에 대입하여 요약문에 어울리는지 확인해 본다.

Reading Skill 글의 중심 내용에 맞게 다음 표를 완성해 봅시다.

상황	1. 장소: __________의 __________ 2. 상황: 일부 사람들이 __________ __________을/를 __________
해결 방법	• Rhonda의 __________ 내용: "__________은/는 __________을/를 위한 __________ __________입니다. __________을/를 __________ 마세요."

1 Rhonda의 심경 변화로 가장 적절한 것은?

① happy → disappointed   ② lonely → pleased

③ disappointed → angry   ④ angry → pleased

⑤ shocked → moved

2 다음 밑줄 친 단어와 바꿔 쓸 수 있는 것을 글에서 찾아 한 단어로 쓰시오.

The dealer made us a <u>reasonable</u> offer for the house.

3 | Prediction | 글의 뒷부분을 추론하여 다음 빈칸에 적절한 단어를 글에서 찾아 쓰시오.

Rhonda was happy to see that two rolls came back. However, in the other bathroom with no note, no toilet paper came back until the cleaners brought more. Maybe she will put the same (1)______________ in the other (2)______________ of the share house, too.

직독직해 Skill 다음을 의미 단위로 끊어 읽고(/), 주어(S)와 동사(V)에 표시해 봅시다.

· She felt upset about the matter.

____

Words

share *n.* 공유, 몫 *v.* 공유하다, 나누다
toilet paper 화장지, 휴지
fair *a.* 공정한, 공평한
upset *a.* 화난
note *n.* 쪽지, 메모
shared *a.* 공유의
item *n.* 물건
change *n.* 변화 *v.* 변하다, 변화시키다
behavior *n.* 행동, 태도

Chapter 02

정보 파악하기

Reading Key · 필요한 정보 중심으로 빠르게 독해하기

A 정보 중심의 빠른 독해가 필요한 지문 ❶

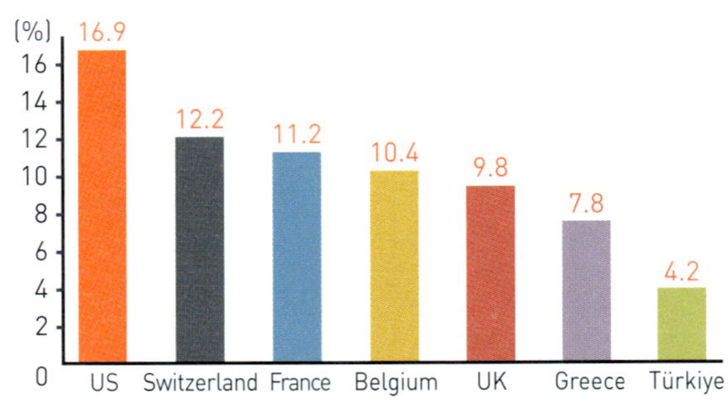

'할인합니다', '여행 서비스' 등의 **광고**나 **안내문**, 또는 **도표**를 다루는 문항에서는 글의 주제를 묻는 문제는 출제되지 않는다. 광고·안내문·도표와 같은 글에서는 글의 주제를 파악하기보다는, '무엇을, 언제 할인하는지', '어떤 여행 서비스를 제공하는지', '무엇이 증가(감소)했는지' 등의 핵심 정보를 빠르게 파악하는 것이 중요하다.

(기출 예제)

Summer Camp

Let's meet at Jeju Island. All middle school students are welcome!

· Dates: July 23 – 25

· Fee: $150 per person

· Activities: Hiking, Swimming, and Surfing

· Every student will receive a backpack.

For more information, please visit us at www.jejusummercamp.com.

□ __________ __________ 에 관해 안내/홍보하는 글

□ 장소, __________, __________, __________, 참가 기념품을 안내함

Words   fee *n.* 요금, 회비   receive *v.* 받다

어떤 **사물·동물에 대한 설명**이나 **인물의 일대기**에 관한 글 역시 다양한 정보로 이루어진 글로, 주제를 찾기보다는 주요 정보 중심으로 빠르게 독해하는 것이 좋다.

(기출 예제)

The addax is a kind of antelope. It lives in some areas in the Sahara Desert. It has twisted horns and short legs. There are only about 500 addaxes in the wild. The length of the addax is 150 – 170 centimeters. Males are slightly taller than females. The addax is mostly active at night because of the heat of the desert.

아닥스(addax)에 관한 설명 내용 완성하기

☐ 영양의 일종   ☐ 사는 곳: ___________

☐ 신체 특징: 나선형 뿔과 ___________ 다리   ☐ 야생 개체수: ___________

☐ 몸길이: ___________

☐ 기타 특징: 1. 수컷이 암컷보다 약간 더 큼

    2. ___________ : 밤에 활동

Words   antelope *n.* 영양 (사슴과 비슷한 동물)   twisted *a.* 꼬인, 비틀어진   length *n.* 길이   male *n.* 남자, 수컷
female *n.* 여자, 암컷

Earth Hour에 관한 다음 안내문의 내용과 일치하는 것은?

Earth Hour

Your ⓐ<u>small actions</u> can save our Earth!

The "lights off" moment began in 2007.

Switch off and ⓑ<u>give an hour for Earth</u>!

Saturday, March 25

ⓒ <u>Turn lights off</u> from 8:30 p.m. to 9:30 p.m.

Just 60 minutes? Yes, just one hour.

Every year, we ⓓ<u>get together</u> across the globe to celebrate Earth Hour and take one symbolic action: ⓔ<u>switch off</u> the lights just for an hour. But it is so much more than that.

It is a symbol of unity. It is a symbol of hope.

Let's show the power of collective action

for our future and planet!

If we are together, we can do more!

Join this event with your family, friends, and neighbors!

① 지구 온난화 해결을 위한 기금 마련을 목적으로 한다.
② 4년에 한 번씩 전 세계인들이 함께 기념한다.
③ 저녁에 한 시간 동안 불을 끄는 행사가 열린다.
④ 전 세계인의 화합을 위해 시작되었다.
⑤ 세계적으로 유명한 수집가들의 수집품들도 전시된다.

Mini Quiz

글을 읽으면서 글의 목적이 가장 잘 드러난 문장을 찾아 밑줄을 그어 봅시다.

Reading 비법

행사 공지글이나 안내문에서는 시간이나 장소 등의 정보를 나타내는 표현들에 유의한다.

Reading Skill 글의 중심 내용에 맞게 다음 표를 완성해 봅시다.

주요 내용	• ____________ ____________ 행사에 관한 안내와 홍보 • 행사 활동: __________ 동안 __________ 하기

1 밑줄 친 ⓐ~ⓔ 중 의미하는 것이 나머지와 <u>다른</u> 것은?

① ⓐ　　　② ⓑ　　　③ ⓒ　　　④ ⓓ　　　⑤ ⓔ

2 다음 문장에서 글의 내용과 일치하지 <u>않는</u> 부분을 찾아 바르게 고쳐 쓰시오.

The Global Lights Off event is held once a month for our Earth.

3 | Making a Poster | 다음 빈칸에 적절한 단어를 글에서 찾아 쓰시오.

Earth Hour

When?: (1) _______________________

Do What?: (2) _______________________

For What?: (3) _______________________

직독직해 Skill 다음을 의미 단위로 끊어 읽고 (/), 주어(S)와 동사(V)에 표시해 봅시다.

· Every year. we get together across the globe to celebrate Earth Hour and take one symbolic action.

READING 15

Naming Contest에 관한 다음 안내문의 내용과 일치하지 <u>않는</u> 것은?

Naming Contest

Show your passion and creativity.

Please create the best name.

The name is for <u>the study cafe</u> of our school.

This new space will open next year.

Only students can use this space.

Students can study alone or in groups.

Sometimes students can play here.

Any student in our school can take part in this contest.

We hope many of you will participate.

We will give great gifts to the winners.

You can submit names from October 1 to November 30.

How: Post a name with its meaning through a QR code.

Prize: 1st Place (1 person) – tablet

2nd Place (2 people) – earphones

3rd Place (3 people) – movie ticket

Announcement of Winners: December 7

① 새 학습 공간의 이름을 공모하는 대회이다.
② 이 학교 학생들은 누구나 참가할 수 있다.
③ 새 공간에서 학생들은 혼자서 또는 그룹으로 공부할 수 있다.
④ QR 코드를 통해서 작품을 게시하면 된다.
⑤ 수상자는 총 3명이다.

Mini Quiz

선택지를 먼저 읽고, 글을 읽으면서 각 선택지에 해당하는 문장에 밑줄을 그어 봅시다.

Reading 비법

특정 행사에 관한 안내문을 읽을 때는 행사 기간, 방법, 상품 등의 세부 정보를 주의 깊게 읽도록 한다.

Reading Skill 글의 중심 내용에 맞게 다음 표를 완성해 봅시다.

주요 내용	• __________ __________ 대회 안내 및 홍보 • 행사 활동: _______ _______의 _______의 _______ _______ 활동

1 밑줄 친 부분에 대해 글에서 언급된 것을 <u>모두</u> 고르면?

① 오픈 시기　　② 건축 재료　　③ 이용 대상
④ 면적　　　　⑤ 건축 비용

2 미나가 대회에 제출한 다음 내용을 보고 해당되는 내용을 간단히 우리말로 쓰시오.

제출자: ○미나
이름: 놀멍쉬멍공멍
제출일: 11월 20일

(1) 대회 안내문의 내용을 따르지 않은 것:

____

(2) (1)과 같이 답한 이유: _______________

____

3 | Q&A | 다음 빈칸에 적절한 단어를 글에서 찾아 쓰시오.

A: Hi, did you hear about the (1)______________ contest?
B: What's that?
A: It is a contest of (2)____________ a name for the new (3)____________ cafe of our school.
B: Wow, that sounds interesting! How can I submit a name?
A: You have to submit it through a (4)____________ code with its (5)____________. Don't forget to submit it by the last day of (6)____________.
B: Thank you very much!

직독직해 Skill 다음을 의미 단위로 끊어 읽고(/), 주어(S)와 동사(V)에 표시해 봅시다.

· We will give great gifts to the winners.

____

READING 16

다음 도표의 내용과 일치하지 <u>않는</u> 것은?　　　　　기출 응용

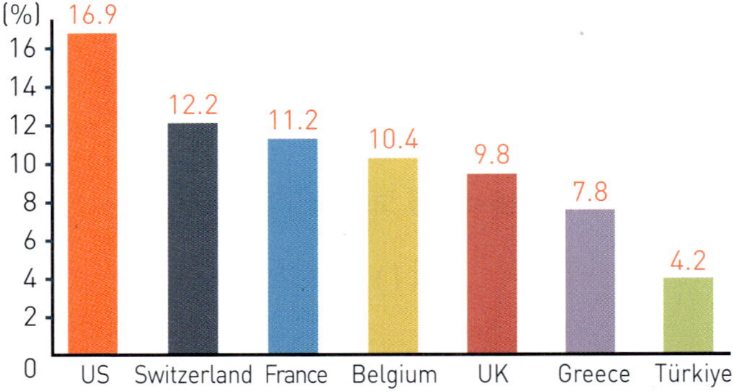

　　The graph above shows the percentage of GDP spent on health care in 2018. Which country spent the most among the countries shown? Which country spent the least among the countries shown? Is there a big difference between the countries? Let's look and compare. ① The US spent the highest percentage of GDP on health care among the countries shown. ② Switzerland spent 12.2 percent of its GDP on health care. That's less than the US. ③ France spent a higher percentage of its GDP on health care than Belgium. ④ Türkiye spent less than 5 percent of its GDP on health care. ⑤ The UK and Greece spent the same percentage of their GDP on health care. They also each spent more than 5 percent of their GDP on health care.

Mini Quiz

글을 읽으면서 무엇을 비교하는 도표인지 가장 잘 설명한 문장을 찾아 밑줄을 그어 봅시다.

Reading 비법

도표의 제목과 가로축, 세로축이 나타내고 있는 내용을 확인하면서 글을 읽는다.

Reading Skill

글의 중심 내용에 맞게 다음 표를 완성해 봅시다.

도표 내용	• 국가들의 __________ 대비 __________ 지출 비율
세부 정보	• __________ 년도 7개 국가 비교 : 미국, __________, __________, __________, __________, __________, __________

1 도표에서 언급된 내용으로 적절한 것은?

① GDP 대비 의료비 지출 비율
② 2018년 각 국가의 GDP
③ 국민들의 연간 병원 이용 횟수
④ 2018년 국가별 국민 행복 지수
⑤ 국가별·연도별 의료비 지출 증가액

2 도표와 일치하지 <u>않는</u> 단어를 찾아 바르게 고쳐 쓰시오.

(1) Belgium spent a lower percentage of its GDP on health care than Greece.
(2) Switzerland spent 1 percent less of its GDP on health care than France.
(3) Türkiye spent the highest percentage of its GDP on health care among the seven countries in 2018.

3 |Comparing| 다음 빈칸에 적절한 단어를 글에서 찾아 쓰시오.

Group 1: more than 10%	Group 2: more than 5% but less than 10%	Group 3: less than 5%
(1) The __________, __________, __________, and __________ spent more than 10 percent of their GDP each on health care in 2018.	(2) The __________ and __________ spent more than 5 percent but less than 10 percent of their GDP each on health care in 2018.	(3) __________ spent less than 5 percent of its GDP on health care in 2018.

직독직해 Skill 다음을 의미 단위로 끊어 읽고(/), 주어(S)와 동사(V)에 표시해 봅시다.

· France spent a higher percentage of its GDP on health care than Belgium.

READING 17

Benjamin Franklin에 관한 다음 글의 내용과 일치하지 <u>않는</u> 것은?

Benjamin Franklin is one of the most important people in American history. He was a publisher, author, inventor, and scientist. He was born in Boston on January 17, 1706. ⓐ<u>He</u> was the 15th of 17 children. His father made soap and candles. He got some formal education but he was mostly self-taught. At the age of 12, he started to work for ⓑ<u>his brother</u>'s newspaper. After ⓒ<u>he</u> worked for four years, he began to write his own stories. Instead of his real name, he wrote under a pen name, Mrs. Silence Dogood. People loved his stories. And they thought that ⓓ<u>the writer</u> might be a married woman. People never thought that ⓔ<u>she</u> was a 16-year-old boy!

① 미국 역사상 가장 중요한 인물 중 한 명이다.
② 1706년 1월 보스턴에서 태어났다.
③ 학교 교육도 받았지만 대부분 스스로 공부했다.
④ 형의 신문사에서 일하는 4년 동안 자신의 이야기를 썼다.
⑤ 글을 쓸 때 진짜 이름 대신 필명을 사용했다.

Mini Quiz

글을 읽으면서 선택지의 내용이 어느 문장에 해당하는지 밑줄을 그어 봅시다.

Reading 비법

인물에 관한 글은 인물에 대한 핵심 정보를 빠르게 파악하면서 글을 읽는다.

Reading Skill 글의 중심 내용에 맞게 다음 표를 완성해 봅시다.

대상	・이름: _______________	
정보	・출생일: _______________	・출생지: __________
	・가족 관계: _______________	・(모든) 직업: _______________

1 밑줄 친 ⓐ~ⓔ 중 가리키는 대상이 나머지와 <u>다른</u> 것은?

① ⓐ   ② ⓑ   ③ ⓒ   ④ ⓓ   ⑤ ⓔ

2 다음 빈칸에 적절한 단어를 글에서 찾아 쓰시오.

Mrs. Silence Dogood was a __________ __________ for Benjamin Franklin when he wrote his __________ __________.

3 | Summary Map | 다음 빈칸에 적절한 단어를 글에서 찾아 쓰시오.

All about Benjamin Franklin

Date of Birth:
(1) __________ __________, in
(2) __________

Place of Birth:
(3) __________ in the USA

Pen Name:
(4) __________

Q: What did he do at the age of 16?
A: He began to
(5) __________ his own
(6) __________.

Words

history *n.* 역사
publisher *n.* 출판업자
author *n.* 작가
inventor *n.* 발명가
scientist *n.* 과학자
formal *a.* 정식의, 정규의
education *n.* 교육
mostly *ad.* 주로, 대부분(의)
self-taught *a.* 독학의, 혼자 공부하는
age *n.* 나이, 연령
newspaper *n.* 신문, 신문사
own *a.* 자신의, 독자적인
pen name *n.* 필명
married *a.* 결혼한, 기혼의

직독직해 Skill 다음을 의미 단위로 끊어 읽고(/), 주어(S)와 동사(V)에 표시해 봅시다.

· At the age of 12, he started to work for his brother's newspaper.

READING 18

글을 읽으면서 중심 소재의 특성이 드러난 문장들을 찾아 밑줄을 그어 봅시다.

Sharks에 관한 다음 글의 내용과 일치하지 <u>않는</u> 것은?

Sharks live in all areas of the seas. We can see them in shallow water to the deep sea. Most sharks live 20 to 30 years, but some species can live far longer. Sharks have big, sharp teeth. ⓐWhile humans use their teeth to bite and chew food, sharks use their teeth to grab food and swallow it all at once. They eat ⁵ animals like fish or seals as well as other prey. For example, tiger sharks like to eat turtles. And blue sharks love squids. Most sharks have good eyesight. They have fantastic night vision and can see colors, too. The bodies of sharks have dark skin on top and light skin on the bottom. ⓑIt helps sharks to hide from threats. It can make hunting prey easier, too.

① 깊은 바다뿐만 아니라 얕은 바다에서도 산다.
② 대부분 20~30년 산다.
③ 이빨이 크고 날카롭다.
④ 사람과 달리 이빨을 음식을 잡는 데 사용한다.
⑤ 시력은 좋지만 색맹이라서 색상 구별은 할 수 없다.

Reading 비법

특정 동물에 대해서 설명하는 글은 해당 동물의 특징을 나타내는 세부 정보를 선택지와 비교하며 읽는 것이 효과적이다.

Reading Skill 글의 중심 내용에 맞게 다음 표를 완성해 봅시다.

대상	• ___________________

특징	• 수명: 대부분, _________년 ~ _________년
	• 신체 특징 – _________________ 이빨
	      – _________을/를 구별하며, 뛰어난 _________ 시력
	      – 위는 _________이고 아래는 _________ 몸통
	• 먹이: _________나 _________와 같은 동물

1 글의 밑줄 친 ⓐ<u>While</u>의 뜻으로 가장 적절한 것은?

① 잠깐   ② ~까지   ③ 반면에

④ ~하는 동안에   ⑤ ~에도 불구하고

2 밑줄 친 ⓑ<u>It</u>이 가리키는 것을 30자 이내의 우리말로 쓰시오.

It: ____

3 |Summary| 다음 빈칸에 적절한 단어를 글에서 찾아 쓰시오.

> **I Am a** (1)_______________
>
> · I live (2)_______________ to (3)_______________ years on average.
> · I live here and there, from (4)_______________ water to the (5)_______________ sea.
> · I grab animals like fish or seals for (6)_______________ with my teeth.
> · Thanks to my different top and bottom skin (7)_______________, I can hide from threats and hunt (8)_______________ easily.

Words

shark *n.* 상어
shallow *a.* 얕은
sharp *a.* 날카로운
teeth *n.* tooth(이빨)의 복수형
while *conj.* 반면에, ~하면서
bite *v.* 물다
chew *v.* 씹다
grab *v.* 잡다, 움켜쥐다
seal *n.* 물개
prey *n.* 먹이, 사냥감
eyesight *n.* 시력
night vision 야간 시력
bottom *n.* 아래
hide *v.* 숨다, 감추다
threat *n.* 위협(받는 상황(존재)), 위험

직독직해 Skill   다음을 의미 단위로 끊어 읽고(/), 주어(S)와 동사(V)에 표시해 봅시다.

· They eat animals like fish or seals as well as other prey.

____

READING 19

Elizabeth Catlett에 관한 다음 글의 내용과 일치하지 <u>않는</u> 것은? 기출 응용

Elizabeth Catlett was born in Washington, D.C., in 1915. Her grandparents were slaves. So she often heard the stories of slaves from her grandmother. A mostly white college turned Catlett down just because she was black. Instead, Catlett studied design and drawing at Howard University, a university for black students. She earned a master's degree in fine arts (MFA) at the University of Iowa. She became one of the first three students to earn an MFA at the university. Throughout her life, she created art. In her art, she showed the injustice or unfairness of society. She also showed the people who suffered from it. She received many prizes in the United States and Mexico. She spent over sixty years in Mexico. She became a Mexican citizen in 1962. Catlett died in 2012 at her home in Mexico.

① 할머니로부터 노예 이야기를 자주 들었다.
② 그녀가 흑인이라는 이유로 다니지 못한 학교도 있었다.
③ Iowa 대학교에서 석사 학위를 받았다.
④ 미국과 멕시코에서 많은 상을 받았다.
⑤ 병든 사람들을 표현하는 예술 작품 활동을 했다.

Mini Quiz

글을 읽으면서 인물의 직업에 대해 알 수 있는 문장을 찾아 밑줄을 그어 봅시다.

Reading 비법

인물에 대한 정보를 드러내는 장소나 시간, 사건 등을 표시하면서 읽는다.

Reading Skill 글의 중심 내용에 맞게 다음 표를 완성해 봅시다.

대상	• __________________________
정보	• 출생 연도와 출생지: __________, __________ • 두각을 나타낸 분야: __________ • 여생을 보낸 곳: __________ • 업적: 사회의 __________이나 __________을 다루는 __________ 활동

1 Elizabeth Catlett에 대해 글에서 언급되지 <u>않은</u> 것은?

① 출생지　　　　② 인종　　　　③ 전공 분야

④ 수상 작품 수　　　⑤ 사망 연도

2 다음 빈칸에 적절한 단어를 글에서 찾아 쓰시오. (단, 필요시 형태를 바꿀 것)

A mostly white college turned Catlett down just because she was black. Maybe she felt that it was u______________.

3 | Summary Map | 다음 빈칸에 적절한 단어를 글에서 찾아 쓰시오.

Elizabeth Catlett's Experience	Elizabeth Catlett as an Artist
· She often heard the stories of (1)______________ from her grandmother. · She was not allowed to enter a college because she was (2)______________.	· She created many works showing people who (3)______________ from social (4)______________ or (5)______________.

직독직해 Skill 다음을 의미 단위로 끊어 읽고(/), 주어(S)와 동사(V)에 표시해 봅시다.

· Instead, Catlett studied design and drawing at Howard University, a university for black students.

묘사된 분위기나 심경 파악하기

Reading Key 인물과 사건 중심으로 빠르게 읽기

Unit 08 분위기·심경 파악하기

인물과 사건 중심으로 빠르게 읽기

A 사건·일화나 상황을 묘사하는 글

즐겁고(joyful) 축제 분위기인(festive)

평화롭고(peaceful) 차분한(calm)

바쁘고(busy) 혼잡한(crowded)

사건이나 상황을 묘사하는 글은 나열식 구조이다. 주제가 있는 글이 아니므로, 한 가지 주제문을 찾기보다는 전반적인 글의 "분위기를 빠르게 파악하며" 읽어야 한다. 예를 들어 즐거운 운동회를 묘사하는 글은 활기찬 분위기를 전달한다.

기출 예제

The Chief said to Jane and Sam, "You're now married." As soon as the wedding ceremony was over, the celebration began. Young boys and girls began dancing to music. They danced in circles and made joyful sounds. Jane joined them. People started clapping and singing. Jane and Sam were two happy people.

> 상황 묘사 1: 족장이 Jane과 Sam의 __________ 을 선언했다.
> 상황 묘사 2: __________ __________ 가 시작되었다.
> 　　　　　　청년들과 아가씨들은 _________에 맞춰 원을 그리며 _________, _________
> 　　　　　　소리를 냈다. 사람들은 _________ 을 치며 노래하고, Jane과 Sam은 행복했다.
> ☐ 글 전반의 분위기: (joyful / scary)

Words chief *n.* 추장, 족장, 우두머리　　married *a.* 결혼한　　ceremony *n.* 의식　　celebration *n.* 기념(축하) 행사　　clap *v.* 손뼉을 치다

B 등장인물의 심경을 묘사하는 글

＋ 단서

wonderful   smile   the best

friendly   better

beautiful   cannot wait to

－ 단서

exhausted   pale

uneasy   terribly wrong

grief   terrible

사건이나 일화를 설명하는 글 중에서도 사건보다는 등장인물의 마음 상태, 즉 심경에 초점을 맞춘 글들이 있다. 이런 글 역시 주제를 찾기보다는 등장인물이 처한 상황과 그때 느꼈을 심경을 파악하며 읽어야 한다.

기출 예제

On the way home, Shirley saw a strange truck across the street. New neighbors! Shirley wanted to know about them. She ran to her father and joyfully asked, "Do you know anything about the new neighbors?" He said, "Yes. They have a girl just your age." How wonderful! She couldn't stop smiling. She and the new girl would become best friends.

단서: (1) Shirley는 새로운 ___________ 에 대해 알고 싶어 했다.

(2) 아빠에게 달려가서 ___________ 물었다.

(3) 그녀는 ___________ 가 멈추지 않았다.

☐ Shirley의 심경: (excited / bored)

Words　strange *a.* 낯선　　neighbor *n.* 이웃　　joyfully *ad.* 기쁘게, 기쁨에 차서

READING 20

글을 읽으면서 계절을 알 수 있는 문장들을 찾아 밑줄을 그어 봅시다.

다음 글의 분위기로 가장 적절한 것은?

ⓐ<u>A new season</u> is coming. There are no more ⓑ<u>biting</u> winds all around. No more chilly air. All the snow is melting away. Birds are singing happily. Their singing makes me open the window. I open the window and get some fresh air. Everything feels and seems new. Flower buds are about to bloom outside the window. It makes me keep smiling. Suddenly, I feel a strong wish to clean my own room and put a new blanket on the bed! A humming comes out of my mouth. Surprisingly, I see myself humming and dancing while cleaning! I didn't like to clean before! But now? I am no longer Grouchy from *The Smurfs*! You see, Grouchy always complains, but not me now! I am enjoying cleaning.

① dull and boring
② cheerful and lively
③ romantic and moving
④ lonely and gloomy
⑤ tense and frightening

Reading 비법

글의 분위기를 유추할 수 있는 동사, 형용사, 부사 등에 유의하여 읽는다.

Reading Skill

글의 중심 내용에 맞게 다음 표를 완성해 봅시다.

시기적 배경의 단서	• 새로운 __________이 오고 있다. • 더 이상 __________과 __________는 없다. • 눈이 __________ 있다.
심경의 단서	1. __________은/는 나를 __________ 한다. 2. __________은/는 나를 __________ 한다. 3. 그것들은 나를 청소를 하면서 __________ 한다.

1 밑줄 친 ⓐA new season이 의미하는 계절을 영어 단어로 쓰시오.

→ ___________________

2 밑줄 친 ⓑbiting의 의미로 가장 적절한 것은?

① mild   ② eatable   ③ freezing
④ hungry   ⑤ hot

3 | Past and Present | 다음 빈칸에 적절한 단어를 |보기|에서 골라 쓰시오.

| 보기 |

| hum   spring   Grouchy   winter   enjoy   hated |

	Before	Now
Season	(1) _____________	(4) _____________
Changes in My Attitude	(2) I _____________ cleaning.	(5) I _____________ cleaning.
	I was (3) _____________ from *The Smurfs*.	I (6) _____________ and dance while cleaning.

직독직해 Skill   다음을 의미 단위로 끊어 읽고(/), 주어(S)와 동사(V)에 표시해 봅시다.

• It makes me keep smiling.

____

Words

season *n.* 계절
no more 더 이상 ∼이 아니다
biting *a.* 살을 에는 듯한
melt *v.* 녹다
flower bud *n.* 꽃봉오리
be about to 막 ∼하려고 하다
bloom *v.* 꽃이 피다
suddenly *ad.* 갑자기
humming *n.* 콧노래, 흥얼거림
no longer 더 이상 ∼이 아니다
Grouchy *n.* 만화 '개구쟁이 스머프'의 투덜이 스머프
complain *v.* 불평하다
dull *a.* 지루한, 단조로운
boring *a.* 재미없는, 따분한
cheerful *a.* 쾌활한, 명랑한
lively *a.* 활기찬
romantic *a.* 낭만적인
moving *a.* 감동적인
lonely *a.* 외로운
gloomy *a.* 우울한
tense *a.* 긴장되는
frightening *a.* 무시무시한

READING 21

다음 글에 드러난 'They'의 심경으로 가장 적절한 것은?

They were very hungry for a month because there was little food to eat. They tried to hunt animals for food. But they were too poor at hunting. However, after starving for three days, Salva and the boys luckily got something to eat. While hunting, one of them caught ⓐ<u>a squirrel</u>. They gathered wood to build a fire. Then they roasted ⓑ<u>it</u> on the fire. None of ⓒ<u>this</u> took place silently. They couldn't hide the joy in their voices. It seemed that it was the best day!

"The fire needs to be bigger."

"It won't last long enough — we need more wood."

"Quick, turn ⓓ<u>it</u> over, it's burning!"

The juice of ⓔ<u>it</u> dripped and sizzled. The air was filled with a delicious smell.

① sad ② angry ③ doubtful
④ excited ⑤ disappointed

글을 읽으면서 등장인물들의 기분을 유추할 수 있는 문장을 찾아 밑줄을 그어 봅시다.

Reading 비법

등장인물의 심경 파악은 먼저 글의 상황을 파악해야 가능하다.

Reading Skill 글의 중심 내용에 맞게 다음 표를 완성해 봅시다.

등장인물	• __________ 와 __________
상황과 사건	• __________ 동안 __________________ • __________ 하는 동안 __________ 이 __________ 를 사냥함

1 밑줄 친 ⓐ~ⓔ 중 의미하는 대상이 나머지와 <u>다른</u> 것은?

① ⓐ　　　② ⓑ　　　③ ⓒ　　　④ ⓓ　　　⑤ ⓔ

2 다음 두 문장이 같은 뜻이 되도록 빈칸에 적절한 단어를 주어진 철자를 바르게 배열하여 쓰시오.

They couldn't hide the joy in their voices.
= They were ___________ .　f　j　l　o　u　y

3 | Summary | 다음 빈칸에 적절한 단어를 | 보기 |에서 골라 쓰시오. (단, 필요시 형태를 바꿔 쓸 것)

| 보기 |

build	delicious	happy

While hunting, a boy caught a squirrel. They (1)___________ a fire to cook it. They were very hungry but (2)___________. The (3)___________ smell spread through the air.

직독직해 Skill　다음을 의미 단위로 끊어 읽고(/), 주어(S)와 동사(V)에 표시해 봅시다.

· None of this took place silently.

____

Words

hunt *v.* 사냥하다
starve *v.* 굶다
luckily *ad.* 운좋게도
catch *v.* 잡다
squirrel *n.* 다람쥐
gather *v.* 모으다
wood *n.* 나무, 장작
build a fire 불을 지피다
roast *v.* 굽다
take place 일어나다
silently *ad.* 조용히
joy *n.* 즐거움, 기쁨
voice *n.* 목소리
need to ~할 필요가 있다
last *v.* 지속되다, 오래가다
quick *a.* 빠른 *ad.* 빨리
turn over 뒤집다
juice *n.* 즙, 육즙
drip *v.* 떨어지다
sizzle *v.* 지글지글 끓다
air *n.* 공기, 대기
delicious *a.* 맛있는
smell *n.* 냄새

READING 22

다음 글에 드러난 'I'의 심경 변화로 가장 적절한 것은?   기출 응용

  I was waiting for my mom to come back from the mall with a special present for me. I was pretty sure that I knew what <u>it</u> was. I was thrilled because I would soon have a new cell phone to communicate with! I really wanted to download cool apps. I was daydreaming about using all of the apps. I was imagining ⁵ playing games with my friends, too! However, my mom smiled and handed me a book. I flipped through the pages. I thought that maybe she had hidden my new phone inside the book. But I slowly realized that my present was not a new cell phone, just a little book. There was not a new cell phone inside the book! ¹⁰

① worried → upset   ② surprised → happy
③ ashamed → proud   ④ upset → satisfied
⑤ excited → disappointed

Mini Quiz

글을 읽으면서 등장인물의 심경 변화가 시작되는 문장을 찾아 밑줄을 그어 봅시다.

Reading 비법

심경 변화나 분위기의 변화를 나타내는 however나 but 등의 연결어에 주의하며 읽는다.

Reading Skill   글의 중심 내용에 맞게 다음 표를 완성해 봅시다.

심경 관련 단서	• 글쓴이(I)가 기다리는 것: __________이/가 __________ 것을 기다림
변화된 심경 관련 단서	• 현실: __________이/가 __________을 글쓴이(I)에게 전달함

1 밑줄 친 it의 기능 중 글에서 언급되지 <u>않은</u> 것을 <u>모두</u> 고르면?

① to communicate　　② to take a walk
③ to download cool apps　　④ to read books
⑤ to play games with friends

2 글의 내용과 일치하도록 다음 질문에 영어로 답하시오.

Q: Why did the writer flip through the pages?

A: ____

3 | Reading Flow | 다음 빈칸에 적절한 단어를 |보기|에서 골라 쓰시오.

┌ 보기 ─
ⓐ me　　ⓑ mom　　ⓒ little book　　ⓓ new cell phone
ⓔ present　　ⓕ communicate
└

I was waiting for my mom to come back home.

↓

I expected a (1)__________ from my mom as a special present.

↓

I was very thrilled because I could soon (2)__________ with it!

↓

Finally, my (3)__________ gave (4)__________ a present.

↓

I realized that my (5)__________ was a (6)__________.

직독직해 Skill 다음을 의미 단위로 끊어 읽고(/), 주어(S)와 동사(V)에 표시해 봅시다.

· I was pretty sure that I knew what it was.

____

Words

mall *n.* 쇼핑몰, 가게
present *n.* 선물
pretty *ad.* 매우, 꽤
be sure that ~을 확신하다
thrilled *a.* 매우 신이 난, 흥분한
soon *ad.* 곧
cool *a.* 멋진
hand *v.* 건네다
flip through 획획 넘기다, 훑어보다
inside *prep.* ~의 안에, 속에

글의 흐름 파악하기

글의 흐름을 파악하고 이어질 내용 예측하기

A 글의 흐름 파악

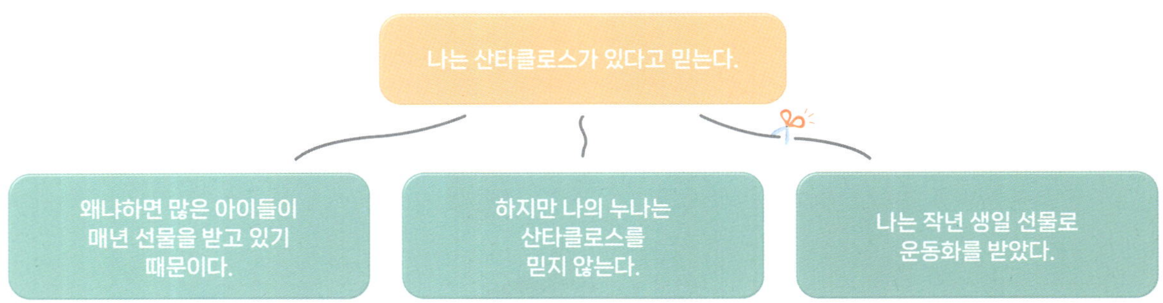

시험에 출제되는 지문은 짜임새가 잘 갖추어진 글들이다. 다양한 글이 있기에 첫 문장이 나온 후 그에 대한 이유가 이어질 수도, 예시가 이어질 수도, 반론이 이어질 수도 있지만 무관한 내용이 나올 수는 없다.

(기출 예제)

How can fish swim up and down smoothly? To rise to the surface, most fish use a swim bladder.

흐름상 이어지기에 <u>어색한</u> 내용은?

a. 물고기 부레의 작동 원리

b. 물고기가 수영을 잘하는 이유

c. 하지만 부레를 사용하지 않는 물고기도 있다는 반례

Words　surface *n.* 수면, 표면　　swim bladder 부레

B 이어질 내용 예측

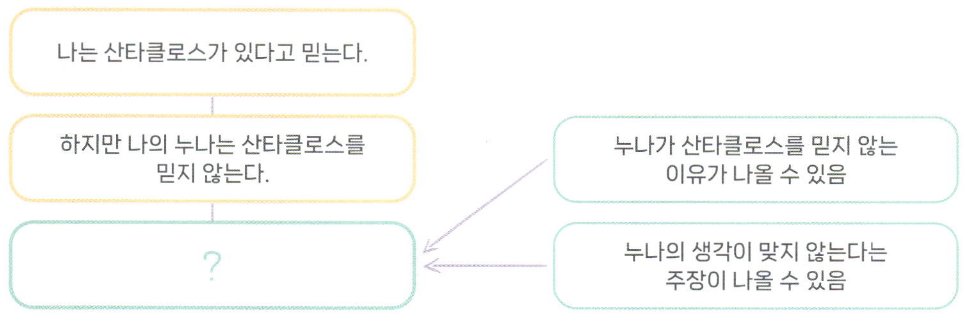

글의 흐름을 파악하는 것에 그치지 않고, 나아가 이어질 내용을 예측하며 적극적으로 읽는 것이 좋다.

기출 예제

Rivers seem to be ideal for natural boundaries between countries.

(A) For example, the Rio Grande has often shifted its course. And it causes problems in deciding the exact boundary.

(B) But river boundaries can change as rivers change course.

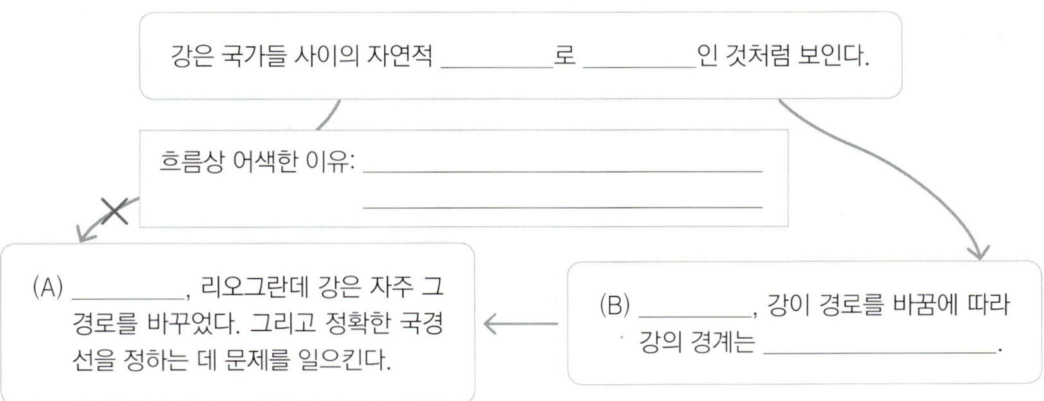

Words   seem *v.* 보이다, ~인 것 같다   ideal *a.* 이상적인   boundary *n.* 경계(선)   shift *v.* (방향을) 바꾸다   course *n.* 경로, 흐름, 수로(水路)

READING 23

주어진 글 다음에 이어질 글의 순서로 가장 적절한 것은?

> Reading books has many benefits. Interestingly, one of them is to reduce stress.

(A) Another study showed that just 30 minutes of reading can lower blood pressure. And it can slow down heart rate. Then worries or tensions may go away. Finally, you become relaxed. 5

(B) Besides, you can enjoy reading anywhere — at home, at the park, and at the library. Also, books do not cost that much. So let's step away from cell phones. Why not open the pages of a book instead?

(C) Some studies found that reading is a great way to reduce 10 stress levels, lowering them by 68%. It is more effective than listening to music (61%). It is also more effective than drinking tea (54%) or going for a walk (42%). And it is <u>far</u> more effective than playing video games (21%). 15

① (A) – (C) – (B)   ② (B) – (A) – (C)   ③ (B) – (C) – (A)
④ (C) – (A) – (B)   ⑤ (C) – (B) – (A)

Mini Quiz

글을 읽으면서 요지가 가장 잘 드러난 문장을 찾아 밑줄을 그어 봅시다.

Reading 비법

글을 읽으면서 글의 순서를 알 수 있는 단서를 찾는다. 예를 들어, another는 '또 다른', besides는 '게다가'라는 의미로, 이러한 단어들은 모두 주로 앞에서 언급된 것 외에 추가로 부연 설명할 때 사용된다.

Reading Skill 글의 중심 내용에 맞게 다음 표를 완성해 봅시다.

주제문	·__________이 많은 __________
근거문	· 근거 1: __________ 지수 – __________퍼센트까지 줄여 줌
	· 근거 2: 30분 독서 – __________과 __________를 낮춰 줌
	· 근거 3: 장소 – __________ 가능
	· 근거 4: 비용 – __________

1 글의 제목으로 가장 적절한 것은?

① How to Lower Blood Pressure
② The Most Effective Exercise for Health
③ Reducing the Costs of Reading Books
④ Many Different Activities to Help You Relax
⑤ Reading a Book: A Good Way to Reduce Stress

2 다음 밑줄 친 부분에 유의하여 두 문장이 같은 뜻이 되도록 빈칸에 적절한 단어를 쓰시오.

It is <u>far</u> more effective than playing video games (21%).
= It is ___________ more effective than playing video games (21%).

3 | Making a Graph | 다음 빈칸에 적절한 단어를 글에서 찾아 쓰시오.

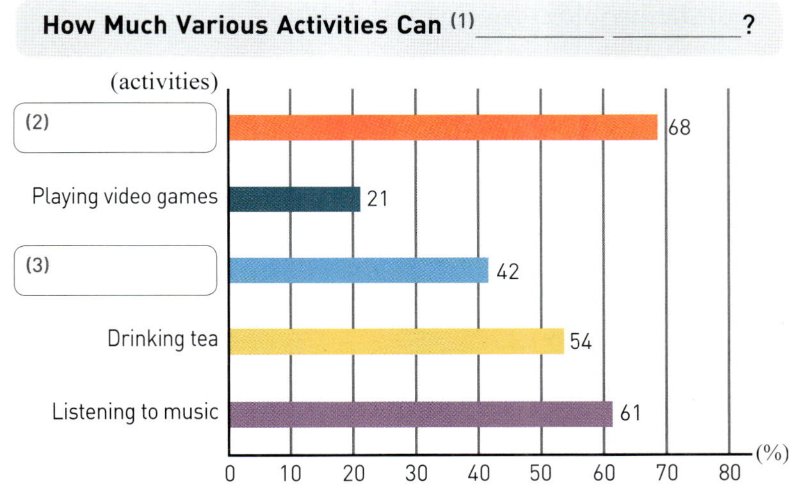

직독직해 Skill 다음을 의미 단위로 끊어 읽고(/), 주어(S)와 동사(V)에 표시해 봅시다.

· Besides, you can enjoy reading anywhere.

Words

benefit *n.* 이득, 이점
interestingly *ad.* 흥미롭게도
reduce *v.* 감소시키다
lower *v.* 낮추다
blood pressure 혈압
heart rate 심장 박동 수
tension *n.* 긴장, 긴장감
anywhere *ad.* 어디서나
cost *v.* 비용이 들다
step away from ~에서 멀어지다, 발을 떼다
find *v.* 알아내다
effective *a.* 효과적인
go for a walk 산책하다

READING 24

주어진 글 다음에 이어질 글의 순서로 가장 적절한 것은?

> A woman went to see a doctor. She said, "I have a problem. When I get into bed, I think that there is somebody under it. I look under the bed, then I think there is somebody on top of it. Top, under, top, under. I think I'm going crazy!"

(A) The doctor was shocked, "What did he do for you?" The woman said, "It was so simple. He told me to cut the legs of the bed. It was much cheaper than your suggestion."

(B) A few days later, they met on the street. "Why didn't you come to visit me again?" the doctor asked. The woman said, "Luckily, my problem disappeared. My brother helped me with the problem for just ten dollars."

(C) The doctor said, "Come to me for three months. Come here once a week and I will help you with your problem. It costs fifty dollars for a visit."

① (A) – (C) – (B)　　② (B) – (A) – (C)　　③ (B) – (C) – (A)
④ (C) – (A) – (B)　　⑤ (C) – (B) – (A)

Mini Quiz

글을 읽으면서 등장인물을 지칭하는 단어를 각각 찾아 밑줄을 그어 봅시다.

Reading 비법

글을 읽으면서 각 단락의 중심 내용을 파악한다.

Reading Skill

글의 중심 내용에 맞게 다음 표를 완성해 봅시다.

문제	· 여자는 __________와 아래에 누군가가 __________고 생각함
해결 방법	· 해결한 사람: __________________________________ · 방법: __________________________________

1 여자의 문제 해결에 소요된 비용으로 적절한 것은?

① 10달러　　② 50달러　　③ 200달러　　④ 300달러　　⑤ 1200달러

2 글의 밑줄 친 It이 가리키는 것을 10자 이내의 우리말로 간단히 정리하여 쓰시오.

It was much cheaper than your suggestion.

→ ____

Words

see a doctor 진료를 받다
crazy *a.* 미친, 제정신이 아닌
shocked *a.* 충격을 받은
cheap *a.* 가격이 싼
later *ad.* 후에, 나중에
visit *v.* 방문하다 *n.* 방문
disappear *v.* 사라지다
once a week 1주일에 1번씩

3 | Summary | 다음 빈칸에 적절한 단어를 글에서 찾아 쓰고 여자의 선택에 ✔표 하시오.

	Suggestions	Her Choice
The doctor	"(1) ____________ ____________ once a (2) ____________ for three months."	☐
Her brother	"Cut the (3) ____________ of the (4) ____________."	☐

직독직해 Skill 다음을 의미 단위로 끊어 읽고(/), 주어(S)와 동사(V)에 표시해 봅시다.

· I will help you with your problem.

____

READING 25

주어진 글 다음에 이어질 글의 순서로 가장 적절한 것은?   기출 응용

> We play most major sports activities with a ball. So, balls are very important in sports.

(A) A ball must have the correct size. Also, it must have the proper weight. However, if it is made of steel, it will be too stiff. Or, if it is made from foam rubber, it will be too soft.

(B) Ball sports have <u>some rules</u> about the balls used. They are rules about the characteristics of the balls, such as size or weight. The balls must have a certain stiffness, too.

(C) Similarly, along with stiffness, a ball needs a proper amount of bounce. A solid rubber ball would be too bouncy for most sports. And a solid clay ball would not bounce at all.

* stiffness: 단단함

① (A) − (C) − (B)   ② (B) − (A) − (C)   ③ (B) − (C) − (A)
④ (C) − (A) − (B)   ⑤ (C) − (B) − (A)

Mini Quiz

글을 읽으면서 글의 요지가 가장 잘 드러난 문장을 찾아 밑줄을 그어 봅시다.

Reading 비법

글 전체적으로 자주 등장하는 단어는 글의 핵심어인 경우가 많다.

Reading Skill   글의 중심 내용에 맞게 다음 표를 완성해 봅시다.

대상	• ______________________
점검 항목	• 1. __________ 2. __________ 3. __________ 4. __________

1 글의 밑줄 친 <u>some rules</u>에 해당되지 <u>않은</u> 것은?

① 정확한 크기　　② 적절한 무게　　③ 단단함의 정도
④ 특정한 색상　　⑤ 튕김의 정도

2 글의 내용과 일치하지 <u>않는</u> 부분을 찾아 바르게 고쳐 쓰시오.

If a ball were made of solid clay, it would bounce too high.

_______________ → _______________

3 ǀ Checklist ǀ 다음 빈칸 ⓐ~ⓖ에 적절한 단어를 ǀ보기ǀ에서 골라 쓰시오.

보기

hard　bounce　size　stiffness　bouncy　soft　weight

Rules about a Ball in Sports

☐ ____ⓐ____ : It must have the correct ____ⓐ____.
☐ ____ⓑ____ : It must be properly heavy or light.
☐ ____ⓒ____ : It must have a certain ____ⓒ____.
　ex A steel ball would be too ____ⓓ____.
　　A foam rubber ball would be too ____ⓔ____.
☐ ____ⓕ____ : It must have a proper amount of ____ⓕ____.
　ex A solid rubber ball would be too ____ⓖ____.

직독직해 Skill 다음을 의미 단위로 끊어 읽고(/), 주어(S)와 동사(V)에 표시해 봅시다.

· And a solid clay ball would not bounce at all.

____

Words

major *a.* 주요한, 중요한
correct *a.* 정확한, 올바른
proper *a.* 적절한, 알맞은
weight *n.* 무게
be made of ~로 만들어지다
steel *n.* 철
foam rubber 발포 고무
characteristic *n.* 특징
certain *a.* 특정한
amount *n.* 양
bounce *n.* 튕김 *v.* 튕기다
solid *a.* 단단한, 순수한(다른 물질이 섞이지 않은)
bouncy *a.* 튕기는, 튀어오르는
clay *n.* 점토, 흙

READING 26

글의 흐름으로 보아, 주어진 문장이 들어가기에 가장 적절한 곳은?

> However, you don't have to worry about that much.

Do you like alpacas? Alpacas live in South American countries like Chile or Peru. They have very soft hair. And they are famous for their cute faces and big bodies. But when you meet these animals, you should always be careful! They have bad habits, so they may spit at you. Why do they spit? (①) First, they want to show that they feel angry or upset. (②) Second, they want to protect themselves from danger. (③) In addition, their spit has a very bad smell because it includes the food they recently ate. (④) Alpacas are usually peaceful animals when they feel safe. (⑤) So, when you see some alpacas, you need to be kind to them.

Mini Quiz

글을 읽으면서 알파카의 긍정적인 면을 나타내는 단어에는 밑줄을 긋고 부정적인 면을 나타내는 단어에는 네모로 표시해 봅시다.

Reading 비법

특정 동물에 대해 설명하는 글에서는, 해당 동물의 특징을 주의 깊게 읽으면서 세부 정보를 파악해야 한다.

Reading Skill 글의 중심 내용에 맞게 다음 표를 완성해 봅시다.

대상	• _________________________
부정적인 면	• 나쁜 습관: __________을 __________
긍정적인 면	• 평소 성향: 대체로 __________

1 알파카에 관한 글의 내용과 일치하지 <u>않는</u> 것은?

① 칠레나 페루 등의 나라에 산다.
② 털은 아주 부드럽다.
③ 작은 몸과 귀여운 얼굴로 유명하다.
④ 기분이 나쁠 때 침을 뱉기도 한다.
⑤ 안전하다고 느낄 때는 평화로운 동물이다.

2 글의 내용과 일치하도록 다음 질문에 영어로 답하시오.

Q: Why does alpacas' spit have a bad smell?
A: It is because ________________________.

3 | Summary Map | 다음 빈칸에 적절한 단어를 | 보기 | 에서 골라 쓰시오.

| 보기 |

spitting   danger   habits   protect   feeling

Alpacas have bad (1)____________ **like** (2)____________.

Reason 1 They want to show their bad (3)____________.

Reason 2 They want to (4)____________ themselves from (5)____________.

직독직해 Skill 다음을 의미 단위로 끊어 읽고(/), 주어(S)와 동사(V)에 표시해 봅시다.

· Second. they want to protect themselves from danger.

READING 27

글의 흐름으로 보아, 주어진 문장이 들어가기에 가장 적절한 곳은?

> But I suggest that you find some water to drink first.

Imagine that you have to stay alone on a desert island. What would you do first? Maybe you would say, "Make an SOS sign," or "Find some food." (①) Water is the most important thing to help you survive. If you don't have enough water in your body, you will die, even in just three days. (②) For this reason, you must find water that is safe to drink. Here are some tips to help you find clean drinking water. (③) First, the water in streams or rivers is usually safe. But you should remember that it may still have some diseases in it. Second, save some rainwater because it is drinkable. (④) Third, there is some water in many foods, such as coconuts and fruit. (⑤) If you keep these tips in mind, you will be safer on a desert island.

Mini Quiz

글을 읽으면서 핵심어에 밑줄을 그어 봅시다.

Reading 비법

필자가 주장하고자 하는 내용은 I suggest that ~, 명령문, 조동사 must나 should 등의 표현에 드러난다.

Reading Skill 글의 중심 내용에 맞게 다음 표를 완성해 봅시다.

상황	• __________에서 __________________하는 상황
주장	• 가장 먼저 __________을/를 찾아라.

1 글에서 필자가 주장하는 바로 가장 적절한 것은?

① 무인도에 혼자 사는 것은 힘들다.

② 조난 시 구조 요청을 해야 한다.

③ 무인도에서는 안전한 물을 찾는 것이 중요하다.

④ 물에는 병균이 많아서 조심해야 한다.

⑤ 깨끗한 물을 찾는 것은 어렵다.

2 글의 내용과 일치하면 T, 일치하지 않으면 F에 표시하시오. 단, F인 경우에는 <u>틀린</u> 부분을 고쳐 바르게 다시 쓰시오.

(1) We need water to live and we would die, even in just three days, without it. [T/ F]

(2) Rainwater sometimes has diseases in it. [T/ F]

F인 경우: ________________________ → ________________________

3 | Q&A | 다음 빈칸에 적절한 단어를 글에서 찾아 쓰시오.

> **Q**: **How do you find clean water on a desert island?**

Tip 1 Find some water in (1)______________ or rivers.

Tip 2 Save some (2)______________.

Tip 3 Eat some (3)______________ like (4)______________ or fruit.

직독직해 Skill 다음을 의미 단위로 끊어 읽고(/), 주어(S)와 동사(V)에 표시해 봅시다.

· If you don't have enough water in your body, you will die, even in just three days.

____

Words

suggest *v.* 제안하다
imagine *v.* 상상하다
desert *a.* 사람이 살지 않는
n. 사막
survive *v.* 생존하다
even *ad.* 심지어
tip *n.* (실용적인) 조언
stream *n.* 개울, 시내
disease *n.* 질병
rainwater *n.* 빗물
drinkable *a.* 마실 수 있는
keep ~ in mind ~을 명심하다

READING 28

글의 흐름으로 보아, 주어진 문장이 들어가기에 가장 적절한 곳은?　기출 응용

> In the short term, using food in this way is effective.

When children are upset, what is a good way to calm them down? One easy and quick way is to give them some food. This helps them change their focus from being upset to something else. They will use their hands and mouth to do something else. (①) ⁵ So, they can forget the things they are angry about. (②) If you give them snacks, such as candy or chocolate, children will feel happier. (③) But, in the longer term, this can be harmful. (④) The children might think that they will get a snack if they show any negative emotions. (⑤) Then, when they feel bad, upset, or even bored, they will want some food to make themselves feel better.

Mini Quiz

글을 읽으면서 연결어에 밑줄을 그어 봅시다.

Reading 비법

핵심 내용을 담고 있지 않은 문장 중 앞뒤 문장과 흐름이 이어지지 않는 문장을 찾아야 한다.

Reading Skill

글의 중심 내용에 맞게 다음 표를 완성해 봅시다.

중심 소재	• 아이가 __________ 때 __________ 을 주는 것
단기적 효과	• 아이가 __________ 함
장기적 효과	• 아이가 __________________ 을/를 보이면 __________ 을 받는다고 생각함

1 글의 제목으로 가장 적절한 것은?

① Why Children Are Angry
② One Way to Calm Down Children
③ Children's Favorite Snacks
④ Good Foods to Make Children Happy
⑤ The Difficulty of Controlling Children's Emotions

2 밑줄 친 This가 의미하는 것을 다음 |조건|에 맞게 쓰시오.

┌─ 조건 ─
(1) 15글자 내외의 우리말로 쓸 것
(2) '~(는) 것'으로 끝나도록 할 것

this → ________________________________

3 | Summary | 다음 빈칸에 적절한 단어를 글에서 찾아 쓰시오.

When children are upset, giving them some (1)____________ is an effective way to calm them down. When children have some food, their focus changes from being (2)____________ to something else. Because they will use their hands and (3)____________. However, in the longer term, it can be (4)____________ because they might want to eat food to control their emotions.

직독직해 Skill 다음을 의미 단위로 끊어 읽고(/), 주어(S)와 동사(V)에 표시해 봅시다.

· The children might think that they will get a snack if they show any negative emotions.

____

다음 글에서 전체 흐름과 관계 없는 문장은?

Can you see any window or clock in a department store? You may not even think about this. Actually, there are no windows or clocks in most department stores. Why is this? It is a secret marketing skill. Windows and clocks make you think about the time. The department store wants people to enjoy shopping without thinking about the time. So, they use this way to make people focus on shopping. ① Also, department stores decorate or hang advertisements on their walls. ② Decorating the walls is hard because it is a big space. ③ If there are some clocks or windows on the walls, it is hard to use the walls. ④ This is the secret of department stores. ⑤ So, the next time you visit a department store, look around carefully. Does the store have windows, clocks, or advertisements on its walls?

Mini Quiz

글을 읽으면서 주제를 가장 잘 나타내는 문장을 찾아 밑줄을 그어 봅시다.

Reading 비법

글의 각 문장은 주제와 연결되어 있어야 한다. 만약 흐름을 찾는 문제에서 주제와 관련이 없어 보이는 문장이 있다면 그 문장을 빼고 읽으면서 앞뒤 문장이 매끄럽게 연결되는지 확인하도록 한다.

Reading Skill 글의 중심 내용에 맞게 다음 표를 완성해 봅시다.

중심 소재	• _________에서 _________와/과 _________을/를 볼 수 없는 이유
목적	• 사람들이 _________을/를 알지 못하게 하여 _________에 집중하도록 함 • 벽을 꾸미거나 _________을/를 전시하는 용도

1 글을 읽고 알 수 있는 것은?

① 백화점에서 볼 수 있는 것들
② 백화점에 시계가 없는 이유
③ 창밖을 보고 시간을 아는 방법
④ 백화점 광고가 다른 광고와 다른 점
⑤ 백화점에서 쇼핑하는 요령

Words

department store *n.* 백화점
marketing *n.* 마케팅
skill *n.* 기술
decorate *v.* 꾸미다, 장식하다
hang *v.* 걸다
advertisement *n.* 광고
look around 둘러보다
get attention 주의를 끌다

2 다음 빈칸에 공통으로 들어갈 적절한 단어를 글에서 찾아 쓰시오.

· Please _____________ your jacket up in the closet.
· May I _____________ up the phone?
· The teens _____________ around outside for a while.

3 | Summary | 글의 내용과 일치하지 <u>않는</u> 단어 2개를 찾아 바르게 고쳐 쓰시오.

In many department stores, there aren't any windows or clocks. As a marketing secret, the store wants to get our attention while we are shopping. We will enjoy our shopping without thinking about prices. They need to use their windows for decoration or to hang some advertisements there.

(1) _____________ → _____________
(2) _____________ → _____________

직독직해 Skill 다음을 의미 단위로 끊어 읽고(/), 주어(S)와 동사(V)에 표시해 봅시다.

· The department store wants people to enjoy shopping without thinking about the time.

____

다음 글에서 전체 흐름과 관계 없는 문장은?　　기출 응용

　Do you think a cup of coffee can help you wake up? Most studies show that caffeine helps you stay awake all day long. And even just 60mg of caffeine can make you react faster. Caffeine is also effective for relieving headaches when ⓐit is used together with medicine. However, caffeine cannot take the place of a good night's sleep. ① Having a good sleep is hard when you worry a lot. ② One study showed that caffeine can increase the chances of people with little sleep making mistakes. ③ Also, ⓑthey did not get higher scores on tests, even after having caffeine, than a group with enough sleep. ④ Therefore, using caffeine cannot fully make up for not having enough sleep. ⑤ To do your work better, you need sleep more than coffee.

Mini Quiz

글을 읽으면서 핵심이 되는 문장을 찾아 밑줄을 그어 봅시다.

Reading 비법

연결어 However, Also, Therefore 등은 앞 문장과 뒤 문장이 어떻게 연결되어 있는지를 잘 보여 주는 힌트가 된다.

Reading Skill　글의 중심 내용에 맞게 다음 표를 완성해 봅시다.

중심 내용	• ___________의 효과
부작용	• 연구 내용 1: _____________이/가 _________함 • 연구 내용 2: _____________을 취한 그룹보다 _________이/가 _________

1 글의 내용을 가장 바르게 이해한 학생은?

① Kevin: 역시 커피는 건강에 좋아.
② Judy: 시험 볼 때 커피를 마시면 실수를 줄일 수 있어.
③ Lucy: 두통약 대신 커피를 마셔야지.
④ James: 잠을 안 자고 커피를 마시면 안 되겠네.
⑤ Minsu: 커피를 마시면 불면증이 생길 거야.

2 밑줄 친 ⓐit과 ⓑthey가 각각 가리키는 것을 글에서 찾아 쓰시오.

ⓐ it: ___________

ⓑ they: the people ___________ ___________ ___________

Words

wake up 깨우다
awake *a.* 깨어 있는
react *v.* 반응하다
headache *n.* 두통
medicine *n.* 약
take the place of ~을 대신
하다
increase *v.* 늘리다, 증가시
키다
fully *ad.* 완전히
make up for 보충하다, 보상
하다

3 | Summary | 글의 내용과 일치하도록 각 네모 안에서 적절한 단어를 고르시오.

> Using caffeine is not the (1) | same / different | as having enough sleep. People having caffeine without enough sleep make (2) | less / more | mistakes and get (3) | lower / higher | scores.

직독직해 Skill 다음을 의미 단위로 끊어 읽고(/), 주어(S)와 동사(V)에 표시해 봅시다.

· Most studies show that caffeine helps you stay awake all day long.

____

내용 추론하기

Reading Key 글의 내용을 단서로 추론하기

A 글에 빈칸이 있는 경우

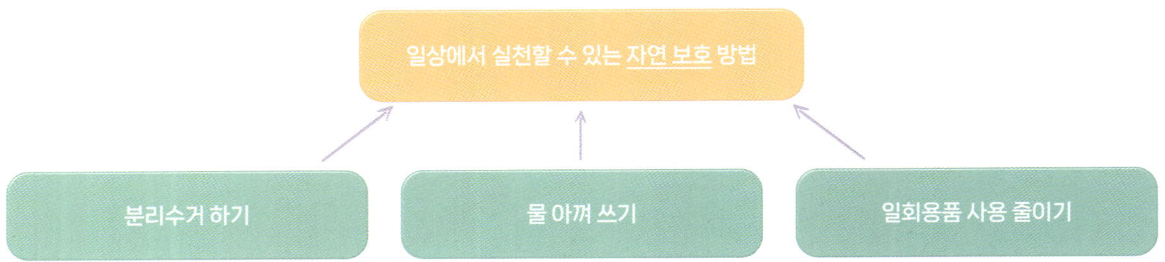

빈칸에 들어갈 말을 추론할 때는, 절대 글을 읽는 사람의 상식이나 생각대로 판단해서는 안 된다. 글의 주제에 맞게, 즉 글의 내용을 단서로 추론해야 한다.

기출 예제

Many communities have their own dance. They express ______________. For example, African people dance slowly. Spanish people dance fast. Scottish people dance together.

빈칸에 들어갈 말로 적절한 것은?

a. the dancers of the group

b. the identity of the group

c. the speed of the group

주제문	춤은 그 사회의 __________을/를 보여 준다.
세부적 내용	아프리카 사람들은 춤을 __________ 춘다. 스페인 사람들은 춤을 __________ 춘다. 스코틀랜드 사람들은 __________ 춤을 춘다.

Words   community *n.* 공동체, 지역 사회   express *v.* 표현하다   identity *n.* 정체성

B 추상적인 표현이 나온 경우

> 어머니는 내가 아기였을 때 사진을 보며 말씀하셨다.
>
> "시간이 정말 화살과 같구나."

추상적인 표현이 중간에 나오는 글들이 있다. 상황에 동떨어진 표현을 갑자기 사용하는 경우는 없으므로, 글의 전체적인 내용과 흐름을 살피면 추상적인 표현의 숨은 뜻을 추론해 낼 수 있다.

기출 예제

Kids learn mostly by example. They model their own behavior after their parents and their older siblings. So be a good role model to your kids. <u>Your actions speak louder than your words.</u>

아이들은 부모와 형제자매를 본받아 자신의 행동을 형성하므로, 아이들에게 좋은 __________가 되어라.

Your actions speak louder than your words.: 말보다 행동이 더 중요하다.
숨겨진 의미: 아이들에게 __________으로 본보기를 보여라.

Words   model after ~을 본받다   sibling *n.* 형제자매

31

다음 빈칸에 들어갈 말로 가장 적절한 것은?

Where does the trash go after you throw it away? You may think it will harm the earth. But, in the fashion field, trash can become new, fancy products thanks to creative thinking. It is a new kind of fashion, called 'upcycling'. The German company 'Freitag' makes bags from many pieces of waterproof cloth and safety belts. They need many pieces of cloth and belts to make their bags. Naturally, tons of trash is used. Their bags soon became famous because they are strong, waterproof, and eco-friendly. Also, all their bags in the world are different because each bag is made from many different types of cloth. This trend in the fashion field is not only unique, but also good for the ______________.

① safety   ② company   ③ environment

④ product   ⑤ creativity

Mini Quiz

글을 읽으면서 글의 중심 내용이 가장 잘 드러난 문장에 밑줄을 그어 봅시다.

Reading 비법

빈칸에 들어갈 단어는 글에 자주 나오는 핵심어가 무엇인지 파악하는 것이 중요하다.

Reading Skill

글의 중심 내용에 맞게 다음 표를 완성해 봅시다.

중심 내용	• ______________의 장점
근거 문장	1. ______________적 2. ______________적

1 Freitag에 관한 글의 내용과 일치하지 <u>않는</u> 것은?

① 가방 제조 회사이다.

② 방수천과 안전벨트 폐기물을 사용하여 제품을 만든다.

③ 제품을 만들면서 수 톤의 쓰레기가 수거된다.

④ 같은 디자인의 제품을 대량 생산한다.

⑤ 제품을 출시하자 곧 유명해졌다.

2 밑줄 친 부분이 의미하는 한 단어를 글에서 찾아 쓰시오.

This trend = _______________

3 ⌐Q&A⌐ 글의 내용과 일치하도록 다음 빈칸에 적절한 단어를 쓰시오.

> Q: What is upcycling?
> A: It is making new items from (1)_____________. With (2)_____________ thinking, unique and (3)_____________ items are made.

직독직해 Skill 다음을 의미 단위로 끊어 읽고(/), 주어(S)와 동사(V)에 표시해 봅시다.

· You may think it will harm the earth.

____

32

다음 빈칸에 들어갈 말로 가장 적절한 것은? 기출 응용

  One late evening in August of 1952, a man opened and closed the piano cover three times in a theater. He pressed the timer on the piano. And he did not press any keys for four minutes and thirty-three seconds. It seems strange, but it was John Cage's 4'33". It was a famous piece of music with only ____________. [5] Cage thought people could feel the music without the artist, so he removed the artist from the music. During the performance, the artist and composer could not make an impact on the music. Even Cage himself had no way to control the sounds in the theater. There was still real-life noise and people also had some feelings and thoughts. He wanted to show that all the things we feel can be music. [10]

① silence　　　② chorus　　　③ lyrics
④ laughing　　　⑤ humming

Reading 비법

빈칸은 글의 요지와 직접적 으로 관계된 경우가 많다. 특 히 빈칸이 글의 중간에 있을 경우 앞뒤 흐름을 이해하고 단서가 되는 단어를 찾아야 한다.

Reading Skill 주제문과 근거 문장을 찾아 다음 표를 완성해 봅시다.

주제문	• Cage는 사람들이 ________ 없이도 ________ 을/를 ________ 있다고 생각했다.
근거 문장	• 연주자는 ________ 동안 어떤 ________ 도 ________ 않았다. • Cage의 4'33″에서는 누구도 ________ 에 ________ 을/를 줄 수 없었다.

1 글의 제목으로 가장 적절한 것은?

① A Piece of Music Without an Artist
② How to Use a Timer Effectively
③ Good Manners in the Theater
④ Painful Noise for Humans
⑤ How to Feel Music

2 |보기|의 각 영영풀이가 나타내는 단어를 글에서 찾아 쓰시오.

> ─| 보기 |─
>
> (1) someone who writes music, in most cases, classical music
> (2) to take something or someone away from a place

(1) ＿＿＿＿＿＿＿ (2) ＿＿＿＿＿＿＿

3 | Q&A | 글의 내용과 일치하도록 다음 질문에 영어로 답하시오.

> Q: What is John Cage's 4'33"?
> A: It is music with (1)＿＿＿＿＿ and without an (2)＿＿＿＿＿.
> Q: What is the result of removing the (2)＿＿＿＿＿ from the music?
> A: People could have some feelings and thoughts in real-life (3)＿＿＿＿＿.
> Q: Could John Cage control the sounds in the theater during 4'33"?
> A: (4)＿＿＿＿＿, he had (4)＿＿＿＿＿ way to control the sounds.

Words

press *v.* 누르다
key *n.* (피아노) 건반
piece *n.* 작품, 곡
artist *n.* 연주자
remove *v.* 제거하다
performance *n.* 공연
composer *n.* 작곡가
make an impact on ~에 영향을 주다
control *v.* 제어하다, 통제하다
real-life *a.* 실제의, 현실의
noise *n.* 소음

직독직해 Skill 다음을 의미 단위로 끊어 읽고(/), 주어(S)와 동사(V)에 표시해 봅시다.

· During the performance, the artist and composer could not make an impact on the music.

READING 33

다음 빈칸에 들어갈 말로 가장 적절한 것은?

YouTube Shorts, TikToks, or Instagram reels. You might watch these kinds of videos. They are all "short-form media." Short-form media has content which is under 10 minutes or under 1,000 words. People become familiar with these short videos because they can get information easily and quickly. With the rise of short-form media, people are turning away from long-form media like books and movies. They _______________ and don't want to know the full content. A study by Microsoft shows that short-form media decreased the attention time of teenagers. In just a few years, it became 8 seconds from over 10 seconds. This is a serious problem, because 8 seconds is shorter than <u>that</u> of a goldfish. In school, students also have difficulty focusing on their classes. Short videos have both good and bad points: They provide quick information but also decrease students' attention time.

① want to get attention ② like reading a lot of books
③ already know the content ④ focus on long-form media
⑤ lose their focus quickly

Mini Quiz
글을 읽으면서 주제문과 근거 문장을 찾아 밑줄을 그어 봅시다.

Reading 비법
빈칸은 보통 주제문과 연결 지어서 유추할 수 있는 경우가 많기 때문에 전체를 포괄하는 주제문을 먼저 찾아야 한다.

Reading Skill 주제문과 근거 문장을 찾아 다음 표를 완성해 봅시다.

주제문	• _________ 미디어의 장단점: _____________와 _________ 시간
근거문	• 장점: 쉽고 _________ 얻을 수 있는 _________ • 단점: _________________________________

1 글을 읽고 알 수 있는 내용이 <u>아닌</u> 것은?

① 쇼트폼(short-form) 미디어의 예시
② 쇼트폼(short-form) 미디어에 익숙해진 이유
③ 롱폼(long-form) 미디어의 문제점
④ 십 대들이 집중할 수 있는 시간
⑤ 쇼트폼(short-form) 미디어가 학생에게 미치는 영향

2 밑줄 친 부분이 가리키는 것을 여섯 자 이내의 우리말로 쓰시오.

that → ______________

3 | Summary Map | 다음 빈칸에 적절한 단어를 글에서 찾아 쓰시오.

Short-Form Media	
Definition	content under (1)______________ minutes or under (2)__________ words
Examples	YouTube Shorts, TikToks, or Instagram reels *cf.* examples of long-term media : (3)__________ and (4)__________
Good Point	We can get (5)__________ easily and quickly.
Bad Point	People do not want to know the full (6)__________. Students show short (7)__________ time.

Words

content *n.* 내용, 콘텐츠
familiar *a.* 익숙한
information *n.* 정보
rise *n.* 출현, 상승
turn away from ~을 외면하다
decrease *v.* 감소시키다, 줄이다
attention *n.* 집중
serious *a.* 심각한
goldfish *n.* 금붕어

직독직해 Skill 다음을 의미 단위로 끊어 읽고(/), 주어(S)와 동사(V)에 표시해 봅시다.

· In school, students also have difficulty focusing on their classes.

____

34

다음 빈칸에 들어갈 말로 가장 적절한 것은? 기출 응용

When children become four years old, they start to ___________. For example, you can ask a four-year-old girl, "What is inside the package of gum?" ⓐ<u>She</u> will say, "Gum." You open the package and show her what's inside. There is a pencil inside. Then, you ask her, "What will your mom think is inside?" Her mom is waiting outside the room, so ⓑ<u>she</u> cannot see what's inside. Still, the girl will say, "Gum." It is because she knows her mother did not see the pencil inside. But children under four will say, "Pencil" in the same example. They cannot imagine their mom did not see inside. They do not know someone needs to see inside to know what is in there. So, they think everyone thinks the same way as they do.

① express their needs
② share their things with others
③ give a name to each object
④ understand other people's thinking
⑤ understand the happiness of learning

Mini Quiz

글을 읽으면서 네 살 미만의 아이들이 생각하는 방식에 밑줄을 그어 봅시다.

Reading 비법

빈칸이 속한 문장을 유심히 읽고 관련된 내용을 찾아야 한다. 특히 빈칸이 가장 첫 문장이나 마지막 문장에 있는 경우 주제문일 확률이 높다.

Reading Skill 글의 중심 내용에 맞게 다음 표를 완성해 봅시다.

껌 통 안에 무엇이 있을지에 대한 질문	
4세 이상 어린이	1번째 대답(__________의 생각) : __________ 2번째 대답(엄마의 생각 추론) : __________
4세 미만 어린이	1번째 대답(__________의 생각) : __________ 2번째 대답(엄마의 생각 추론) : __________

1 다음 각각의 빈칸에 들어갈 말이 순서대로 바르게 짝지어진 것은?

> Children __________ the age of four cannot yet __________ a world beyond their own reality.

① over ······ understand ② over ······ misunderstand
③ under ······ imagine ④ under ······ misunderstand
⑤ who are ······ discover

Words

package *n.* (껌 등의) 통
gum *n.* 껌
reality *n.* 현실
misunderstand *v.* 오해하다

2 글의 밑줄 친 ⓐ와 ⓑ가 각각 가리키는 것을 우리말로 간단히 쓰시오.

ⓐ: __________________   ⓑ: __________________

3 | Summary Map | 다음 |보기|에서 알맞은 말을 골라 예시로 제시된 상황과 그 결과를 정리한 표를 완성하시오.

| 보기 |

> Pencil　　Gum　　mom　　package　　thinking

Condition	1. Show the inside of a gum (1)__________ with a pencil inside. 2. Ask two groups of children, "What will your mom think is inside?"
Result	Four-Year-Old Kids
	Under-Four-Year-Old Kids

Result	Four-Year-Old Kids	They answered "(2)__________" because they know their (3)__________ didn't see the inside of the package.
	Under-Four-Year-Old Kids	They answered "(4)__________" because they cannot understand other people's (5)__________.

직독직해 Skill

다음을 의미 단위로 끊어 읽고(/), 주어(S)와 동사(V)에 표시해 봅시다.

· It is because she knows her mother did not see the pencil inside.

글을 읽으면서 주제문과 해당 예
시문에 밑줄을 그어 봅시다.

READING 35

밑줄 친 a red light가 다음 글에서 의미하는 바로 가장 적절한 것은?

Imagine that you are late for school. But all the traffic lights you meet are red. You may think, "Anything that can go wrong will go wrong." This idea is called Murphy's Law. However, some scientists say that we don't have to think so negatively. They say that the reason for the way we think is selective memory. Our brains cannot remember all the things we did. Only strong memories remain in the brain, so we remember a failure or bad things much more than positive things. For example, our brain does not focus on crossing the street easily when there is a green light. But, at <u>a red light</u>, we should stop and wait for a few minutes. This small difference makes us think we meet more red lights than green lights. If this thinking is repeated often, we mostly remember the bad things and finally think that we always fail.

① small differences
② negative thinking
③ positive sign to keep safe
④ remembering things selectively
⑤ bad things we remember strongly

Reading 비법

밑줄 친 부분의 문자적인 의
미가 아닌 글의 전체적인 내
용 속에서 밑줄 친 부분의 함
축적인 의미를 찾아야 한다.
밑줄 친 부분은 글의 요지와
연관된 경우가 많으므로 전체
적인 주제를 파악해야 한다.

Reading Skill 주제문과 예시 문장을 찾아 다음 표를 완성해 봅시다.

주제문	• __________(이)나 __________ 일이 더 강력해서 뇌가 더 잘 __________하는 것을 __________ __________(이)라고 한다.
예시문	• __________은/는 __________ 신호등에서 길을 건너는 것은 __________ 않는다. • __________은/는 __________ 신호등에서 몇 분 __________ 것을 더욱 기억한다.

1 글의 제목으로 가장 적절한 것은?

① Traffic Lights: How to Cross the Street Safely
② Murphy's Law: The Result of Selective Memories
③ Negative Thinking Makes Us Fail
④ The Secret of Memory: Trying to Remember All Things
⑤ Late for School: A Bad Habit

Words

traffic light 신호등
go wrong 잘못되다
law *n.* 법, 법칙
negatively *ad.* 부정적으로
selective *a.* 선택적인
memory *n.* 기억
remain *v.* 남다, 남아 있다
positive *a.* 긍정적인
cross *v.* 건너다
repeat *v.* 반복하다

2 글의 내용과 일치하도록 다음 질문에 영어로 답하시오.

Q: Why do we think we will always fail?
A: It's because we _________ only the _________ _________.

3 | Comparing | 다음 빈칸에 적절한 단어를 |보기|에서 골라 쓰시오.

보기

| remember | focus | green | bad | red | failure |

An Example of Good Memory

Our brain does not ___ⓐ___ on crossing the street easily at a ___ⓑ___ light.

Selective Memory

We mostly remember ___ⓒ___ things or a ___ⓓ___.

An Example of Bad Memory

Our brain ___ⓔ___ bad things longer when we should stop at a ___ⓕ___ light.

직독직해 Skill 다음을 의미 단위로 끊어 읽고(/), 주어(S)와 동사(V)에 표시해 봅시다.

• Only strong memories remain in the brain.

READING 36

밑줄 친 by reading a body language dictionary가 다음 글에서 의미하는 바로 가장 적절한 것은?

기출 응용

When we talk to people, we also use our body language. Some people think body language is like a dictionary. They use body language like a set of rules. With this dictionary approach, they cannot find the many sides of social understanding. They might see someone with their arms crossed and think they're angry, or 5 see someone smiling and think they're happy. But when people communicate by just memorizing certain signals, they cannot see the bigger picture. It's more complicated than that. Trying to use body language <u>by reading a body language dictionary</u> is like trying to speak French by reading a French dictionary. Our body language might be thought of as robotic and confusing if we don't use it naturally.

① with an expert's help
② by comparing body language and learning French
③ by learning body language in a social context
④ without understanding its social meaning
⑤ in the way people learn their native language

Mini Quiz

2행에 있는 like a dictionary 와 관련된 단어와 표현에 밑줄을 그어 봅시다.

Reading 비법

글 전체에서 반복적으로 제시되는 어구를 통해 글의 중심 소재를 파악해야 한다.

Reading Skill 글의 중심 내용에 맞게 다음 표를 완성해 봅시다.

중심 내용	• __________ 사용시의 유의점
근거 문장	• __________을/를 __________하여 의사소통하는 것은 __________을/를 보지 못하는 것

1 글에서 필자가 주장하는 바로 가장 적절한 것은?

① 몸짓 언어도 외국어처럼 꾸준히 배워야 한다.

② 나라마다 다양한 몸짓 언어를 가지고 있다.

③ 몸짓 언어를 사용할 때 사회적 맥락을 고려해야 한다.

④ 몸짓 언어 사전을 통해 다양한 몸짓 언어를 알 수 있다.

⑤ 팔짱을 낀 사람들은 대부분 화난 것이다.

2 글의 내용과 일치하도록 다음 빈칸에 적절한 단어를 쓰시오.

> Effective body language includes more than the total of each signal, and we can find the many sides of __________ __________ in it.

Words

body language 몸짓 언어
approach *n.* 접근
social *a.* 사회적인
crossed *a.* 교차한
memorize *v.* 암기하다, 기억하다
signal *n.* 신호
complicated *a.* 복잡한
robotic *a.* 로봇 같은
confusing *a.* 혼란스러운
naturally *ad.* 자연스럽게
expert *n.* 전문가
total *n.* 합계, 전체

3 | Summary Map | 다음 빈칸에 적절한 단어를 |보기|에서 골라 쓰시오.

┌ 보기 ┐
| robotic | communicate | memorizing | picture |

Meaning of the 'Dictionary Approach'	to (1)__________ by just (2)__________ each body language signal
Effects of the 'Dictionary Approach'	1. We cannot see the bigger (3)__________. 2. Our body language might be thought of as (4)__________, so people may be confused.

직독직해 Skill 다음을 의미 단위로 끊어 읽고(/), 주어(S)와 동사(V)에 표시해 봅시다.

· They might see someone with their arms crossed and think they're angry.

____

긴 글 독해하기

Reading Key 긴 글의 구조 파악하기

A 주제와 부연 설명 구별하기

반려동물을 키우는 것은 쉽게 활용 가능한 건강 대책이다.

주제 부분은
자세히 읽기

- 반려동물 주인들은 더 낮은 혈압, 심장병 위험 감소, 더 낮은 스트레스를 나타낸다.
- 또한 직장에서도 동물은 이점이 될 수 있다.
- 직장인들의 스트레스 수치가 더 낮아진다.
- 직업 만족도와 직장 분위기에 긍정적인 영향을 미친다.

부연 설명/예시는
빠르게 읽기

글이 길수록 예시나 부연 설명이 반드시 들어 있으므로 이에 유의하여 주제에 집중해야 한다. 모든 내용이 다 중요한 것이 아니기 때문에 부연 설명과 핵심을 구별하고, 중심 내용에 집중하며 읽는 것이 좋다.

기출 예제

Scientists in Germany did an interesting experiment. They found that hearing scary warnings like "This is going to hurt" before a shot can make us feel pain even before the needle touches our skin! The scientists used a special machine to look at people's brains and found that when people hear words that mean something painful is coming, the part of their brain that feels pain becomes really active.

This shows that words really do matter. When we hear or say negative or painful words, our brains start to feel that pain. But don't worry. We can control our own health by changing the way we talk to ourselves! If we think positive thoughts, say positive words, and hang out with positive people, our bodies will feel better. We might even have lower blood pressure and stress hormones! So let's choose our words wisely and try to think positively all the time!

Words experiment *n.* 실험　　scary *a.* 무서운, 겁나는　　warning *n.* 경고, 주의　　shot *n.* 주사 (한 대)　　needle *n.* (주사) 바늘, 침

세부 내용	• 실험 결과 – "이거 아플 거예요"라는 말을 들으면 주사 바늘이 피부에 닿기도 전에 __________을/를 느낀다. – __________은/는 중요하다. – __________ 또는 __________ 말을 들으면 뇌가 고통을 느끼기 시작한다. – 자신에게 말하는 방식의 변화를 통해 __________을/를 제어할 수 있다. – __________ 생각과 말을 하고 __________ 사람들과 어울리면 더 건강해질 수 있다.
주제문	우리의 말을 __________ 선택하고 항상 __________ 생각하도록 노력하자.

B 시간 순서에 따른 흐름 이해하기

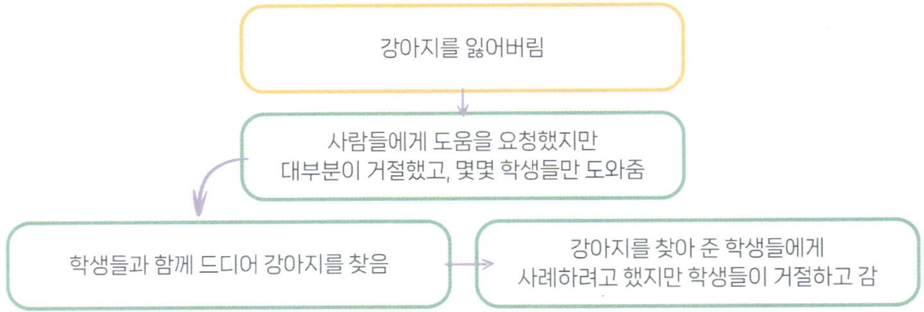

긴 글 일화는 사건 전개 또는 시간 순서대로 흐름을 이해한다. 이와 같은 글은 시간의 흐름이나 사건의 전개에 따라 단락의 순서를 쉽게 파악할 수 있을 정도로 그 흐름이 명확하다.

기출 예제

Tim Burke was a talented baseball player who dreamed of playing professionally from a young age. He worked hard to make his dream come true and played for the Montreal Expos. Although Tim loved playing baseball, he loved his family even more. Tim and his wife wanted to have children but found out they couldn't. So they decided to adopt children who needed a home. They adopted four children with special needs from different countries. Tim was a loving father who wanted to give his children the best life possible.

(A) So Tim made the difficult decision to stop playing baseball, even though he had worked so hard to become a professional player. He wanted to spend more time with his family and be the best father and husband he could be. Tim knew that his family was the most important thing to him, and he was happy to make this decision.

Words talented *a.* (타고난) 재능이 있는   professionally *ad.* 직업적으로   come true 이루어지다, 실현되다   adopt *v.* 입양하다
special needs 특수 교육   possible *a.* 가능한   professional player 프로 선수, 직업 선수   decision *n.* 결정

(B) But Tim's job as a baseball player meant he had to travel a lot. He had to travel to different cities and countries to play games, sometimes spending long periods away from home. This made it difficult for him to spend as much time with his family as he wanted.

(C) One day, a reporter asked Tim why he was quitting baseball. Tim replied that although he loved playing baseball, his family needed him more. He wanted to be there for his kids and his wife, and he knew he couldn't do that if he kept playing baseball.

Tim Burke는 노력하여 프로 야구선수의 ___________을 이뤘지만 아이가 있는 가정을 이루고 싶어서 특수 교육이 필요한 4명의 아이를 해외 ___________함

(A) Tim은 가족과 더 많은 시간을 보내고 좋은 아버지와 남편이 되고 싶어서 야구를 ___________ 하기로 어렵게 결정함

(B) Tim은 원정 경기를 다녀야 했기 때문에 좋은 아버지와 남편이 되기 어려움을 느낌

(C) (은퇴의 이유를 질문 받자,) Tim은 야구하는 것을 사랑하지만, ___________이 자신을 훨씬 더 필요로 한다고 대답함

올바른 순서: ___________ — ___________ — ___________

다음 글을 읽고, 물음에 답하시오.

What is an important thing in ⓐ<u>learning</u> something? High IQ? A good teacher? Enough study time? They are all ⓑ<u>related</u>. But a learning style gives you an answer to how you can learn best. To find your own learning style, there is a simple question. If you want to learn how to play a new board game, what will you do? First, you can read the manual carefully and take notes. Second, you can listen to others' explanations and ask questions. Third, you can watch others play and try it yourself. Your own actions can show your learning style.

There are three types of learning styles. The first type is visual learning. People with a visual learning style learn by reading and taking notes. For them, drawing a diagram or pictures is ⓒ<u>helpful</u> for learning. The second type of people focuses on sounds. They learn through hearing and saying something. So, reading the text aloud can be a good way for them to learn something. The last type of person uses their body. They learn by ⓓ<u>moving</u> their body. They can use role-plays to learn something. Every student uses their own learning style to learn. Knowing one's own learning style helps the student learn more ⓔ<u>ineffectively</u>. So, understand how you learn and use it as much as possible!

1 윗글의 제목으로 가장 적절한 것은?

① Moving the Body to Lose Weight
② A Good Teacher Makes a Good Student
③ Drawing Diagrams as a Learning Strategy
④ A Simple Question: Are You Good at Studying?
⑤ A Good Answer to How to Learn: Know Your Learning Style

2 밑줄 친 ⓐ ~ ⓔ 중에서 문맥상 낱말의 쓰임이 적절하지 <u>않은</u> 것은?

① ⓐ   ② ⓑ   ③ ⓒ   ④ ⓓ   ⑤ ⓔ

Words
related *a.* (~에) 관련된
manual *n.* 설명서
explanation *n.* 설명
visual *a.* 시각의
diagram *n.* 도표
role-play 역할극
ineffectively *ad.* 비효율적으로, 헛되게

3 글의 내용과 일치하도록 다음 빈칸에 적절한 단어를 글에서 찾아 쓰시오.

Your own actions in learning something can show your ___________ ___________.

4 | Summary Map | 다음 도표의 각 유형에 맞는 내용을 |보기|에서 골라 네모에 기호를 쓰시오.

Three Types of Learning Styles

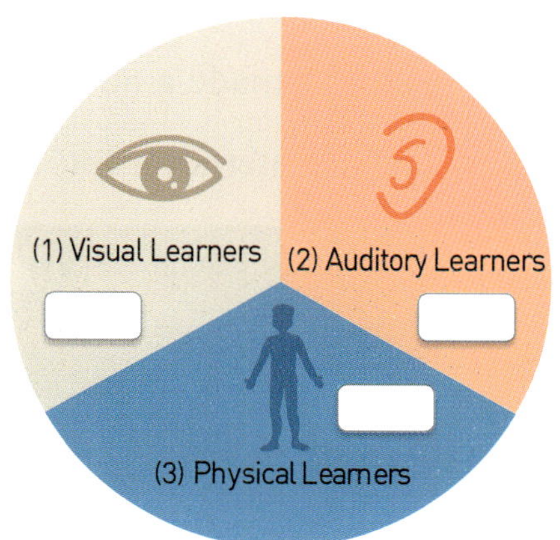

| 보기 |
a. to use charts and diagrams
b. to use role-plays
c. to use listening
d. to read aloud
e. to take notes
f. to say something
g. to use pictures
h. to do it oneself

Reading Skill 글의 주제문을 찾아 다음 표를 완성해 봅시다.

| 주제문 | • 여러분의 ___________ ___________을/를 아는 것은 효과적인 ___________에 중요하다. |

Reading 비법
글의 제목을 묻는 문제의 답을 찾기 위해서는 전체를 포괄하는 주제문을 찾는 것이 중요하다.

직독직해 Skill 다음을 의미 단위로 끊어 읽고(/), 주어(**S**)와 동사(**V**)에 표시해 봅시다.

• But a learning style gives you an answer to how you can learn best.

다음 글을 읽고, 물음에 답하시오.

Is hacking always bad? There are good hackers, white hat hackers. They use their hacking skills to find some problems with ⓐ<u>security</u>. They are different from black hat hackers. They follow the law when they hack. The name "white hat" hacker is from old American movies about the country's "Wild West" days. Heroes in those movies wore white hats, and the ⓑ<u>bad</u> guys wore black hats. So, today's good hackers became 'white hat' hackers.

Marc Maiffret is one of the famous white hat hackers. He found a big ⓒ<u>weak</u> point in Microsoft software. Because of this problem, black hat hackers could get into the software and steal its data. But he helped Microsoft ⓓ<u>solve</u> the problem. He made a new program to ⓔ<u>attack</u> the software. Since we use the Internet a lot, a white hat hacker like Maiffret plays an important role in protecting our personal information.

Mini Quiz

글을 읽으면서 중심 소재를 찾아 밑줄을 긋고, 중심 소재에 대해서 어떤 정보들이 있는지 파악해 봅시다.

1 윗글의 제목으로 가장 적절한 것은?

① How to Become a Hacker
② Marc Maiffret, Our Hero
③ Why Are Black Hat Hackers Famous?
④ The White Hat Hacker: The Protector of Software
⑤ The Meaning of White and Black Hats in American Movies

2 밑줄 친 ⓐ ~ ⓔ 중에서 문맥상 낱말의 쓰임이 적절하지 <u>않은</u> 것은?

① ⓐ   ② ⓑ   ③ ⓒ   ④ ⓓ   ⑤ ⓔ

3 다음 빈칸에 적절한 단어를 글에서 찾아 쓰시오.

> Q: Where does the expression "white hat" hacker come from?
> A: It comes from old __________ __________ . In the
> __________ , the __________ wore __________ __________ .

Words

security *n.* 보안
follow *v.* 따르다, (법을) 준수하다
law *n.* 법
hack *v.* 해킹을 하다
steal *v.* 훔치다
data *n.* 자료, 정보
solve *v.* 해결하다
attack *v.* 공격하다
(↔ protect 보호하다)
since ~ 때문에
play a role 역할을 하다
personal *a.* 개인적인

4 | Details | 다음 빈칸에 적절한 단어를 글에서 찾아 쓰시오. (단, 필요시 형태를 바꿔 쓸 것)

> **White hat hackers should ...**
>
> (1) follow the __________ when hacking.
>
> (2) use their hacking skills to find __________ problems.
>
> (3) suggest solutions to __________ our personal information.

Reading Skill   글의 중심 내용에 맞게 다음 표를 완성해 봅시다.

핵심어	• __________________
부연 설명	• 유래: ____________________
	• 역할: _____________ , _____________ , _____________

Reading 비법

장문은 글을 전체적으로 보고 반복적으로 언급되는 핵심 어구를 찾아내서 요지를 파악해야 한다.

직독직해 Skill   다음을 의미 단위로 끊어 읽고(/), 주어(S)와 동사(V)에 표시해 봅시다.

• They use their hacking skills to find some problems with security.

39

다음 글을 읽고, 물음에 답하시오.

(A) In a thick, green forest, there lived a huge elephant and a tiny family of ants. The elephant looked down on all the small animals. ⓐ <u>He</u> was proud of his strength and wanted to show it off. On the other hand, the ant family was always busy finding food.

(B) The ant slowly crawled into the elephant's body and started biting ⓑ <u>him</u>. Soon, the elephant couldn't move. The elephant tried to get the ant out, but ⓒ <u>he</u> continued biting him. The elephant was a big animal, but he couldn't do anything against the tiny ant.

(C) He shouted in pain and started to cry. Finally, he apologized to the ant. The ant said, "This is how we feel when you hurt us!" The ant stopped biting and came out of the elephant's body. From that day on, ⓓ <u>he</u> didn't hurt other small animals anymore.

(D) One day, when the ant family was going to work, the elephant sprayed a lot of water on them. "Ouch! You should not hurt others like this!" cried one of the ants. The elephant said, "Oh, stupid ant! Keep quiet, or I will kill you." The poor ant was scared, but he decided to teach ⓔ <u>him</u> a lesson.

1 주어진 글 (A) 다음에 이어질 글의 순서로 가장 적절한 것은?

① (B)–(D)–(C) ② (C)–(B)–(D)
③ (C)–(D)–(B) ④ (D)–(B)–(C)
⑤ (D)–(C)–(B)

2 밑줄 친 ⓐ ~ ⓔ 중에서 가리키는 대상이 나머지 넷과 <u>다른</u> 것은?

① ⓐ ② ⓑ ③ ⓒ ④ ⓓ ⑤ ⓔ

3 코끼리에 관한 내용으로 적절하지 <u>않은</u> 것은?

① 작은 동물들을 무시했다.
② 자신의 힘에 자부심을 가지고 있었다.
③ 개미가 무는 것을 견디지 못했다.
④ 끝까지 뉘우치거나 반성하지 않았다.
⑤ 개미 가족에게 물을 뿌려 다치게 했다.

4 글이 주는 교훈으로 적절한 것은?

① Fight fire with fire.
② The more, the better.
③ No pain, no gain.
④ Speak of the devil.
⑤ Put yourself in someone else's shoes.

Words

thick *a.* 울창한, 빽빽한
huge *a.* 거대한
tiny *a.* 아주 작은
look down on ~을 무시하다
be proud of ~을 자랑스러워하다
show off 뽐내다
crawl *v.* 기다
continue *v.* 계속하다
against *prep.* ~에 대항하여
shout *v.* 소리 지르다, 소리치다
pain *n.* 고통
apologize *v.* 사과하다
spray *v.* 뿌리다
stupid *a.* 어리석은, 바보 같은
lesson *n.* 교훈

5 |Summary| 다음 빈칸에 적절한 단어를 글에서 찾아 쓰시오.

There once lived a huge (1)__________ and a tiny family of (2)__________. When the ant family was going to work, the elephant (3)__________ water on them and hurt them. So, one of the ants crawled into his body and bit him. He shouted in (4)__________ and finally said sorry to the ant. From that day on, he didn't hurt others anymore.

Reading 비법

글의 순서를 파악해야 할 때 다음에 어떤 일이 일어날지 생각하면서 읽도록 한다.

Reading Skill

글의 내용에 맞게 다음 표를 완성해 봅시다.

단락 요약 (가급적 6하 원칙을 준수할 것)	(A) __________________________
	(B) __________________________
	(C) __________________________
	(D) __________________________

직독직해 Skill

다음을 의미 단위로 끊어 읽고(/), 주어(S)와 동사(V)에 표시해 봅시다.

· Keep quiet. or I will kill you.

Wise English Sayings

“The only way to do great work is to love what you do.”
(훌륭한 일을 하는 유일한 방법은 당신이 하는 일을 사랑하는 것이다.)

Steve Jobs

“I have not failed. I've just found 10,000 ways that won't work.”
(나는 실패한 적이 없다. 나는 다만 효과가 없는 만 가지 방법을 찾았을 뿐이다.)

Thomas Edison

“The biggest adventure you can ever take is to live the life of your dreams.”
(여러분이 할 수 있는 가장 큰 모험은 여러분이 꿈꾸는 삶을 사는 것이다.)

Oprah Winfrey

“All our dreams can come true if we have the courage to pursue them.”
(우리가 그것들을 추구할 용기가 있다면, 우리의 모든 꿈은 이루어질 수 있다.)

Walt Disney

“Success is not final, failure is not fatal: it is the courage to continue that counts.”
(성공은 최종적인 것이 아니며, 실패는 치명적이지 않다: 중요한 것은 계속하는 용기이다.)

Winston Churchill

다음 글을 읽고, 물음에 답하시오.   기출 응용

(A) One day a poor man gave a bunch of grapes to a prince as a gift. He was very excited to bring a gift for ⓐ <u>him</u> because he was too poor to buy anything else. He put the grapes near the prince and said, "Oh. Prince, please take this small gift from me." He was so happy because he could give him his small gift. 5

(B) The prince said, "I thought that if I shared the grapes with you, you would make funny faces and say the grapes were bad. That would hurt the feelings of the poor man. So I thought it would be better if I ate all the grapes happily by myself to please ⓑ <u>him</u>. I didn't want to hurt the poor man's feelings." 10 Everyone around him was impressed.

(C) The prince thanked him politely. As the man looked at him, the prince ate one grape. Then ⓒ <u>he</u> ate another one. Slowly the prince finished the whole bunch of grapes by himself. He did not give any grapes to anyone near ⓓ <u>him</u>. The poor man 15 was very pleased and left. The close friends of the prince were very surprised.

(D) Usually, the prince shared everything he had with others. He would share with them whatever he was given, and they would eat it together. This time, it was different. ⓔ <u>He</u> ate the bunch of 20 grapes all by himself. One of the friends asked, "Prince! Why did you eat all the grapes by yourself and not share them with us?" He smiled and said that he did it because the grapes were too sour. 25

Mini Quiz
글을 읽으면서 순서를 추론할 수 있는 단서에 밑줄을 그어 봅시다. (대명사, 연결어 등)

1 주어진 글 (A) 다음에 이어질 글의 순서로 가장 적절한 것은?

① (B)–(D)–(C) ② (C)–(B)–(D)
③ (C)–(D)–(B) ④ (D)–(B)–(C)
⑤ (D)–(C)–(B)

Words

bunch *n.* 송이
excited *a.* 기쁜, 흥분한
by oneself 혼자서
impressed *a.* 감명받은
politely *ad.* 정중하게
pleased *a.* 기쁜
close *a.* 가까운
whatever *pron.* 무엇이든
sour *a.* 시큼한, 신

2 밑줄 친 ⓐ ~ ⓔ 중에서 가리키는 대상이 나머지 넷과 <u>다른</u> 것은?

① ⓐ   ② ⓑ   ③ ⓒ   ④ ⓓ   ⑤ ⓔ

3 왕자에 관한 내용으로 적절하지 <u>않은</u> 것은?

① 포도 한 송이를 선물로 받았다.
② 가난한 남자의 기분을 상하게 하고 싶지 않았다.
③ 포도를 혼자 다 먹지 못했다.
④ 곁에 있던 누구에게도 포도를 권하지 않았다.
⑤ 평소에 다른 사람과 뭐든지 나누는 사람이다.

4 글을 읽고 각 학생들이 느낀 점으로 가장 적절한 것은?

① 가연: 나누면서 사는 삶이 중요해.
② 나은: 신하들의 충성심이 정말 대단한 것 같아.
③ 다현: 받는 사람에게 필요한 선물을 해야 해.
④ 은아: 왕자가 타인을 배려하는 모습이 감명 깊었어.
⑤ 재훈: 작은 것에도 행복을 느끼는 왕자를 본받아야지.

5 | Sequence | 다음 빈칸에 적절한 단어를 글에서 찾아 쓰시오.

One day a poor man gave a bunch of grapes to a (1)_________ as a gift.

↓

When the prince got the gift from the poor man, he thanked him politely and began eating the grapes. The prince slowly finished eating them without sharing the grapes with the others. The poor man was very happy and his friends were (2)_________.

↓

The prince normally shared everything with others and they ate together. However, when he got the grapes from the poor man, he ate them all (3)__________ __________. When his friend asked him why he did not share the grapes, the prince said with a smile that the grapes were too (4)__________.

↓

The prince knew that if they ate the grapes, they would make fun of the poor man and (5)__________ the feelings of that poor man. So, the prince ate all the grapes himself. Everyone was impressed by his kindness.

Reading 비법

순서를 추론할 때에는 연결어, 대명사 등의 단서를 찾아가면서 읽어야 한다.

Reading Skill 글의 내용에 맞게 다음 표를 완성해 봅시다.

단락 요약 (가급적 6하 원칙을 준수할 것)	(A) ________________________________
	(B) ________________________________
	(C) ________________________________
	(D) ________________________________

직독직해 Skill 다음을 의미 단위로 끊어 읽고(/), 주어(S)와 동사(V)에 표시해 봅시다.

· He would share with them whatever he was given.

Wise English Sayings

"Believe you can and you're halfway there."
(할 수 있다고 믿으면 절반은 간 것이다.)

Theodore Roosevelt

"You don't have to see the whole staircase, just take the first step."
(계단 전체를 볼 필요는 없고, 첫걸음만 내딛으면 된다.)

Martin Luther King Jr.

"Success is not the key to happiness. Happiness is the key to success. If you love what you are doing, you will be successful."
(성공이 행복의 열쇠는 아니다. 행복은 성공의 열쇠이다. 만약 여러분이 하고 있는 일을 사랑한다면, 여러분은 성공할 것이다.)

Albert Schweitzer

"The only limit to our realization of tomorrow will be our doubts of today."
(우리가 내일을 실현하는 데 있어 유일한 한계는 오늘에 대한 의심일 것이다.)

Franklin D. Roosevelt

"The best way to predict your future is to create it."
(미래를 예측하는 가장 좋은 방법은 그것을 창조하는 것이다.)

Abraham Lincoln

MEMO

MEMO

MEMO

MEMO

김선우 이해성 김해 의대관 학원
김성은 네오시스템영어전문학원
김소민 창원다올영어수학학원
김재훈 창원 더케이영어학원
김주은 더큰샘학원
김준 가우스 SME전문학원
김태리 전문과외
김현우 창녕대성고등학교
김현주 삼성영어셀레나 프리미엄신명점
나현호 펜덕스 어학원 율하센터
박영하 네오시스템영어학원
박재형 인투잉글리쉬어학원
박정주 창원 타임영어전문학원
배송이 JS어학원
배승빈 에스영어전문학원
배현령 배선영어
백민경 Michelle
손선영 이화멘토영어학원
신형섭 크림슨어학원
심정은 제시카영어교습소
안혜경 티오피에듀학원
양경화 봄영어
양기영 다니엘어학원
우지아 종로엠스쿨
윤지연 에이프릴어학원
이근호 레이첼 잉글리쉬
이수길 명성학원
이아현 다름학원
이연홍 Rhee's English Class
이원평 코치클래스 영어학원
이인아 인잉글리쉬
이지훈 엠베스트SE학원 신진주 캠퍼스
임나영 삼성영어셀레나 남양영어교습소
임진희 진해어썸영어학원
장은정 케이트어학원
장재훈 ASK 배움학원
장지영 잉글리시아이 명동사랑채점
정상락 비싱글리시아이대운점영어교습소
정수정 지탑영어
최승관 창선고등학교
최지영 시퀀스영수학원
최환준 Jun English
최효정 인에이블영수학원
하동권 네오시스템영어학원
한지용 성민국영수학원
허민정 허달영어
황다영 헤럴드어학원
황은영 에이블어학원

Kailey Pak 케일리 영어
강민표 현일고등학교
강유진 지니쌤영어
강은석 미래인재학원
강혜성 EiE 고려대 어학원
계지숙 Happy Helen English
김광현 그린빌
김도량 다이너마이트잉글리쉬
김도영 김도영영어학원
김상호 전문과외
김주훈 아너스영어
김지훈 알앤비
김혜지 스카이 프라임 에듀

문상현 안동 에이원영어
박경애 포항 대성초이스학원
박계민 영광중학교
박규정 베네치아 영어 교습소
박지은 능률주니어랩꿈터학원
배세왕 BK영수전문학원
변민준 한솔플러스영어수학학원 약목점
손누리 이든샘영수학원
유진욱 공부의힘 영어수학전문학원
윤재호 이상렬 일등단과학원
이강정 이룸단과학원
이상원 필즈학원
이지ען 전문과외
이지은 Izzy English
장가은 앨리스영어학원
장미 잉글리시아이 원리학원
전영아 N&K영어학원
정보경 울진고등학교
정선린 포항항도중학교
최동희 전문과외
최미선 영천영어전문과외

김도엽 스카이영어전문학원
김동익 이룸교육원
김병남 위즈덤 영어
김상연 공감영어학원
김서witty 디엔영어
김수인 광주 모조잉글리쉬
김신 와이(Y) 아카데미
김영연 전문과외
김원경 전문과외
김유경 프라임아카데미
김유희 김유희 영어학원
김윤희 수프림 영어공부방
김인화 김인화영어학원
나혜영 윤선생우리집앞영어교실
문장엽 엠제이영어수학전문학원
박주형 봉선동 한수위 영어학원
봉병주 철수와영수
신지수 온에어영어학원
양신애 윤학당오름국어영어학원
오승리 이지스터디
오평안 상무 지산한길어학원
우진일 블루페스 영어학원
유현주 유즈영어교습소
윤상혁 하이엔드 영어 학원
이남주 장원학원
이민정 롱맨어학원
이현창 진월유앤아이어학원
임지상 외대어학원
전솔 서강고등학교
정지선 이지스터디
채성문 마하나임 영수학원
한기석 이(E)영어교습소
한방엽 베스트영수학원

강정임 CanTalk English
고은진 헬렌영어
곽민경 조성애세움영어수학학원
구영모 대구여자상업고등학교
권보현 씨즈더데이어학원
권오길 공부를 디자인한다

권익재 제이슨영어교습소
권하련 아너스이엠에스학원
김근아 블루힐영어학원
김기목 목쌤영어교습소
김나래 더베스트영어학원
김다영 헬렌영어학원
김미나 전문과외
김민재 열공열강 영수학원
김병horn LU영어
김상완 YEP영어학원
김연정 유니티영어
김예slateslate슬 헬렌 영어
김유환 잉글과한글
김정혜 제니퍼영어
김종석 에이블영수학원
김준석 크누KNU입시학원
김지영 김지영 영어
김진호 강성영어
김철우 메라키 영어 교습소
김하나 하나로운영어
김희정 이선생영어학원
노태경 전문과외
문창숙 지앤비(GnB)스페셜입시학원
민승규 민승규영어학원
박고은 스테듀입시학원
박라율 열공열강영어수학학원
박소현 공터영어 테크노폴리스센터
박연희 좀다른영어
박예빈 영재키움영어수학전문학원
박지환 전문과외
방성모 방성모영어학원
배정연 이앤하이공부방
백재민 에소테리카 영어학원
서정인 서울입시학원
신혜경 전문과외
심경아 Shim's English
심유진 대구유신학원
엄재경 하이엔드영어학원
오다인 헬렌영어 프리미어 1관,2관
원현지 원샘영어교습소
위은령 브릿지영어
유지연 에스피영어학원
윤이강 윤이강 영어
이근성 헬렌영어학원
이동현 쌤마스터입시학원
이미경 전문과외
이수희 EAON 영어학원
이승민 KEREC
이승현 학문당입시학원
이지민 아이플러스 수학
이지현 아이플러스 수학
이진영 전문과외
이현욱 이헌욱 영어학원
임지민 헬렌영어학원
임형주 사범대단과학원
장지연 이지영어
장현진 고려대EIE어학원(현풍)
전윤애 올링글리쉬
전윤영 뮤엠영어 경동초점
전지민 헬렌영어학원
정대운 유신학원
정소영 씨즈더데이월암어학원

정연주 대한민국 입시학원
정용희 에스피영어
정은경 전문과외
조혜연 연쌤영어수학학원
진보라 메이킹학원
최정임 컬럼비아 영어학원
최현희 다온수학학원
최효진 너를 위한 영어
한정아 능인고등학교
황윤슬 사적인영어

Tony Park 전문과외
강은혜 노마드국어영어학원
고우리 영어의 꿈
권현이 디디샘영어
길민주 전문과외
김경이 영어서당학원
김근범 딱쌤학원
김기형 상승학원
김영철 빅뱅잉글리시캠퍼스
김유진 굿티쳐강남학원
김주리 위드제이영어
김하나 위드유학원
나규성 비전21학원
남영종 엠베스트SE 대전 전민점
노현서 앨리잉글리쉬아카데미
민지원 민쌤영어교습소
박난정 제일학원
박성희 청담프라임학원
박효진 박효진 영어
박효춘 수잔스튜터링
심효령 삼부가람학원
안수정 궁극의 사고
오봉주 새미래영수학원
유수민 제일학원
윤영숙 전문과외
이고은 고은영어
이길형 빌드업영어
이대희 청명대입학원
이보배 비비영어
이성구 청명대입학원
이수미 이수미어학원
이영란 일인주의 학원
이원성 파스칼베스티안학원
이재근 이재근영어수학학원
이홍원 홍T영어
임혜지 마이더스 손 영어학원
장유리 테스영어
정동현 대성외국어
정라라 영어문화원 정라라 영어교습소
정예슬 유레카원학원
정윤희 Alex's English
정혜수 쌜리영어
조재형 에듀플렉스
조현 퍼스트학원
채송은 위캔영어학원
최성호 에이스영어교습소
최현우 파스칼베스티안학원
한왕호 김태헌영어학원
한형식 서대전여자고등학교
황지현 공부자존감영어입시학원

강민주 전문과외
강하늘 뉴스터디종합학원
고경원 JS 영수학원
김도담 도담한영어교실
김도윤 코어영어 교습소
김동혁 코어영어수학전문학원
김동휘 장정호 영어전문학원
김미혜 더멘토영어
김병택 탑으로가는 영어 교습소
김서영 대치명인학원(해운대)
김성미 다올영어
김소림 엘라영어학원
김소연 전문과외
김수정 리더스어학원
김연주 링구아어학원
김은숙 강동초등학교
김재경 부산진구 탑클래스 영어학원
김지애 김지애영어연구소
김진규 의문을열다
김효은 김효은 영어전문학원
남재호 제니스학원
류미향 류미향입시영어
박미진 MJ영어학원
박수진 제이엔씨 영어학원
박영주 전문과외
박지우 영어를 ON하다
박지은 박지은영어전문과외방
박창현 오늘도,영어그리고수학
배찬원 에이플러스 영어교습소
변혜련 전문과외
성장우 전문과외
손소희 호이겐스학원
손지안 정관 아슬란학원
송석준 비상아이비츠 해랑학원
송초롱 괴정최상위영어
심혜정 명품수학
안영실 개금국제학원
안정희 GnB어학원양성캠퍼스
양희주 링구아어학원 해운대
오세창 범천반석단과학원
오정안 쏘트
오지은 이루다영어
윤경은 쌤드루
윤지영 잉글리쉬무무영어교습소
윤진희 전문과외
이기연 미네르바국제아카데미
이미정 탑에듀영어교습소
이상석 상석영어
이순실 종로엠스쿨(하단분원)
이윤호 메트로 영어
이재우 무한꿈터
이지현 Serena영어
이혜정 로엠학원
임정연 침팬지영어학원 마린시티점
장민지 탑클래스영어학원
정승덕 성균관 영어
정영훈 J&C영어전문학원(제이엔씨)
조정훈 입시영어전문 THOUGHT
채지영 리드앤톡영어도서관학원
최승빈 다온학원
최우성 초이English&Pass

최이내	전문과외
최효선	해피트리어학원
탁아진	에이블영어.국어학원
한영희	미래탐구 해운대

서울

kimhyerim	아르테에비뉴
가혜림	벨쌤.com
강민정	네오 과학학원
강보경	크라센어학원
강성호	대원고등학교
강정훈	더(the)상승학원
강준수	전문과외
강현숙	토피아어학원 중계캠퍼스
공리아	리더스 잠실
구나현	플러스잉글리쉬영어교습소
구대만	잇올 스파르타 독재학원
구민모	키움학원
구지은	DYB최선Mate 본사
권혜령	전문과외
김경수	탑킴입시앤영어
김나결	레이쌤영어교습소
김남철	마이티마우스학원
김명열	대치명인학원
김미은	오늘도맑음 영어교습소
김미정	전문과외
김병준	iLO ENGLISH
김보경	클라우드캐슬영어교습소
김빛나	뮤엠영어피닉스영어교습소
김상희	스카이플러스학원
김선경	대치마크영어
김성근	배움자리학원
김성연	대치열린학원
김소정	브로든 영어
김승환	Arnold English Class
김연아	올리비아 영어교습소
김영삼	YS영어공부방
김은영	루시아 잉글리시
김은정	전문과외
김은진	에이스영어교습소
김정민	더블유 영어학원
김정수	토즈 스터디센터
김종현	김종현영어
김지헌	다원교육 목동
김태홍	이투스247학원 송파점
김하은	전문과외
김현영	대치웰영어학원
김현정	진심영어
김현지	전문과외
김혜림	대치 청담 어학원
김혜영	스터디원
김희정	스터디 코치
나선아	전문과외
노은경	이은재어학원
노종주	전문과외
노진숙	최선어학원
노현희	전문과외
노혜정	최강학원
도선혜	중계동 영어 공부방
류하영	전문과외
맹혜선	휘경여자고등학교
명가은	명가은영어학원
문명기	문명기 영어학원

문민아	탄탄대로 입시컨설팅
문지현	반포헨리학원
박광운	영어교습소
박기철	한진연 입시전략연구소
박남규	알짜영어교습소
박미애	명문지혜학원
박미정	위드멘토학원
박병석	주영학원
박선경	씨투엠학원
박소영	JOY English
박소하	전문과외
박솔	SOLE ENGLISH
박수정	YBM잉글루 박수정 영어학원
박숭규	이지수능교육
박은경	오늘영어교습소
박정미	드림영어하이수학학원
박정효	성북메가스터디
박준용	은평 G1230 학원
박지연	영어공부연구소
박진경	JAYz ENGLISH
박찬경	펜타곤영어학원
박현정	1등급학원
반향진	세레나영어수학
배수현	남다른이해
배련경	전문과외
변지예	북두칠성학원
서예은	스터디브릭스학원 내신관
서은조	방배중학교
손종민	미즈원어학원
신경훈	탑앤탑 수학영어 학원
신연우	목동 씨앤씨학원
신정애	당산점 와와학습코칭학원
신지혜	비욘드 어드밴스
신호현	아로새김학원
신희경	신쌤 영어
심나현	성북메가스터디
안미영	스카이플러스학원
안웅희	이엔엠국영수전문학원
양세희	양세희수능영어 학원
양하나	목동 씨앤씨 바이올렛T
어홍주	이-베스트 영어학원
엄태열	대치차오름학원
오남숙	헬리오 오쌤 영어
오은경	전문과외
용혜영	SWEET ENGLISH 영어전문 공부방
우승희	우승희영어학원
유경미	무무&차(천광학원)
윤성	대치동 새움학원
윤은미	CnT 영어학원
윤지인	반포잉글리쉬튜터링
이계훈	이지영어학원
이광희	가온에듀 2관
이국재	공감학원
이남규	신정송현학원
이명순	Top Class English
이미나	위드미영어교습소
이미영	티엠하버드영어학원
이상수	넥서스학원
이석원	숭실중학교
이석호	한샘영재학원
이성택	엠아이씨영어학원
이수정	영샘영어

이승미	금천정상어학원
이아진	AJ INSTITUTE
이연주	Real_YJ English
이윤형	아만다영어학원
이은선	드림영어하이수학학원
이은영	DNA영어학원
이은정	전문과외
이은주	대치써미트영어학원
이자임	자몽영어교습소
이정인	프레임 학원
이정혜	수시이룸교육
이주희	윌링어학원
이지민	대치명인학원 은평캠퍼스
이지연	석률학원
이철웅	비상하는 또또학원
이혜숙	사당대성보습학원
이혜정	이루리학원
이희영	이샘영어 아카데미 교습소
이희진	목동씨앤씨
임서은	형설학원
임소례	윤선생영어교실 신내키움
임은희	전문과외
장서희	전문과외
장소당	최선어학원
전계령	신촌 메가스터디학원
전수진	절대영어학원
전지영	탑클래스영수학원
정가람	촘촘영어
정경록	미즈원어학원
정민혜	정민혜밀착영어학원
정성준	팁탑영어
정유하	YNS 열정과신념 영어학원
정재욱	씨알학원
정지희	대치하이영어전문학원
정해림	서울숭의초등학교 영어전담
조미영	튼튼영어 마스터클럽 구로학원
조민석	더원영수학원
조민재	정성학원
조봉현	조셉영어국어학원
조연아	연쌤 영어
조용수	EMC이승환영어전문학원
조용현	바른스터디학원
조은성	종로학원
조인회	가디언 어학원(본원)
진영민	브로든영어학원
채상우	클레영어
채에스더	문래중학교
천수진	메리트영어
천예은	폴티스 영어학원
최가은	지엔영어
최민주	전문과외
최수린	목동 CNC 국제관
최안나	영어의완성 영어교습소
최유송	목동 씨앤씨학원(CNC)
최유정	강북청솔학원
최정문	한성학원
최형미	전문과외
최희재	SA어학원
편선경	IGSE Academy
하다님	연세마스터스 학원
하제원	더블랙에듀
한인혜	레나잉글리쉬

한혜주	박홍학원
함규민	클레어영어교실
허미영	삼성영어 창일교실 학원
현승준	강남종로학원 교대점
홍대균	홍대균 영어
홍영민	성북상상학원
홍희진	이티영어학원
황상희	어나더레벨 영어전문학원
황선애	앤스영어학원
황혜진	이루다 영어

세종

김보경	더시에나
방종영	세움학원
백승희	백승희영어
손대령	강한영어학원
송지원	베이 교육컨설팅
안성주	더타임학원
안초롱	21세기학원
이지현	OEC 올리비아 영어 교습소
이현지	전문과외
허욱	전문과외

울산

강상배	전문과외
김경수	핀포인트영어학원
김경현	에린영어
김광규	EIE 온양어학원
김주희	하이디 영어교습소
김한중	스마트영어전문학원
서예원	해법멘토영어수학학원
송회철	꿈꾸는고래
양혜정	양혜정영어
엄여은	준쌤영어교습소
윤주이	인생영어학원
이서경	이서경영어
이수현	제이엘영어교습소
이윤미	제이앤에스 영어수학
임재희	임재희영어전문학원
정은선	한국esl어학원
조충일	YBM잉글루 울산언양 제1캠퍼스
최나비	더오름high-end학원
한건수	한스영어
허부배	비즈단과학원
황희정	장검 앵커어학원

인천

강재민	스터디위드제이쌤
고미경	쎄리영어학원
김갑헌	카일쌤영어학원
김미경	전문과외
김선나	태풍영어학원
김영태	에듀터학원
김영호	조주석수학&영어클리닉학원
김옥경	잉글리쉬 베이
김지연	송도탑영어학원
김지	Jenna's English
김현미	송도탑영어학원
김현희	에이플러스원영어수학학원
나일지	두드림하이영어학원
남미경	뮤엠구월서초영어교습소
문지현	고대어학원
박민아	하이영어
박소연	링컨 영어

박정우	영수원칙학원
박주현	Ashley's English Corner
박진영	인천외국어고등학교
배이슬	비상영수학원
서유화	K&C American School
성하율	타이탄 영어
송현민	Kathy's Class
신나리	이루다교육학원
신은주	명문학원
신현경	전문과외
심현정	전문과외
오희정	엠베스트SE논현캐슬
원정연	공탑학원
윤선	밀턴 영어학원
윤효주	프렌잉글리시청라레이크블루
윤희영	세실영어
이가희	S&U영어
이동규	인천상아초등학교
이미선	고품격EM EDU
이수진	전문과외
이윤주	Triple One
이은정	인천 논현 고등학교
이주현	레이첼영어
이진희	이진희 영어
이한아	선한영수
장승혁	지엘학원
전혜원	제일고등학교
정도영	대신학원
정춘기	정상어학원 남동분원
조슈아	와이즈에듀학원
조윤정	원당중학교
최민지	빅뱅영어
최수련	업앤업영어교습소
최지유	J(제이)영수전문학원
최창영	학산에듀
한은경	호크마학원
황성현	인천외국어고등학교

전남

강용문	JK영수
강유미	정상어학원 목포남악분원
고경희	에이블 잉글리쉬
곽혜진	H&J ENGLISH
김미선	여수개인교습
김아름	전문과외
김은정	BestnBest
류성준	타임영어학원
박동규	정상학원
박민지	벨라영어
박현아	정상어학원 목포남악분원
서창현	목포백련초등학교
손빛나	프렌잉글리시 여수웅천학원
손성호	아름다운 11월학원
양명승	엠에스어학원
오은주	순천금당고등학교
이상호	스카이입시학원
이영주	재키리 영어학원
임동묵	문향고등학교
조소을	수잉글리쉬
차형진	상아탑학원
황상윤	K&H 중고등 영어 전문학원

전북

길지만	비상잉글리시아이영어학원

기본 독해부터 수능 독해까지 한번에 완성

내신대비
워크북

Reading∞
master 중등

수능
plus
내신

Level 1

이투스북

Reading ∞ master 중등

수능 plus 내신

Level 1

PART 01 Review Test
PART 02 핵심 직독직해

다음 글을 읽고, 물음에 답해 봅시다.

Polar bears are warm-blooded animals, but they don't feel cold in the freezing Arctic temperatures. They ___ⓐ___ warm in the Arctic thanks to their special hair and black skin. First, their hair is mostly clear and colorless, ___(A)___ an empty tube. (①) The hair is filled ___(B)___ air, and it traps the sun's heat. (②) Polar bears' hair is also oily. When they shake their body after swimming, the water comes off their body right away. (③) This stops them ___(C)___ getting wet. (④) It soaks up the sunlight, so they don't easily get cold. (⑤) Moreover, ⓑ <u>검은 피부 아래에는 두꺼운 체지방층이 있다.</u> It keeps them warm while swimming.

1

윗글의 ①~⑤ 중 주어진 문장이 들어갈 위치로 가장 적절한 곳은?

> Second, polar bears have black skin underneath their fur.

①   ②   ③   ④   ⑤

2

윗글의 빈칸 ⓐ에 들어갈 말로 가장 적절한 것은?

① stop   ② keep   ③ trap
④ want   ⑤ enjoy

3

윗글의 빈칸 (A), (B), (C)에 들어갈 말로 가장 적절한 것은?

	(A)	(B)	(C)
①	by	of	to
②	by	with	from
③	like	with	from
④	like	with	to
⑤	like	of	from

4 (서술형)

윗글의 밑줄 친 ⓑ와 일치하도록 주어진 단어들을 바르게 배열하여 문장을 완성하시오.

➡ Moreover, underneath the black skin ______
___________________________.

(thick, of, a, body, layer, fat, is)

5 (서술형)

윗글의 내용과 일치하도록 다음 요약문의 빈칸에 적절한 말을 윗글에서 찾아 쓰시오.

> Polar bears can survive the freezing Arctic temperatures thanks to their special ________ and black ________.

Iguazú National Park is a very big national park in Argentina. You can enjoy many types of activities there. First, you can see the Iguazú Falls. ⓐ <u>It's the world's biggest waterfalls with about 275 different waterfalls.</u> You can experience the (A) <u>high</u> point, the Devil's Throat, by taking a boat tour, helicopter ride, or just by walking on the trails. You can also see wild animals in the park. There are many kinds of animals such as jaguars, fish, turtles, and monkeys. Last, you can go (B) <u>hike</u> to different places. You can hike around the rainforest, below the falls, and ⓑ<u>even</u> on top of the falls. ⓒ 비옷을 가져가는 것만 기억해라, 그렇지 않으면 젖을 수 있다.

1

윗글의 내용과 일치하는 것은?

① 이구아수 국립공원은 아르헨티나에서 가장 큰 국립공원이다.

② 이구아수 폭포는 단일 규모로 275m에 이르는 가장 큰 폭포이다.

③ '악마의 목구멍'은 위험해서 일반인들의 접근이 불가능하다.

④ 이구아수 국립공원에서는 재규어나 아나콘다 같은 야생동물들을 볼 수 있다.

⑤ 폭포 아래까지 하이킹을 할 수 있다.

2

윗글의 밑줄 친 (A)와 (B)의 적절한 형태가 바르게 짝지어진 것은?

	(A)		(B)
①	higher	·····	to hike
②	higher	·····	hiking
③	highest	·····	to hike
④	highest	·····	hiking
⑤	highest	·····	to hiking

3

윗글의 밑줄 친 ⓑeven과 의미가 같은 것은?

① The score is <u>even</u>.

② <u>Even</u> a child can do that.

③ 4 is called an <u>even</u> number.

④ It's <u>even</u> colder than yesterday.

⑤ His book is <u>even</u> better than we expected.

4 〔서술형〕

윗글의 밑줄 친 문장 ⓐ에서 어법상 틀린 부분을 찾아 바르게 고쳐 쓰시오.

___________ ➡ ___________

5 〔서술형〕

윗글의 밑줄 친 ⓒ와 일치하도록 문장을 완성하시오.

➡ Just _________ _________ _________
your raincoat, _________ you may get wet.

다음 글을 읽고, 물음에 답해 봅시다.

Sometimes a different view ① <u>annoys</u> us. ______ ⓐ ______ , Pablo Picasso, a famous artist, tried to see the world differently. In his famous work *Three Musicians*, he painted three music players. But he did not draw three people. Instead, he used ______ ⓑ ______ . When you first see this work, you may not ② <u>notice</u> the players. ⓒ <u>아무것도 이해되지 않을 것이다.</u> But when you keep ⓓ <u>look</u> at the painting, you can see them in it! It's like a puzzle. Picasso's work shows a ③ <u>special</u> way of painting. His work used shapes, objects, and colors so differently from the real world. His paintings look very ④ <u>unique</u>. To understand the work, you should view things completely ⑤ <u>differently</u>. This can be a whole new joy. It is the joy of viewing the world differently.

1

윗글의 밑줄 친 ①~⑤ 중 문맥상 낱말의 쓰임이 적절하지 <u>않은</u> 것은?

① ② ③ ④ ⑤

2

윗글의 빈칸 ⓐ에 문맥상 들어갈 말로 가장 적절한 것은?

① In contrast　　② Therefore
③ That is　　　　④ For example
⑤ In addition

3

윗글의 빈칸 ⓑ에 들어갈 말로 가장 적절한 것은?

① real objects
② vivid colors
③ abstract shapes
④ unusual materials
⑤ pictures of the musicians

4 서술형

윗글의 밑줄 친 ⓒ와 일치하도록 주어진 단어들을 바르게 배열하여 문장을 쓰시오.

➡ _______________________________

(you, sense, to, makes, nothing)

5 서술형

윗글의 밑줄 친 ⓓ look의 적절한 형태를 쓰시오.

➡ _______________________________

다음 글을 읽고, 물음에 답해 봅시다.

For ancient Egyptians, cats were ⓐ<u>the most</u> special animal. They first kept cats as ________. (①) Egyptians believed cats were magical creatures. (A)<u>They</u> thought ⓑ<u>that</u> cats brought good luck. (②) To honor the cats, rich families put jewelry on (B)<u>them</u>. They also gave high-quality food to the cats. (③) Cats were an important part of ancient Egyptian life. When cats died, their owners ⓒ<u>would</u> shave their eyebrows. (C)<u>They</u> showed their sadness until their eyebrows grew back. (④) When a human killed a cat, he or she ⓓ<u>killed</u>, too. (⑤) Cats were ⓔ<u>clearly</u> more than just ________ to them.

1

윗글의 밑줄 친 ⓐ~ⓔ 중 어법상 틀린 것은?

① ⓐ   ② ⓑ   ③ ⓒ   ④ ⓓ   ⑤ ⓔ

2

윗글의 ①~⑤ 중 주어진 문장이 들어갈 위치로 가장 적절한 곳은?

> The ancient Egyptians protected cats even by law.

①   ②   ③   ④   ⑤

3

윗글의 빈칸에 공통으로 들어갈 말로 가장 적절한 것은?

① toys   ② pets
③ prey   ④ families
⑤ guardians

4 서술형

다음 영어 설명에 해당하는 단어를 윗글에서 찾아 쓰시오.

> to treat (someone) with respect and admiration

→ ________________________

5 서술형

윗글의 밑줄 친 (A), (B), (C)가 가리키는 것을 각각 쓰시오.

(A) They → ________________________
(B) them → ________________________
(C) They → ________________________

다음 글을 읽고, 물음에 답해 봅시다.

When you go camping, you make sure to bring enough food. Astronauts ⓐ <u>do the same thing</u> when they go to space. They prepare food. ___ⓑ___ on Earth, ① <u>astronauts</u> eat three meals a day. (A) <u>There is many different foods for astronauts in space.</u> Dried food is very common. There are canned potatoes and meats. A spacecraft can ② <u>store</u> some fresh fruit and vegetables. (B) <u>There is also an oven in a spacecraft and it can make food warmly.</u> But there is no ③ <u>refrigerator</u>. So all the food comes in ④ <u>packets</u> for easy storage. Salt comes as ⑤ <u>liquid</u>. Ordinary salt would simply float away. Sauces ___ⓑ___ ketchup, mustard, and mayonnaise are also available in tubes. (C) <u>With these various space foods, astronauts can stay health in space.</u>

1

윗글의 내용과 일치하는 것은?

① 우주비행사들은 건조된 음식만 먹는다.
② 우주선은 신선한 과일과 채소를 저장할 수 없다.
③ 우주선에는 오븐과 냉장고가 없다.
④ 우주에서는 소금이 액체로 나온다.
⑤ 우주비행사들은 우주에서 건강을 유지하기가 어렵다.

2

윗글의 빈칸 ⓑ에 공통으로 들어갈 말로 가장 적절한 것은?

① With(with)
② Like(like)
③ Such as(such as)
④ Except(except)
⑤ Instead(instead)

3

윗글의 밑줄 친 ①~⑤에 대한 영어 설명이 알맞지 <u>않은</u> 것은?

① a person who travels in a spacecraft into outer space
② a building or room in which things are sold
③ a device that is used to keep things cold
④ a small, thin package
⑤ a substance that is able to flow freely like water

4 서술형

윗글의 밑줄 친 ⓐ do the same thing이 의미하는 바를 우리말로 쓰시오.

➡ __________________________

5 서술형

윗글의 밑줄 친 (A), (B), (C)에서 어법상 틀린 것을 각각 찾아 바르게 고쳐 쓰시오.

(A) __________ ➡ __________
(B) __________ ➡ __________
(C) __________ ➡ __________

Do you know anybody with no failure at all? Or can you think of anyone in sports history with a record of only wins? Probably not. Roger Federer,   (A) , is the world's greatest tennis player with twenty Grand Slam titles. But he actually played in   ⓐ   than sixty Grand Slam tournaments.   (B) , he lost in more than 2/3 of the tournaments. He lost many more tournaments than he won. ⓑ 여전히 우리는 그를 실패자가 아니라 챔피언으로 생각합니다. Failure makes success. So don't be afraid of failure. Losing a game or not (C) <u>pass</u> a test is okay. No one is perfect. Try (D) <u>accept</u> your failure and move on from it.

1

윗글의 빈칸 (A)와 (B)에 문맥상 들어갈 말로 가장 적절한 것은?

	(A)	(B)
①	for example	…… Nevertheless
②	for example	…… In other words
③	however	…… In other words
④	on the other hand	…… In addition
⑤	on the other hand	…… Nevertheless

2

윗글의 빈칸 ⓐ에 들어갈 말로 가장 적절한 것은?

① many   ② very
③ much   ④ most
⑤ more

3

윗글의 밑줄 친 (C)와 (D)의 적절한 형태가 바르게 짝지어진 것은?

	(C)	(D)
①	passed	…… accept
②	to pass	…… accepting
③	to pass	…… to accept
④	passing	…… to accept
⑤	passing	…… to accepting

4 서술형

윗글의 밑줄 친 분수를 영어로 알맞게 표현하시오.

➡ ______________ - ______________

5 서술형

윗글의 밑줄 친 ⓑ와 일치하도록 주어진 단어들을 바르게 배열하여 문장을 완성하시오.

➡ Still, ______________________,

______________________.

(as, of, champion, not, as, him, a, we, failure, a, think)

다음 글을 읽고, 물음에 답해 봅시다.

Dear Mr. Kang,

I am a tour guide at Fun&Joy Zoo. Thank you for (A)| visit / visiting | our zoo for your field trip! I hope you will have a wonderful day here. I would like to ask you ⓐa favor. Before your visit, please advise your students not (B)| to throw / throwing | waste in the zoo. Trash cans are in place all around the zoo. Plastic bags and other _________ can be very harmful to our animals. Like small children, animals love to test things with their mouths. ⓑThey may mistake this trash for food and swallow it. It can make them very sick. So, for the health of our lovely animals, students should not (C)| throw / to throw | waste in the zoo. I thank you for your cooperation.

Sincerely,

Danna Smith

1

윗글의 내용과 일치하는 것은?

① Danna Smith teaches students at school.
② Danna Smith is worried about their animals getting sick.
③ Mr. Kang works at the zoo as a tour guide.
④ Mr. Kang thanks Danna Smith for her cooperation.
⑤ Mr. Kang and his students visited for their field trip at Fun&Joy Zoo.

2

윗글 (A), (B), (C)의 각 네모 안에서 어법에 맞는 표현으로 가장 적절한 것은?

	(A)	(B)	(C)
①	visit	throwing	to throw
②	visiting	throwing	throw
③	visit	to throw	throw
④	visiting	to throw	throw
⑤	visit	to throw	to throw

3

윗글의 빈칸에 들어갈 말로 가장 적절한 것은?

① food   ② bird
③ trash   ④ love
⑤ trees

4 서술형

윗글의 밑줄 친 ⓐa favor의 내용을 20자 내외의 우리말로 쓰시오.

➡

____

5 서술형

윗글의 밑줄 친 ⓑ를 우리말로 해석하시오.

➡ ___________________________

다음 글을 읽고, 물음에 답해 봅시다.

Answers p. 42

ⓐ Don't click the Send button right away when you send emails. Nothing terrible will happen (A) before / after you click the Send button. There can be misspellings or errors of fact in your writing. However, it doesn't matter ＿＿＿＿ you don't click the Send button. Why? You can take some time to fix mistakes. And nobody will be able to know the difference. So, never hurry to click the Send button. ⓑ Looking again and fixing should come first; sending should come later. If you see any mistakes (B) before / after sending an email, it can be a big problem. So, don't forget to read your writing carefully (C) before / after you click the Send button. ⓒ The same goes for sending school assignments or business letters by email.

1

윗글의 (A), (B), (C)의 각 네모 안에서 문맥에 맞는 단어로 가장 적절한 것은?

	(A)	(B)	(C)
①	before	before	before
②	before	after	before
③	after	before	after
④	after	before	before
⑤	after	after	after

2

윗글의 빈칸에 들어갈 말로 가장 적절한 것은?

① if
② that
③ unless
④ although
⑤ as soon as

3

윗글의 밑줄 친 ⓒThe same goes가 의미하는 바로 가장 적절한 것은?

① 이메일을 서둘러 보내지 마라.
② 이메일을 제출 기한 내에 보내라.
③ 이메일을 보내고 나서 확인해라.
④ 이메일을 보내기 전에 검토해라.
⑤ 이메일을 보낼 때는 반드시 'Send' 버튼을 눌러라.

4 서술형

윗글의 밑줄 친 ⓐ의 이유를 다음과 같이 쓸 때, 빈칸에 적절한 말을 한 단어로 쓰시오.

> Your emails may have some ＿＿＿＿＿ such as misspellings or errors of fact.

➡ ＿＿＿＿＿＿＿＿＿＿

5 서술형

윗글의 밑줄 친 ⓑLooking again이 의미하는 바를 윗글에서 찾아 다음 빈칸을 완성하시오.

➡ to ＿＿＿＿ ＿＿＿＿ ＿＿＿＿ ＿＿＿＿

다음 글을 읽고, 물음에 답해 봅시다.

We started a new tutor-tutee project in science class last month. It was a kind of peer teaching. My science teacher said, "This project will be helpful for the tutees. It will also be good for the tutors!" I liked science best. I was good at science, so I volunteered ① as a student teacher. I taught my friend. He was poor ② at science. At first, I thought I was spending too ③ many time with the tutee. I also thought it was a waste of time. ④ But later, I found out I was wrong. As a tutor, I began to understand the material better and more clearly. I also got a better grade on the final exam ⓐ thanks to the project. I realized ⑤ that I could learn more by _______ ⓑ _______.

1

윗글의 빈칸 ⓑ에 들어갈 말로 가장 적절한 것은?

① teaching myself
② teaching others
③ helping my teacher
④ teaching each other
⑤ getting help from others

2

윗글의 'I'에 관한 내용으로 일치하지 <u>않는</u> 것은?

① 과학을 가장 좋아하고 잘한다.
② 새로운 과학 프로젝트에 선발되었다.
③ 또래 친구에게 과학을 가르쳐 주었다.
④ 과학 프로젝트를 하면서 친구와 많은 시간을 보냈다.
⑤ 기말시험에서 더 좋은 성적을 받았다.

3

윗글의 밑줄 친 ⓐ thanks to와 바꿔 쓸 수 있는 것은?

① without   ② because
③ but for   ④ except for
⑤ because of

4 서술형

윗글의 밑줄 친 ①~⑤ 중 어법상 틀린 것을 찾아 바르게 고쳐 쓰시오.

(   ) ➡ ___________________

5 서술형

윗글의 내용과 일치하지 <u>않는</u> 단어를 찾아 바르게 고쳐 쓰시오.

A tutor-tutee was a new science project that ended last month. It was that tutor students taught tutee students.

___________________ ➡ ___________________

다음 글을 읽고, 물음에 답해 봅시다.

● Answers p. 42

Nature is a source of discovery. Observing nature can make human life better. It means that our life can be easier and ⓐ<u>comfortable</u>. ___(A)___, special paint can keep your house clean. The rough surface of the paint pushes away dust. After using this paint, you can wash the outside of your house less often. This discovery came from looking at ⓑ<u>lotus leaves</u>. (①) As people know, lotus lives in muddy ponds. ___(B)___, its leaves always look clean. (②) Look at a lotus leaf under a microscope. (③) Then you can know the answer. (④) There are many tiny bumps on it. (⑤) They look like small nails and make the surface rough. So it can keep dust off. Always try to observe nature closely!

1

윗글의 빈칸 (A), (B)에 들어갈 말로 가장 적절한 것은?

	(A)		(B)
①	As a result	……	Besides
②	In addition	……	However
③	In addition	……	Therefore
④	For example	……	Therefore
⑤	For example	……	However

2

윗글의 밑줄 친 ⓑ<u>lotus leaves</u>에 관한 내용으로 일치하지 <u>않는</u> 것은?

① They always look clean.
② Their surface is rough.
③ They look like small nails.
④ They can be seen in muddy ponds.
⑤ They are a source of special paints.

3

윗글의 ①~⑤ 중 주어진 문장이 들어갈 위치로 가장 적절한 곳은?

> Why is this possible?

①   ②   ③   ④   ⑤

4 서술형

윗글의 밑줄 친 ⓐ<u>comfortable</u>의 적절한 형태를 쓰시오.

➡ ___________________

5 서술형

윗글의 내용과 일치하도록 다음 요약문의 빈칸에 적절한 말을 윗글에서 찾아 두 단어로 쓰시오.

> People can live better lives by ___________
> ___________ .

다음 글을 읽고, 물음에 답해 봅시다.

We communicate with others through language. But we use ⓐ hand gestures for communication, too. We often use them in daily life. We can also use them when we travel abroad. However, ⓑ not all hand gestures have the same meaning in every culture! Therefore, we should be careful about when and how we use them. The thumbs up is a good example. This gesture is very popular and well known. People often use it all over the world. It is a beloved emoji, too. It usually means agreement or "okay" in many countries like Korea and Japan. _________, it may be an insult in Thailand. And it may mean "no" or show rudeness in Australia. Gestures such as a thumbs up have different meanings in many cultures or countries. So, to avoid misunderstandings, be careful how you use them!

1

윗글의 내용과 일치하도록 할 때, 다음 질문에 대한 답으로 가장 적절한 것은?

> Q: Why should Koreans be careful when they use a thumbs-up gesture in Thailand?
> A: It's because _________________.

① it is only used in Korea
② it is unknown in Thailand
③ it can cause misunderstanding
④ it has a specially good meaning
⑤ it means "being rude" in Thailand

2

윗글의 빈칸에 들어갈 말로 가장 적절한 것은?

① Thus
② However
③ Otherwise
④ Nevertheless
⑤ Furthermore

3

윗글의 밑줄 친 ⓐhand gestures에 대해 <u>잘못</u> 말한 학생은?

① 미주: 의사소통의 한 수단이지.
② 지훈: 일상생활에서 흔히 사용해.
③ 소연: 국내외 여행에서도 사용할 수 있어.
④ 영민: 엄지척 제스처는 모두가 잘 사용해.
⑤ 수지: 일본 사람들은 엄지척 제스처를 싫어할 수도 있어.

4 서술형

윗글의 밑줄 친 ⓑ를 우리말로 해석하시오.

→ _______________________________________

5 서술형

윗글의 제목을 다음과 같이 쓸 때, 각 빈칸에 적절한 말을 윗글에서 찾아 쓰시오.

> The _________ Hand Gesture with _________ Meanings from Country to Country

다음 글을 읽고, 물음에 답해 봅시다.

Do you often feel that there is not enough time? It is the feeling of having too much to do when you do not have enough time. It is ⓐ *time famine*. ①It makes you feel nervous. ②It makes you annoyed, too. You may experience ③this when you study for exams. One study shows that time famine can make students feel more stressed than when they get a low score. But do not worry. There is a way to overcome ④this. You can feel more ________ by saving time. To save time, make a to-do list. ⑤It helps you to focus on the more urgent things. Also, use time-saving services. For instance, you can use a food delivery service instead of eating out or cooking meals.

1

윗글의 주제로 가장 적절한 것은?

① 시간 기근 현상과 대처 방법
② 시간을 아끼는 두 가지 방법
③ 할 일 목록 만들기의 장점과 단점
④ 시간 기근 현상으로 인해 나타나는 증상
⑤ 시간 기근에서 오는 스트레스 해소 방법

2

윗글의 빈칸에 들어갈 말로 가장 적절한 것은?

① worried　　② nervous
③ relaxed　　④ annoyed
⑤ anxious

3

윗글의 내용과 일치하도록 다음 문장의 빈칸에 들어갈 말로 가장 적절한 것은?

> ________ can be an example of saving time.

① Taking a nap
② Staying up late
③ Making dinner myself
④ Writing down what to do today
⑤ Setting an alarm before bedtime

4 서술형

윗글의 밑줄 친 ①~⑤ 중 가리키는 대상이 <u>다른</u> 하나를 고르고, 그 대상이 가리키는 것을 글에서 찾아 쓰시오.

(　　) ⇒ ________________________

5 서술형

윗글의 밑줄 친 ⓐtime famine을 이겨낼 수 있는 방법으로 제시된 2가지를 우리말로 쓰시오.

⇒ ________________________

____

13

Answers p. 43

다음 글을 읽고, 물음에 답해 봅시다.

Rhonda was living in a share house. When the cleaners came on weekends, they left some toilet paper in the two bathrooms. (①) However, all the toilet paper was gone by Monday. The toilet paper was for everyone, but some took more than their fair ⓐ share. (②) She felt upset about ⓑ the matter. So, she decided to put a note in one of the bathrooms. (③) It said, "Do not take all the toilet paper, please. It is a shared item. It is for everyone." (④) She was glad to see that one roll came back in a few hours and ___(A)___ the next day. (⑤) However, in ___(B)___ bathroom with no note, no toilet paper came back until the cleaners brought more.

1

윗글의 내용과 일치하는 것은?

① Rhonda는 다른 사람들과 함께 공동 생활을 하는 집에 살고 있었다.

② 셰어 하우스 주민들은 화장실 화장지를 직접 구매하여 써야 한다.

③ Rhonda는 청소부들에게 화가 났다.

④ Rhonda는 한 화장실에 화장지를 두었다.

⑤ 나머지 화장실에도 똑같은 변화가 일어났다.

2

윗글의 ①~⑤ 중 주어진 문장이 들어갈 위치로 가장 적절한 곳은?

> Then there was a surprising change.

①   ②   ③   ④   ⑤

3

윗글의 밑줄 친 ⓐshare와 의미가 같은 것은?

① They shared the pizza.

② This is your share of the pizza.

③ He shares a house with two other students.

④ Share your problems with your teacher.

⑤ Go Bank's share price fell 9% yesterday.

4 서술형

윗글의 밑줄 친 ⓑthe matter가 의미하는 바를 우리말로 쓰시오.

➡ ____________________

____

5 서술형

윗글의 빈칸 (A), (B)에 적절한 말을 아래에서 골라 쓰시오.

> another   the other

(A): ____________________

(B): ____________________

다음 글을 읽고, 물음에 답해 봅시다.

Earth Hour

Your small actions can ___ⓐ___ our Earth!
The "lights off" moment began ①in 2007.
Switch off and give an hour for Earth!
Saturday, March 25
Turn lights off ②at 8:30 p.m. to 9:30 p.m.
Just 60 minutes? Yes, just one hour.
Every year, we get together ③across the globe (A) celebrate Earth Hour and take one symbolic action: ___ⓑ___.
But it is so much more than that.
It is a symbol of unity. It is a symbol of hope.
Let's (B) show the power of collective action ④for our future and planet!
If we are together, we can do more!
Join this event ⑤with your family, friends, and neighbors!

1

윗글을 읽고 답할 수 <u>없는</u> 질문은?

① What is the event for?
② Who organizes the event?
③ What action do we take?
④ How often does the event take place?
⑤ How long does the event last every year?

2

윗글의 밑줄 친 ①~⑤ 중 어법상 틀린 것은?

①   ②   ③   ④   ⑤

3

윗글의 밑줄 친 (A)와 (B)의 적절한 형태가 바르게 짝지어 진 것은?

	(A)		(B)
①	celebrate	······	show
②	celebrate	······	shows
③	celebrates	······	shows
④	to celebrate	······	show
⑤	to celebrate	······	shows

4 〔서술형〕

다음 영어 설명을 참조하여 윗글의 빈칸 ⓐ에 들어갈 단어를 쓰시오. (단, 주어진 철자로 시작할 것)

> to keep (someone or something) safe; to stop (someone or something) from dying or being hurt, damaged, or lost

➡ s___________

5 〔서술형〕

문맥상 윗글의 빈칸 ⓑ에 적절한 말을 괄호 안의 단어를 활용하여 |조건|에 맞게 쓰시오.

┌ 조건 ├
1. 동사원형으로 시작할 것
2. 필요한 단어를 추가하여 8단어로 쓸 것

➡

(switch, the lights, just for, hour)

다음 글을 읽고, 물음에 답해 봅시다.

Naming Contest

Show your passion and (A) activity/creativity .

Please create the best name.

The name is for the study cafe of our school.

This new space will open next year.

Only students can ① use this space.

Students can study alone or ② in groups.

Sometimes students can play here.

③ Any student in our school can take part in this contest.

We hope ④ many of you will (B) manage / participate .

We will give great gifts to the winners.

You can (C) submit / receive names from October 1 to November 30.

How: Post a name with ⑤ their meaning through a QR code.

Prize: 1st Place (1 person) – tablet

2nd Place (2 people) – earphones

3rd Place (3 people) – movie ticket

Announcement of Winners: December 7

1

윗글을 읽고 공모전에 대해 알 수 없는 것은?

① 네이밍 대상
② 참가 자격
③ 심사 위원
④ 제출 방법
⑤ 제출 기한

2

윗글 (A), (B), (C)의 각 네모 안에서 문맥에 맞는 단어로 가장 적절한 것은?

	(A)	(B)	(C)
①	activity	participate	submit
②	activity	manage	receive
③	creativity	participate	receive
④	creativity	manage	submit
⑤	creativity	participate	submit

3

윗글의 밑줄 친 ①~⑤ 중 어법상 틀린 것은?

① ② ③ ④ ⑤

4 서술형

다음 영어 설명에 해당하는 단어를 윗글에서 찾아 쓰시오.

> to give a document, proposal, etc. to someone so that it can be considered or approved

➡ ___________________

5 서술형

윗글의 내용과 일치하도록 빈칸 (1)~(3)에 적절한 단어를 쓰시오. (각각 2단어로 쓸 것)

> The naming contest for the ___(1)___ will be held for ___(2)___ . The winners will be announced on ___(3)___ .

(1) ___________________
(2) ___________________
(3) ___________________

다음 글을 읽고, 물음에 답해 봅시다.

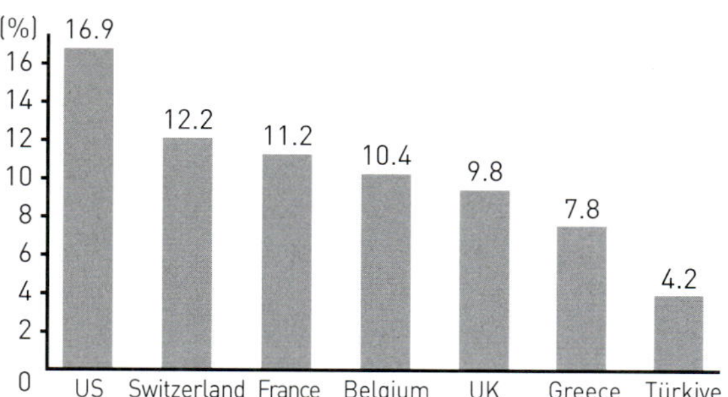

The graph above shows the percentage of GDP spent on health care in 2018. Which country spent the most among the countries shown? Which country spent the least among the countries shown? ⓐ그 나라들 사이에 큰 차이가 있나요? Let's look and compare. The US spent (A)high percentage of GDP on health care among the countries shown. Switzerland spent 12.2 percent of its GDP on health care. That's _________ than the US. France spent a (B)high percentage of its GDP on health care than Belgium. Türkiye spent _________ than 5 percent of its GDP on health care. The UK and ①Greece each spent ②more than ③5 percent of their GDP on health care. The UK spent ④one percent ⑤more of its GDP on health care than Greece did.

1

윗글의 빈칸에 공통으로 들어갈 말로 가장 적절한 것은?

① much
② less
③ more
④ least
⑤ most

2

윗글의 밑줄 친 (A)와 (B)의 적절한 형태가 바르게 짝지어진 것은?

	(A)		(B)
①	high	⋯⋯	higher
②	higher	⋯⋯	high
③	higher	⋯⋯	higher
④	the highest	⋯⋯	higher
⑤	the highest	⋯⋯	highest

3

윗글의 밑줄 친 ①~⑤ 중 도표의 내용과 일치하지 <u>않는</u> 것은?

①   ②   ③   ④   ⑤

4 서술형

윗글의 내용과 일치하도록 밑줄 친 부분을 바르게 고쳐 쓰시오.

> The US spent 16.9 percent of its GDP on health care. That's about four more than <u>the UK</u>.

_______________ ➡ _______________

5 서술형

윗글의 밑줄 친 ⓐ와 일치하도록 주어진 단어들을 바르게 배열하여 문장을 완성하시오.

➡ _______________

(difference, is, between, a, there, the countries, big)

다음 글을 읽고, 물음에 답해 봅시다.

Benjamin Franklin is one of the most important ① people in American history. He was a publisher, author, inventor, and scientist. He ② born in Boston on January 17, 1706. He was the 15th of 17 children. His father made soap and candles. He got some (A) formal / informal education but he was ③ mostly self-taught. ⓐ At the age of 12, he started to work for his brother's newspaper. ④ After he worked for four years, he began to write his own stories. (B) Because of / Instead of his real name, he wrote under a pen name, Mrs. Silence Dogood. People loved his stories. And they thought that the writer ⑤ might be a married woman. People (C) always / never thought that she was a 16-year-old boy!

1

윗글의 내용과 일치하도록 할 때, 빈칸 (A), (B)에 들어갈 말로 가장 적절한 것은?

Benjamin Franklin was a(n) ___(A)___ person in American history in the 18th century and started to ___(B)___ at the age of 16.

	(A)		(B)
①	famous	……	work
②	important	……	work
③	famous	……	study
④	important	……	write
⑤	friendly	……	write

2

윗글의 밑줄 친 ①~⑤ 중 어법상 <u>틀린</u> 것은?

①　　②　　③　　④　　⑤

3

윗글 (A), (B), (C)의 각 네모 안에서 문맥에 맞는 단어로 가장 적절한 것은?

	(A)		(B)		(C)
①	formal	……	Because of	……	always
②	formal	……	Instead of	……	never
③	formal	……	Because of	……	never
④	informal	……	Because of	……	never
⑤	informal	……	Instead of	……	always

4 서술형

다음 영어 설명에 해당하는 단어를 윗글에서 찾아 쓰시오.

a person whose job is writing books; writer

➡ ______________________

5 서술형

윗글의 밑줄 친 문장 ⓐ를 |조건|에 맞게 다시 쓰시오.

조건
1. 접속사 when을 사용할 것
2. 6단어로 쓸 것

➡ ________________________, he started to work for his brother's newspaper.

다음 글을 읽고, 물음에 답해 봅시다.

Sharks live in all areas of the seas. We can see them in shallow water to the deep sea. Most sharks live 20 to 30 years, but some species can live ⓐ<u>very</u> longer. Sharks have big, sharp teeth. (①) While humans use their teeth to bite and chew food, sharks use their teeth to grab food and swallow it all at once. (②) They eat animals ⓑ<u>like</u> fish or seals as well as other prey. (③) And blue sharks love squids. (④) Most sharks have good eyesight. (⑤) They have fantastic night vision and can see colors, too. The bodies of sharks have dark skin on top and light skin on the bottom. ⓒ<u>그것은 상어가 위협으로부터 숨도록 돕는다.</u> It can make hunting prey ⓓ<u>easily</u>, too.

1

윗글을 읽고 답할 수 <u>없는</u> 질문은?

① Where do sharks live?
② How long do sharks live?
③ What do sharks use to catch food?
④ How many sharp teeth do sharks have?
⑤ What do sharks eat?

2

윗글의 ①~⑤ 중 주어진 문장이 들어갈 위치로 가장 적절한 곳은?

For example, tiger sharks like to eat turtles.

①　　　②　　　③　　　④　　　⑤

3

윗글의 밑줄 친 ⓑlike와 같은 의미로 쓰인 것은?

① He always acts <u>like</u> my teacher.
② They don't <u>like</u> eating raw fish.
③ Just eat what you <u>like</u> and take a rest.
④ I enjoy extreme sports <u>like</u> ice climbing.
⑤ They <u>like</u> to walk in the park every day.

4 〔서술형〕

윗글의 밑줄 친 ⓐ와 ⓓ를 바르게 고쳐 쓰시오.

ⓐ ➡ ___________________
ⓓ ➡ ___________________

5 〔서술형〕

윗글의 밑줄 친 ⓒ와 일치하도록 |조건|에 맞게 문장을 쓰시오.

┌ 조건 ┐
1. 문장의 주어를 it으로 하여 5형식 문장으로 쓸 것
2. 괄호 안의 단어를 활용하되 필요한 한 단어를 추가하여 문장을 완성할 것
3. 필요시 단어의 형태를 바꾸어 쓸 것

➡ ___________________

(help, sharks, to hide, threats)

다음 글을 읽고, 물음에 답해 봅시다.

Elizabeth Catlett was born ①in Washington, D.C., in 1915. Her grandparents were slaves. So she often heard the stories of slaves ②about her grandmother. ⓐ A mostly white college turned Catlett down just because of she was black. Instead, Catlett studied design and drawing ③at Howard University, a university for black students. She earned a master's degree ④in fine arts (MFA) at the University of Iowa. ⓑ그녀는 그 대학에서 미술 석사 학위를 받은 최초의 세 명의 학생들 중 한 명이 되었다. ⑤Throughout her life, she created art. In her art, she showed the (A) [injustice / justice] or unfairness of society. She also showed the people who (B) [honored / suffered] from it. She received many prizes in the United States and Mexico. She spent over sixty years in Mexico. She became a Mexican (C) [citizen / artist] in 1962. Catlett died in 2012 at her home in Mexico.

1

윗글의 제목으로 가장 적절한 것은?

① Many Black Artists in Mexico
② Elizabeth Catlett's Grandparents
③ A Slave's Life in the United States
④ Elizabeth Catlett's Life as an Artist
⑤ Famous Artworks of Elizabeth Catlett

2

윗글의 밑줄 친 ①~⑤ 중 어법상 **틀린** 것은?

① ② ③ ④ ⑤

3

윗글 (A), (B), (C)의 각 네모 안에서 문맥에 맞는 단어로 가장 적절한 것은?

	(A)	(B)	(C)
①	justice	honored	artist
②	justice	suffered	citizen
③	injustice	honored	artist
④	injustice	suffered	citizen
⑤	injustice	suffered	artist

4 (서술형)

윗글의 밑줄 친 문장 ⓐ에서 어법상 **틀린** 부분을 찾아 바르게 고쳐 쓰시오.

____________ ➡ ____________

5 (서술형)

윗글의 밑줄 친 ⓑ와 일치하도록 주어진 단어들을 바르게 배열하시오.

➡ She ____________ an MFA at the university.

(one, to earn, of, three, the first, students, became)

다음 글을 읽고, 물음에 답해 봅시다.

A new season is ①coming. There are no more biting winds all around. No more chilly air. All the snow is ②melting away. Birds are ③singing happily. (A) Their singing makes me opens the window. I open the window and get some fresh air. (B) Everything feels and seems newly. Flower buds are about to (C) bloom / cover / drop outside the window. ⓐ그것은 나를 계속 웃게 만든다. Suddenly, I feel a strong ⓑwish to clean my own room and put a new blanket on the bed! A humming comes out of my mouth. Surprisingly, I see myself humming and dancing while ④cleaning! I didn't like to clean before! But now? I am no longer Grouchy from *The Smurfs*! You see, Grouchy always (D) complains / helps, but not me now! I am enjoying ⑤cleaning.

1

윗글의 밑줄 친 ①~⑤ 중 쓰임이 다른 것은?

①   ②   ③   ④   ⑤

2

윗글 (C), (D)의 각 네모 안에서 문맥에 맞는 단어로 가장 적절한 것은?

      (C)   (D)
① bloom ······ complains
② bloom ······ helps
③ cover ······ helps
④ drop ······ complains
⑤ drop ······ helps

3

윗글의 밑줄 친 ⓑwish와 바꿔 쓸 수 있는 것은?

① fear   ② pride
③ desire   ④ surprise
⑤ expectation

4 서술형

윗글의 밑줄 친 (A), (B)에서 어법상 틀린 것을 각각 찾아 바르게 고쳐 쓰시오.

(A): _____________ ➡ _____________

(B): _____________ ➡ _____________

5 서술형

윗글의 밑줄 친 ⓐ와 일치하도록 |조건|에 맞게 문장을 쓰시오.

┌─ 조건 ─
1. 문장의 주어를 it으로 하여 5형식 문장으로 쓸 것
2. 필요시 단어의 형태를 바꾸어 쓸 것
└

➡ _____________________________

(make, keep, me, smile)

다음 글을 읽고, 물음에 답해 봅시다.

They were very hungry for a month because there was (A) a lot of / little / a few food to eat. They tried to hunt animals for food. But they were too poor at hunting. However, ⓐ after starving for three days, Salva and the boys luckily got nothing to eat. While hunting, one of them caught a squirrel. ⓑ They wanted to build a fire. So they gathered wood. Then they roasted it on the fire. None of this took place silently. They couldn't hide the ⓒ in their voices. It seemed that it was the (B) best / worst day!

"The fire needs to be bigger."

"It won't ⓓ last long enough — we need more wood."

"Quick, turn it over, it's burning!"

The juice of it dripped and sizzled. The air was filled with a delicious smell.

1

윗글 (A), (B)의 각 네모 안에서 문맥에 맞는 말로 가장 적절한 것은?

    (A)   (B)
① a few   ⋯⋯ best
② a few   ⋯⋯ worst
③ little   ⋯⋯ best
④ little   ⋯⋯ worst
⑤ a lot of ⋯⋯ best

2

윗글의 빈칸 ⓒ에 들어갈 말로 가장 적절한 것은?

① anger   ② joy
③ sorrow   ④ jealousy
⑤ disappointment

3

윗글의 밑줄 친 ⓓlast와 의미가 같은 것은?

① Hurry up! That is the last train.
② I read an English novel last night.
③ She came in last in the marathon.
④ The popularity is going to last for years.
⑤ He has changed a lot since I last saw him.

4 　서술형

윗글의 밑줄 친 ⓐ에서 문맥상 어색한 부분을 찾아 바르게 고쳐 쓰시오.

_________________ ➡ _________________

5 　서술형

윗글의 밑줄 친 ⓑ의 두 문장을 |조건|에 맞게 한 문장으로 완성하시오.

┌ 조건 ┐
1. 문장의 동사를 gathered로 할 것
2. 6단어로 쓸 것
└─────────┘

➡ They ________________________________ .

다음 글을 읽고, 물음에 답해 봅시다.

I was waiting for my mom to come back from the mall with a special ⓐ present for me. I was pretty sure that I knew what it was. I was ⓑ_______ because I would soon have a new cell phone to communicate with! I really wanted to (A) download / upload cool apps. I was daydreaming about using all of the apps. ⓒ 나는 친구들과 게임하는 것도 상상하고 있었다! (B) However / Therefore, my mom smiled and handed me a book. I flipped through the pages. I thought that maybe she had (C) covered / hidden my new phone inside the book. But I slowly realized that my present was not a new cell phone, just a little book. There was not a new cell phone inside the book!

1

윗글의 밑줄 친 ⓐ와 의미가 같은 것은?

① You should be present at the meeting.
② He's going to present his report today.
③ I'm satisfied with my present situation.
④ We got an unexpected present from Alice.
⑤ The camp will present special experiences.

2

윗글의 빈칸 ⓑ에 들어갈 말로 가장 적절한 것은?

① proud   ② upset
③ worried   ④ thrilled
⑤ disappointed

3

윗글 (A), (B), (C)의 각 네모 안에서 문맥에 맞는 단어로 가장 적절한 것은?

	(A)	(B)	(C)
①	download	However	hidden
②	download	Therefore	hidden
③	download	Therefore	covered
④	upload	However	covered
⑤	upload	Therefore	hidden

4 〈서술형〉

다음 문장과 의미가 같도록 빈칸에 적절한 말을 쓰시오.

My mom smiled and handed me a book.
= My mom smiled and handed _______ _______ _______ _______.

5 〈서술형〉

윗글의 밑줄 친 ⓒ와 일치하도록 |조건|에 맞게 문장을 완성하시오.

┌ 조건 ┐
1. 진행형 문장으로 쓸 것
2. 괄호 안의 단어를 활용하되 필요한 단어를 추가하여 6단어로 쓸 것

➡ I was _______________________
_______________________, too!
(imagine, play games, my friends)

● Answers p. 47

다음 글을 읽고, 물음에 답해 봅시다.

Reading books has many ___ⓐ___. Interestingly, one of them ①are to reduce stress. Some studies found that ⓑ <u>독서는 스트레스 수준을 68% 줄이는 좋은 방법이다</u>. It is more effective than listening to music (61%). It is also more effective than drinking tea (54%) or going for a walk (42%). And it is ②<u>far</u> more effective than playing video games (21%). ③<u>Another</u> study showed that just 30 minutes of reading can ④<u>lower</u> blood pressure. And it can slow down heart rate. Then worries or tensions may go away. Finally, you become ___ⓒ___. ⑤<u>Besides,</u> you can enjoy reading anywhere — at home, at the park, and at the library. Also, books do not cost that much. So let's step away from cell phones. Why not open the pages of a book instead?

1

윗글의 내용과 일치하지 <u>않는</u> 것을 <u>모두</u> 고르면?

① 책을 읽으면 스트레스를 줄일 수 있다.
② 독서를 함으로써 혈압을 낮출 수 있다.
③ 독서는 심장 박동에는 영향을 미치지 않는다.
④ 스트레스를 줄이는 데는 산책이 차를 마시는 것보다 효과적이다.
⑤ 책은 비용이 그렇게 많이 들지 않는다.

2

윗글의 밑줄 친 ①~⑤ 중 어법상 <u>틀린</u> 것은?

①　　②　　③　　④　　⑤

3

윗글의 빈칸 ⓒ에 들어갈 단어로 적절한 것은?

① tense
② bored
③ worried
④ relaxed
⑤ excited

4 〔서술형〕

다음 영어 설명을 참조하여 윗글의 빈칸 ⓐ에 들어갈 단어를 쓰시오. (단, 주어진 철자로 시작할 것)

> a good or helpful result or effect; an advantage or profit gained from something

→ b________________

5 〔서술형〕

윗글의 밑줄 친 우리말 ⓑ에 맞게 주어진 단어들을 바르게 배열하시오.

→ reading ________________________________

________________, lowering them by 68%
(a great way, stress, is, to, levels, reduce)

다음 글을 읽고, 물음에 답해 봅시다.

A woman went to see a doctor. She said, "I have a problem. When I get into bed, I think that there is somebody under it. I look under the bed, then I think there is somebody on top of it. Top, under, top, under. I think I'm going crazy!" The doctor said, "Come to me for three months. You need to come here once a week. Then I will help you with your problem. It costs fifty dollars for a visit." A few days later, they met on the street. "Why didn't you come to visit me again?" the doctor asked. The woman said, "Luckily, my problem ⓐ<u>disappeared</u>. My brother helped me with the problem for just ten dollars." The doctor was ⓑ<u>shock</u>, "What did he do for you?" The woman said, "It was so simple. He told me to cut the legs of the bed. It was much ⓒ<u>cheap</u> than your suggestion."

1

윗글을 읽고 답할 수 <u>없는</u> 질문은?

① What is the woman's problem?
② How was the doctor going to help the woman?
③ How many more times did the woman have to visit the doctor?
④ Who helped the woman with her problem after all?
⑤ How much did the woman pay to get rid of the problem?

2

윗글의 밑줄 친 ⓐ와 바꿔 쓸 수 있는 것은?

① seemed　　　　② brought
③ was raised　　④ was known
⑤ was solved

3

윗글의 밑줄 친 ⓑ와 ⓒ의 적절한 형태가 바르게 짝지어진 것은?

	ⓑ		ⓒ
①	shocks	⋯⋯	cheap
②	shocked	⋯⋯	cheaper
③	shocked	⋯⋯	cheapest
④	shocking	⋯⋯	cheap
⑤	shocking	⋯⋯	cheaper

4 〈서술형〉

윗글의 다음 두 문장을 |조건|에 맞게 한 문장으로 완성하시오.

┌ 조건 ┐
1. 명령문으로 쓸 것
2. 9단어로 쓸 것

You need to come here once a week. Then I will help you with your problem.

= _________________________________

you with your problem.

5 〈서술형〉

윗글의 내용과 일치하도록 다음 빈칸에 적절한 단어를 쓰시오.

The woman's problem disappeared by ___(1)___ , not by ___(2)___ . He said to her, " ___(3)___ ."

(1) (2단어) _______________________
(2) (2단어) _______________________
(3) (6단어) _______________________

다음 글을 읽고, 물음에 답해 봅시다.

We play most major sports activities with a ball. (①) So, balls are very important in sports. (②) They are rules about the characteristics of the balls, ⓐsuch like size or weight. (③) The balls must have a certain stiffness, too. (④) A ball must have the correct size. (⑤) Also, it must have the proper weight. However, if it is made ⓑof steel, it will be too ___(A)___. Or, if it is made ⓒfrom foam rubber, it will be too ___(B)___. Similarly, ⓓalong with stiffness, a ball needs a proper ⓔamount of bounce. A solid rubber ball would be ___(C)___ for most sports. And a solid clay ball would ___(D)___ at all.

1

윗글의 ①~⑤ 중 주어진 문장이 들어갈 위치로 가장 적절한 곳은?

Ball sports have some rules about the balls used.

①   ②   ③   ④   ⑤

2

윗글의 밑줄 친 ⓐ~ⓔ 중 어법상 틀린 것은?

① ⓐ   ② ⓑ   ③ ⓒ   ④ ⓓ   ⑤ ⓔ

3

윗글의 빈칸 (A), (B)에 들어갈 말로 가장 적절한 것은?

	(A)		(B)
①	soft	·····	heavy
②	light	·····	elastic
③	stiff	·····	soft
④	heavy	·····	hard
⑤	elastic	·····	soft

4　서술형

윗글을 다음과 같이 한 문장으로 요약할 때, 빈칸에 적절한 말을 글에서 찾아 쓰시오.

In sports activities played with a ball, there are several rules about the ball: the correct ___(1)___, the proper ___(2)___, a certain stiffness, and the ___(3)___ bounce.

(1) ________________________

(2) ________________________

(3) ________________________

5　서술형

문맥상 윗글의 빈칸 (C)와 (D)에 적절한 말을 |조건|에 맞게 완성하시오.

┌ 조건 ┐
1. 단어 bounce, not, too를 사용하되, 필요시 단어의 형태를 바꾸어 쓸 것
2. 각각 2단어로 쓸 것

(C) ________________________

(D) ________________________

PART 01 Review Test

다음 글을 읽고, 물음에 답해 봅시다.

Answers p. 48

Do you like alpacas? Alpacas live in South American countries like Chile or Peru. (①) They have very soft hair. And they are famous for their cute faces and big bodies. (②) They have bad habits, so they may spit at you. (③) Why do they spit? (④) First, they want ⓐ to show that they feel angry or upset. (⑤) Second, they want to protect ⓑ them from danger.   (A)   , their spit has a very bad smell ⓒ because it includes the food they recently ate. However, you don't have to worry about that much. Alpacas are ⓓ usually peaceful animals when they feel safe.   (B)   , when you see some alpacas, you need ⓔ to be kind to them.

1

윗글을 읽고 답할 수 없는 질문은?

① Where do alpacas live?
② What are alpacas famous for?
③ What do alpacas usually eat?
④ Why should we be nice to alpacas?
⑤ What do alpacas do when they feel unsafe?

2

윗글의 ①~⑤ 중 주어진 문장이 들어갈 위치로 가장 적절한 곳은?

> But when you meet these animals, you should always be careful!

①   ②   ③   ④   ⑤

3

윗글의 빈칸 (A)와 (B)에 들어갈 말이 바르게 짝지어진 것은?

	(A)		(B)
①	Therefore	······	So
②	In addition	······	So
③	In addition	······	For example
④	Therefore	······	However
⑤	Therefore	······	On the contrary

4 서술형

윗글의 밑줄 친 ⓐ~ⓔ 중 어법상 틀린 것을 찾아 바르게 고쳐 쓰시오.

(   ) ➡ ____________________

5 서술형

윗글의 밑줄 친 문장을 우리말로 해석하시오.

➡ ____________________

Imagine that you have ① to stay alone on a desert island. What would you do first? Maybe you would say, "Make an SOS sign, or "Find some food". But I suggest that you find some ② water drink first. Water is the most important thing to help you ___ⓐ___. If you don't have ③ enough water in your body, you will die, even in just three days. (A) [For example / For this reason], you must find water that is safe to drink. Here are some tips to help you find clean drinking water. First, the water in streams or rivers ④ is usually safe. But you should remember that it may still have some diseases in it. Second, save some rainwater (B) [although / because / while] it is drinkable. Third, there is some water in many foods, ⑤ such as coconuts and fruit. ⓑ 여러분이 이러한 조언들을 명심한다면, 여러분은 무인도에서 더욱 안전해질 것이다.

1

윗글의 제목으로 가장 적절한 것은?

① Tips for Changing Rainwater into Clean Water
② How to Stay Safe in a Dangerous Desert
③ Making an SOS Sign: The First Thing I Should Do
④ How to Find Some Water on a Desert Island
⑤ Food: What You Need Most on a Desert Island

2

윗글의 밑줄 친 ①~⑤ 중 어법상 틀린 것은?

①   ②   ③   ④   ⑤

3

윗글 (A), (B)의 각 네모 안에서 문맥에 맞는 단어로 가장 적절한 것은?

	(A)	(B)
①	For example	although
②	For example	because
③	For example	while
④	For this reason	although
⑤	For this reason	because

4 (서술형)

다음 영어 설명을 참조하여 윗글의 빈칸 ⓐ에 들어갈 단어를 주어진 철자로 시작하여 쓰시오.

> to remain alive; to continue to live

➡ s________________

5 (서술형)

윗글의 밑줄 친 우리말 ⓑ에 맞게 괄호 안의 단어들을 바르게 배열하여 문장을 완성하시오.

➡ If you ________________________,
________________________ on a desert island.

(be, in mind, you, safer, these tips, will, keep)

다음 글을 읽고, 물음에 답해 봅시다.

When children are upset, what is a good way ⓐ to calm them down? One easy and ① quickly way is to give them some food. This helps them ⓑ change their focus from being upset to something else. They will use their hands and mouth to do something else. So, they can (A) forget / remember the things they are angry about. If you give them snacks, ② such as candy or chocolate, children will feel ③ more happily. In the short term, ④ use food in this way is (B) effective / ineffective. But, in the longer term, this can be (C) harmful / useful. The children might think that ⓒ 그들이 부정적인 감정을 보이면 간식을 받을 것이다. Then, when they feel bad, upset, or even ⑤ boring, they will want some food to make themselves ⓓ feel better.

1

윗글의 밑줄 친 ⓐ와 쓰임이 같은 것은?

① Her dream is to be a violinist.
② Children like to eat chocolates.
③ I went to France to meet Lisa.
④ He was too sick to go to school.
⑤ We needed some water to drink.

2

윗글의 밑줄 친 ①~⑤ 중 어법상 올바른 것은?

①   ②   ③   ④   ⑤

3

윗글 (A), (B), (C)의 각 네모 안에서 문맥에 맞는 단어로 가장 적절한 것은?

	(A)	(B)	(C)
①	forget	effective	harmful
②	forget	ineffective	harmful
③	forget	effective	useful
④	remember	effective	harmful
⑤	remember	ineffective	useful

4 서술형

윗글의 밑줄 친 ⓑ와 ⓓ의 적절한 형태를 각각 쓰시오.

ⓑ ➡ ___________________

ⓓ ➡ ___________________

5 서술형

윗글의 밑줄 친 우리말 ⓒ와 일치하도록 |조건|에 맞게 문장을 쓰시오. (단, 필요하면 형태를 바꿀 것)

조건
1. 문장의 주어를 they로 하고 조건절을 뒤에 쓸 것
2. 괄호 안의 단어들을 활용하되 필요한 단어를 추가하여 11단어로 쓸 것

➡ ___________________

____

(get, show, any, negative, emotions, will, a, snack)

다음 글을 읽고, 물음에 답해 봅시다.

Can you see any window or clock in a department store? You may not even think about this. Actually, there are no windows or clocks in most department stores. Why is this? It is a secret marketing skill. Windows and clocks make you ⓐ<u>think</u> about the time. ⓑ<u>백화점은 사람들이 시간에 대해 생각하지 않고 쇼핑을 즐기기를 원한다.</u> So, they use this way to make people focus on shopping. Also, department stores decorate or hang advertisements on their walls. If there are some clocks or windows on the walls, it is ＿＿(A)＿＿ the walls. This is the ＿＿(B)＿＿ of department stores. So, the next time you visit a department store, look around carefully. Does the store have windows, clocks, or advertisements on its walls?

1

윗글을 다음과 같이 요약할 때, 빈칸에 들어갈 말로 가장 적절한 것은?

> Department stores do not have windows or clocks because they think windows or clocks ＿＿＿＿＿ people's shopping.

① help
② increase
③ upgrade
④ interfere with
⑤ satisfy

2

윗글의 밑줄 친 ⓐ의 형태로 적절한 것은?

① think
② thinks
③ to think
④ thinking
⑤ have thought

3

윗글의 빈칸 (A)에 들어갈 말로 적절한 것은?

① useful to cover
② simple to build
③ hard to use
④ easy to decorate
⑤ difficult to paint

4 （서술형）

다음 영어 설명을 참조하여 윗글의 빈칸 (B)에 들어갈 단어를 글에서 찾아 쓰시오. (주어진 철자로 시작할 것)

> a fact or piece of information that is kept hidden from other people

➡ s＿＿＿＿＿＿＿＿＿

5 （서술형）

윗글의 밑줄 친 ⓑ와 일치하도록 |조건|에 맞게 문장을 완성하시오.

> | 조건 |
> 1. 현재시제로 쓰고 문장의 목적어를 people로 할 것
> 2. 괄호 안의 단어들을 활용하되, 필요하면 형태를 바꿀 것
> 3. 필요한 단어를 추가하여 7단어로 쓸 것

➡ The department store ＿＿＿＿＿＿＿＿＿＿＿＿

＿＿＿＿＿＿＿＿＿＿ about the time.

(want, enjoy, shop, without, think)

다음 글을 읽고, 물음에 답해 봅시다.

Do you think a cup of coffee can help you wake up? Most studies show that caffeine helps you (A) <u>stay</u> awake all day long. And even just 60mg of caffeine can make you (B) <u>react</u> faster. Caffeine is also (C) effective / ineffective for relieving headaches when it is used together with medicine. However, ⓐ <u>caffeine can take the place of a good night's sleep.</u> One study showed that caffeine can increase the ⓑ <u>chances</u> of people with little sleep making mistakes. Also, they did not get (D) lower / higher / fewer scores on tests, even after having caffeine, than a group with enough sleep. Therefore, ⓒ______ cannot fully make up for ______ⓓ______ . To do your work better, you need sleep more than coffee.

1

윗글의 밑줄 친 (A), (B)의 형태로 적절한 것끼리 짝지어진 것은?

     (A)   (B)
① stay ······ react
② stay ······ to react
③ to stay ······ reacting
④ staying ······ to react
⑤ staying ······ react

2

윗글의 밑줄 친 ⓑchances와 바꿔 쓸 수 있는 것은?

① lucks   ② goals
③ disadvantages   ④ possibilities
⑤ researches

3

윗글 (C), (D)의 각 네모 안에서 문맥에 맞는 단어로 가장 적절한 것은?

     (C)   (D)
① effective ······ higher
② effective ······ lower
③ effective ······ fewer
④ ineffective ······ higher
⑤ ineffective ······ lower

4 서술형

윗글의 밑줄 친 ⓐ에서 문맥상 어색한 부분을 찾아 바르게 고쳐 쓰시오.

__________ ➡ __________

5 서술형

윗글의 빈칸 ⓒ와 ⓓ에 적절한 말을 주어진 단어들을 사용하여 써 넣어 문장을 완성하시오. (단, 필요하면 형태를 바꿀 것)

➡ Therefore, ⓒ__________ cannot fully make up for ⓓ__________ .
(have enough sleep, not, use caffeine)

다음 글을 읽고, 물음에 답해 봅시다.

Where does the trash go after you throw it away? You may think it will (A) harm / save the earth. But, in the fashion field, trash can become new, fancy products (B) such as / thanks to creative thinking. It is a new kind of fashion, called '   ⓐ   '. The German company 'Freitag' makes bags from many pieces of waterproof cloth and safety belts. They need (C) little / many pieces of cloth and belts to make their bags. Naturally, tons of trash is used. Their bags soon became famous   ⓑ   they are strong, waterproof, and eco-friendly. Also, all their bags in the world are different   ⓑ   each bag is made from many different types of cloth. This trend in the fashion field is not only unique, but also good for the environment.

1

윗글의 'Freitag'에 관한 내용으로 일치하지 <u>않는</u> 것은?

① It's a German company.
② It is famous for its strong bags.
③ It uses tons of trash to make products.
④ Its bags are waterproof and eco-friendly.
⑤ Its products are made of one unique cloth.

2

윗글 (A), (B), (C)의 각 네모 안에서 문맥에 맞는 단어로 가장 적절한 것은?

	(A)	(B)	(C)
①	harm	such as	little
②	harm	such as	many pieces of
③	harm	thanks to	many pieces of
④	save	such as	little
⑤	save	thanks to	many pieces of

3

윗글의 빈칸 ⓑ에 공통으로 들어갈 말로 적절한 것은?

① that   ② when
③ because   ④ although
⑤ whether

4 서술형

다음 영어 설명을 참조하여 윗글의 빈칸 ⓐ에 적절한 단어를 쓰시오.

the process of converting waste materials or unwanted products into new materials and products of greater quality

➡ ___________________________

5 서술형

다음 빈칸에 공통으로 들어갈 가장 적절한 단어를 윗글에서 찾아 쓰시오.

· This jacket is ________, so it prevents water.
· Our sunscreens filter UVB rays and it is also ________.
· Please pack extra clothing, ________ mask, and a first-aid kit.

➡ ___________________________

One late evening in August of 1952, a man opened and closed the piano cover three times in a theater. He pressed the timer on the piano. And he did not press ① any keys for four minutes and thirty-three seconds. It seems ② strangely, but it was John Cage's 4'33". It was a famous piece of music with ③ only silence. Cage thought people could feel the music (A) regardless / with / without the artist, so he removed the artist from the music. ④ During the performance, the artist and composer could not make an impact on the music. Even Cage ⓐ himself had no way to (B) control / create the sounds in the theater. There was ⑤ still real-life noise and people also had some feelings and thoughts. ⓑ 그는 우리가 느끼는 모든 것이 음악이 될 수 있다는 것을 보여 주고 싶었다.

1

윗글의 밑줄 친 ①~⑤ 중 어법상 틀린 것은?

①   ②   ③   ④   ⑤

2

윗글 (A), (B)의 각 네모 안에서 문맥에 맞는 단어로 가장 적절한 것은?

	(A)		(B)
①	regardless	……	control
②	with	……	control
③	with	……	create
④	without	……	control
⑤	without	……	create

3

윗글의 밑줄 친 ⓐ와 쓰임이 같은 것은?

① She always talks about herself.
② I recorded the music myself.
③ Remember to love yourself all the time.
④ He likes to look at himself in the mirror.
⑤ Heaven helps those who help themselves.

4 (서술형)

윗글의 밑줄 친 우리말 ⓑ와 일치하도록 주어진 단어들을 바르게 배열하여 문장을 완성하시오.

➡ He wanted ________________

________________ .

(we, music, that, feel, to show, can be, all the things)

5 (서술형)

윗글의 내용과 일치하도록 주어진 단어들을 사용하여 |조건|에 맞게 문장을 완성하시오. (단, 필요하면 형태를 바꿀 것)

┤ 조건 ├
(1) 긍정문과 부정문을 한 번씩 사용할 것
(2) 각 빈칸에 can을 사용할 것
(3) 괄호 안의 단어들을 활용하되 필요한 단어를 추가하여 각각 4단어로 쓸 것

➡ In John Cage's 4'33", you ________________ from the artist, but you ________________ in real-life noise in the theater.
(hear, sounds, feel, any, the music)

다음 글을 읽고, 물음에 답해 봅시다.

YouTube Shorts, TikToks, or Instagram reels. You might watch these ①kinds of videos. They are all "short-form media." Short-form media ②have content which is under 10 minutes or under 1,000 words. People become (A) familiar / strange with this short videos because they can get information easily and quickly. With the rise of short-form media, people are turning away from long-form media ⓐlike books and movies. They lose their focus quickly and don't want ③to know the full content. A study by Microsoft shows that short-form media (B) maintained / decreased / increased the attention time of teenagers. In Just ④a few years, it became 8 seconds from over 10 seconds. This is a serious problem, because ⓑ8 seconds is shorter than that of a goldfish. ⓒ학교에서, 학생들은 또한 수업에 집중하는 데 어려움을 겪는다. Short videos have ⑤both good and bad points: They provide quick information but also decrease students' attention time.

1

윗글 (A), (B)의 각 네모 안에서 문맥에 맞는 단어로 가장 적절한 것은?

	(A)		(B)
①	familiar	......	maintained
②	familiar	......	decreased
③	familiar	......	increased
④	strange	......	decreased
⑤	strange	......	increased

2

윗글의 밑줄 친 ①~⑤ 중 어법상 **틀린** 것은?

①   ②   ③   ④   ⑤

3

윗글의 밑줄 친 ⓐlike와 의미가 같은 것은?

① They like posting clips on their social media.
② I don't want to be treated like a child.
③ We always like to take on new challenges.
④ He has taught subjects like math and science.
⑤ The fiction I like most is *The Adventures of Sherlock Holmes*.

4 （서술형）

윗글의 밑줄 친 ⓑ와 의미가 같도록 적절한 말을 넣어 문장을 완성하시오.

> 8 seconds is shorter than that of a goldfish
> = The ____(1)____ of a goldfish is ____(2)____ 8 seconds

→ (1) ________________ ________________
  (2) ________________ ________________

5 （서술형）

윗글의 밑줄 친 우리말 ⓒ와 일치하도록 |조건|에 맞게 문장을 완성하시오. (단, 필요하면 형태를 바꿀 것)

조건
1. 문장의 주어를 students로 할 것
2. 괄호 안의 단어들을 활용하되 필요한 단어를 추가하여 8단어로 쓸 것

→ In school, ________________________________

________________________________.

(focus, have, their, classes, also, difficult)

다음 글을 읽고, 물음에 답해 봅시다.

When children become four years old, they start ⓐunderstand other people's thinking. For example, you can ask a four-year-old girl, "What is inside the package of gum?" She will say, "Gum." ⓑ<u>You open the package and show to her what's inside.</u> There is a pencil inside. Then, you ask her, "What will your mom think is inside?" (①) Her mom is waiting outside the room, ____ⓒ____ she cannot see what's inside. (②) Still, the girl will say "Gum". (③) But children under four will say, "Pencil" in the same example. (④) They cannot imagine their mom did not see inside. (⑤) They do not know someone needs ⓓsee inside to know what is in there. So, they think everyone thinks the same way ⓔ<u>as</u> they do.

1

윗글의 ①~⑤ 중 주어진 문장이 들어갈 위치로 가장 적절한 곳은?

> It is because she knows her mother did not see the pencil inside.

①   ②   ③   ④   ⑤

2

윗글의 빈칸 ⓒ에 들어갈 말로 적절한 것은?

① if   ② so
③ unless   ④ though
⑤ because

3

윗글의 밑줄 친 ⓔas와 쓰임이 같은 것은?

① She is as tall <u>as</u> their parents.
② Please do <u>as</u> I ask this time.
③ I got angry <u>as</u> she told me a lie.
④ They have worked <u>as</u> travel guides.
⑤ He called me <u>as</u> I was watching TV.

4 〔서술형〕

윗글의 밑줄 친 ⓐ, ⓓ를 각각 적절한 형태로 쓰시오.

ⓐ ➡ ______________________

ⓓ ➡ ______________________

5 〔서술형〕

윗글의 밑줄 친 ⓑ에서 <u>틀린</u> 부분을 찾아 바르게 고쳐 쓰시오.

You open the package and show to her what's inside.

______________ ➡ ______________

다음 글을 읽고, 물음에 답해 봅시다.

Imagine that you are late for school. But all the traffic lights you meet are red. You may think, "Anything that can go wrong will go wrong." This idea ⓐ call Murphy's Law. (A) Besides / However / Therefore , some scientists say that we don't have to think so negatively. They say that the reason for the way we think is ___ⓑ___ . ⓒ우리의 뇌는 우리가 한 모든 것을 기억할 수 없다. Only strong memories (B) change / disappear / remain in the brain, so we remember a failure or bad things much more than positive things. For example, our brain does not focus on crossing the street easily when there is a green light. But, at a red light, we should stop and wait for a few minutes. This small difference makes us think we meet more red lights than green lights. If this thinking is repeated often, we mostly remember the bad things and finally think that we always fail.

1

윗글로 보아, Murphy's Law에 해당하지 <u>않는</u> 것을 <u>모두</u> 고르면?

① 지각했는데 타야 할 버스가 늦게 왔다.
② 길을 건너는데 신호등이 녹색으로 바뀌었다.
③ 시험 직전에 읽은 부분에서 문제가 출제되었다.
④ 내가 계산하려고 선 줄이 가장 늦게 줄어들었다.
⑤ 토스트가 떨어졌는데 잼을 바른 쪽이 바닥으로 떨어졌다.

2

윗글의 밑줄 친 ⓐ call의 형태로 적절한 것은?

① calls
② called
③ is called
④ is calling
⑤ to be called

3

윗글 (A), (B)의 각 네모 안에서 문맥에 맞는 단어로 가장 적절한 것은?

	(A)	(B)
①	Besides	change
②	However	disappear
③	However	remain
④	Therefore	change
⑤	Besides	remain

4 （서술형）

다음 영어 설명을 참조하여 윗글의 빈칸 ⓑ에 적절한 말을 주어진 철자로 시작하여 쓰시오.

> the tendency to remember only what one wants to remember

➡ s_______________ m_______________

5 （서술형）

윗글의 밑줄 친 우리말 ⓒ와 일치하도록 주어진 단어들을 바르게 배열하여 문장을 완성하시오.

➡ Our brains _______________________

_______________________________________ .

(did, the things, remember, we, all, cannot)

다음 글을 읽고, 물음에 답해 봅시다.

When we talk to people, we also use our body language. Some people think body language is like a dictionary. They use body language like a set of rules. With this dictionary approach, they cannot find the many sides of social understanding. ⓐ그들은 팔짱을 끼고 있는 누군가를 볼 수 있다 and think they're angry, or see someone (A)smile and think they're happy. But when people communicate by just memorizing certain signals, they cannot see the bigger picture. It's ⓑ ______ than that. Trying to use body language by reading a body language dictionary is likes trying to speak French by reading a French dictionary. Our body language might be thought of as robotic and (B)confuse if we don't use it naturally.

1

윗글을 다음과 같이 요약할 때, 다음 빈칸 (A), (B)에 들어갈 말로 가장 적절한 것은?

> Body language ____(A)____ a set of rules. Memorizing certain signals is ____(B)____ to understand body language. You should consider many sides of social understanding.

	(A)	(B)
①	is	enough
②	is	not enough
③	is not	not enough
④	is not	necessary
⑤	has been	necessary

2

윗글의 밑줄 친 (A), (B)의 형태로 적절한 것끼리 짝지어진 것은?

	(A)	(B)
①	smile	confused
②	smiles	confusing
③	smiled	confused
④	smiling	confused
⑤	smiling	confusing

3

윗글의 빈칸 ⓑ에 들어갈 말로 적절한 것은?

① easier   ② smaller
③ more desirable ④ less difficult
⑤ more complicated

4 서술형

윗글의 밑줄 친 우리말 ⓐ와 일치하도록 |조건|에 맞게 문장을 완성하시오. (단, 필요하면 형태를 바꿀 것)

> ┤ 조건 ├
> 1. 적절한 소유격을 사용할 것
> 2. 괄호 안의 단어들을 활용하되 필요한 단어를 추가하여 6단어로 쓸 것

➡ They might ________________________________

____.

(arms, someone, with, cross, see)

5 서술형

다음 빈칸에 적절한 말을 윗글에서 찾아 쓰시오.

> ______________ body language signals is not enough. We should understand and use body language within ______________ context.

다음 글을 읽고, 물음에 답해 봅시다.

What is an important thing in learning something? High IQ? A good teacher? Enough study time? They are all (A)| separate / related / relative |. But a learning style gives you an answer to ____ⓐ___. ① To find your own learning style, there is a simple question. If you want to learn ② what to play a new board game, what will you do? First, you can read the manual carefully and take notes. Second, you can listen to others' explanations and ask questions. Third, you can watch others ③ play and try it yourself. Your own actions can show your learning style.

There are three types of learning styles. The first type is visual learning. People with a visual learning style learn by reading and taking notes. For them, drawing a diagram or pictures is helpful for learning. The second type of people focuses on (B)| content / sounds |. They learn through hearing and saying something. So, reading the text aloud can be a good way for them ④ to learn something. The last type of person uses their body. They learn by moving their body. They can use ____ⓑ___ to learn something. Every student uses their own learning style to learn. Knowing one's own learning style helps the student ⑤ learns more effectively. So, understand how you learn and use it as much as possible!

1

윗글 (A), (B)의 각 네모 안에서 문맥에 맞는 단어로 가장 적절한 것은?

	(A)		(B)
①	separate	⋯⋯	content
②	related	⋯⋯	sounds
③	related	⋯⋯	content
④	relative	⋯⋯	sounds
⑤	relative	⋯⋯	content

2

윗글의 빈칸 ⓐ에 들어갈 말로 적절한 것은?

① how you can learn best
② how fast you can learn games
③ what you should do before learning
④ why you should read the learning manual
⑤ how you can have enough study time

3

윗글의 밑줄 친 ①~⑤ 중 어법상 **틀린** 것은? (2개)

①   ②   ③   ④   ⑤

4 서술형

다음 영어 설명을 참조하여 윗글의 빈칸 ⓑ에 적절한 말을 쓰시오. (단, 복수형으로 쓸 것)

> an activity in which people do and say things while pretending to be someone else in a particular situation

➡ __________________

5 서술형

윗글의 내용과 일치하도록 다음 빈칸에 적절한 단어를 |보기에서 골라 쓰시오.

보기
| learning   effective   helpful |

It is __________ for students to know their own __________ style for __________ learning.

다음 글을 읽고, 물음에 답해 봅시다.

Is hacking always bad? There are good hackers, white hat hackers. They use their hacking skills ⓐ to find some problems with (A) charity / security . They are different from black hat hackers. They (B) follow / make the law when they hack. The name "white hat" hacker is from old American movies about the country's "Wild West" days. Heroes in those movies wore white hats, and the bad guys wore black hats. So, today's good hackers became 'white hat' hackers.

(①) Marc Maiffret is one of the famous white hat hackers. (②) Because of this problem, black hat hackers could get into the software and steal its data. (③) But he helped Microsoft (C) cause / solve the problem. (④) He made a new program to protect the software. (⑤) Since we use the Internet a lot, ⓑ Maiffret과 같은 화이트 햇(하얀 모자) 해커는 우리의 개인 정보를 보호하는 데 중요한 역할을 한다.

1

윗글의 ①~⑤ 중 주어진 문장이 들어갈 위치로 가장 적절한 곳은?

> He found a big weak point in Microsoft software.

①　　　②　　　③　　　④　　　⑤

2

윗글의 밑줄 친 ⓐ to find와 쓰임이 같은 것은?

① We like to ride bicycles.
② His goal is to help the poor.
③ I called him to ask for help.
④ He was happy to win first place.
⑤ She planned to travel to America.

3

윗글 (A), (B), (C)의 각 네모 안에서 문맥에 맞는 단어로 가장 적절한 것은?

	(A)	(B)	(C)
①	charity	follow	cause
②	charity	make	solve
③	security	follow	cause
④	security	follow	solve
⑤	security	make	cause

4　서술형

윗글의 밑줄 친 우리말 ⓑ와 일치하도록 주어진 단어들을 사용하여 문장을 완성하시오. (단, 필요하면 형태를 바꿀 것)

➡ a white hat hacker like Maiffret ___________ ___________ our personal information
(protecting, role, important, play, an, in)

5　서술형

윗글의 내용과 일치하도록 다음 문장에서 틀린 단어를 찾아 바르게 고쳐 쓰시오.

> White hat hackers are people who stop black hat hackers from keeping people's information on the Internet.

___________ ➡ ___________

다음 글을 읽고, 물음에 답해 봅시다.

In a thick, green forest, there lived a huge elephant and a tiny family of ants. The elephant looked down on all the small animals. He was ① proud of his strength and wanted to ② show it off. On the other hand, the ant family was always busy ⓐ find food.

One day, when the ant family was going to work, the elephant sprayed a lot of water on them. "Ouch! You should not hurt others like this!" cried one of the ants. The elephant said, "Oh, stupid ant! ⓑ If you don't keep quiet, I will kill you. The poor ant was (A) nervous / scared / confident , but he decided to teach him a lesson.

The ant slowly ③ crawled into the elephant's body and started biting him. Soon, the elephant couldn't move. The elephant tried to get the ant out, but he (B) continued / stopped / remembered biting him. The elephant was a big animal, but he couldn't do anything ④ for the tiny ant.

He ⑤ shouted in pain and started to cry. Finally, he apologized to the ant. The ant said, "This is how we feel when you hurt us!" The ant stopped biting and came out of the elephant's body. From that day on, he didn't hurt other small animals anymore.

1

윗글의 밑줄 친 ①~⑤ 중 문맥상 어색한 것은?

①   ②   ③   ④   ⑤

2

윗글의 밑줄 친 ⓐ의 형태로 적절한 것은?

① find   ② finds
③ to find   ④ finding
⑤ found

3

윗글 (A), (B)의 각 네모 안에서 문맥에 맞는 단어로 가장 적절한 것은?

    (A)   (B)
① nervous ····· stopped
② scared ····· continued
③ scared ····· stopped
④ confident ····· continued
⑤ confident ····· remembered

4 〔서술형〕

윗글의 밑줄 친 문장 ⓑ를 |조건|에 맞게 다시 쓰시오.

┌─ 조건 ┐
1. 명령문으로 시작할 것
2. 7단어로 줄여 쓸 것

➡ _______________________________

5 〔서술형〕

윗글의 내용과 일치하도록 다음 빈칸에 적절한 단어를 넣어 문장을 완성하시오.

After feeling his __________, the elephant realized how he __________ other small animals and __________ to the ant.

40

다음 글을 읽고, 물음에 답해 봅시다.

One day a poor man gave a bunch of grapes to a prince ① as a gift. He was very ⓐ to bring a gift for him because he was too (A) rich / sick / poor to buy anything else. He put the grapes near the prince and said, "Oh. Prince, please take this small gift from me." He was so happy ② because he could give him his small gift.

The prince thanked him politely. As the man looked at him, the prince ate one grape. Then he ate another one. Slowly the prince finished the whole bunch of grapes by himself. He did not give any grapes to anyone near him. The poor man was very pleased and left. The close friends of the prince were very ⓑ .

Usually, the prince shared everything he had with others. He would share with them ③ whatever he was given, and they would eat it together. This time, it was (B) the same / different / enough . He ate the bunch of grapes all by himself. One of the friends asked, "Prince! Why did you eat all the grapes by ④ you and not share them with us?" He smiled and said that he did it because the grapes were too sour.

The prince said, "I thought that if I shared the grapes with you, you would make funny faces and say the grapes were bad. That would hurt the feelings of the poor man. So I thought it would be better if I ate all the grapes happily by myself ⑤ to please him. I

didn't want to hurt the poor man's feelings." Everyone around him was ⓒ .

1

윗글을 다음과 같이 요약할 때, 빈칸에 들어갈 말로 가장 적절한 것은?

> The prince ate all the sour grapes. It was because he didn't want to _________ a poor man that brought the grapes.

① amaze　　② disappoint　③ shock
④ surprise　　⑤ thank

2

윗글의 밑줄 친 ①~⑤ 중 어법상 틀린 것은?

①　　②　　③　　④　　⑤

3

윗글 (A), (B)의 각 네모 안에서 문맥에 맞는 단어로 가장 적절한 것은?

	(A)		(B)
①	rich	·····	different
②	sick	·····	the same
③	sick	·····	enough
④	poor	·····	different
⑤	poor	·····	the same

4 서술형

다음에 주어진 단어들을 사용하여 윗글의 빈칸 ⓐ, ⓑ, ⓒ 에 들어갈 적절한 형태를 쓰시오. (단, 한 번씩만 사용할 것)

> surprise　　impress　　excite

ⓐ _______________________

ⓑ _______________________

ⓒ _______________________

READING 01

1 They keep warm in the Arctic thanks to their special hair and black skin.

2 The hair is filled with air, and it traps the sun's heat.

3 When they shake their body after swimming, the water comes off their body right away.

4 It soaks up the sunlight, so they don't easily get cold.

5 Moreover, underneath the black skin is a thick layer of body fat.

READING 02

1 You can enjoy many types of activities there.

2 They're the world's biggest waterfalls with about 275 different waterfalls.

3 You can experience the highest point, the Devil's Throat, by taking a boat tour, helicopter ride, or just by walking on the trails.

4 You can hike around the rainforest, below the falls, and even on top of the falls.

5 Just remember to bring your raincoat, or you may get wet.

03·04

글을 의미 단위로 끊어 읽고 주어와 동사 에 표시하며 해석하시오.

Answers p. 53

READING 03

1 Sometimes a different view pleases us.

2 For example, Pablo Picasso, a famous artist, tried to see the world differently.

3 When you first see his work, you may not notice the players.

4 But when you keep looking at the painting, you can see them in it!

5 His work used shapes, objects, and colors so differently from the real world.

READING 04

1 For ancient Egyptians, cats were the most special animal.

2 To honor the cats, rich families put jewelry on them.

3 When cats died, their owners would shave their eyebrows.

4 The ancient Egyptians protected cats even by law.

5 Cats were clearly more than just pets to them.

READING 05

1 When you go camping, you make sure to bring enough food.

2 Like on Earth, astronauts eat three meals a day.

3 There is also an oven in a spacecraft and it can make food warm.

4 So all the food comes in packets for easy storage.

5 Sauces like ketchup, mustard, and mayonnaise are also available in tubes.

READING 06

1 Or can you think of anyone in sports history with a record of only wins?

2 Roger Federer, for example, is the world's greatest tennis player with twenty Grand Slam titles.

3 In other words, he lost in more than two-thirds of the tournaments.

4 Still, we think of him as a champion, not as a failure.

5 Try to accept your failure and move on from it.

● Answers p. 54

글을 의미 단위로 끊어 읽고 주어와 동사 에 표시하며 해석하시오.

READING 07

1   Thank you for visiting our zoo for your field trip!

2   Before your visit, please advise your students not to throw waste in the zoo.

3   Plastic bags and other trash can be very harmful to our animals.

4   Like small children, animals love to test things with their mouths.

5   They may mistake this trash for food and swallow it.

READING 08

1   Don't click the Send button right away when you send emails.

2   However, it doesn't matter if you don't click the Send button.

3   Looking again and fixing should come first; sending should come later.

4   So, don't forget to read your writing carefully before you click the Send button.

5   The same goes for sending school assignments or business letters by email.

● Answers p. 55

글을 의미 단위로 끊어 읽고 주어와 동사 에 표시하며 해석하시오.

READING 09

1   We started a new tutor-tutee project in science class last month.

2   I was good at science, so I volunteered as a student teacher.

3   At first, I thought I was spending too much time with the tutee.

4   As a tutor, I began to understand the material better and more clearly.

5   I also got a better grade on the final exam thanks to the project.

READING 10

1   Observing nature can make human life better.

2   After using this paint, you can wash the outside of your house less often.

3   This discovery came from looking at lotus leaves.

4   They look like small nails and make the surface rough.

5   Always try to observe nature closely!

READING 11

1 We communicate with others through language.

2 Therefore, we should be careful about when and how we use them.

3 It usually means agreement or "okay" in many countries like Korea and Japan.

4 Gestures such as a thumbs up have different meanings in many cultures or countries.

5 So, to avoid misunderstandings, be careful how you use them!

READING 12

1 It is the feeling of having too much to do when you do not have enough time.

2 It makes you feel nervous.

3 One study shows that time famine can make students feel more stressed than when they get a low score.

4 There is a way to overcome this.

5 For instance, you can use a food delivery service instead of eating out or cooking meals.

글을 의미 단위로 끊어 읽고 주어와 동사에 표시하며 해석하시오.

READING 13

1 When the cleaners came on weekends, they left some toilet paper in the two bathrooms.

2 However, all the toilet paper was gone by Monday.

3 So, she decided to put a note in one of the bathrooms.

4 She was glad to see that one roll came back in a few hours and another the next day.

5 However, in the other bathroom with no note, no toilet paper came back until the cleaners brought more.

READING 14

1 Your small actions can save our Earth!

2 Switch off and give an hour for Earth!

3 But it is so much more than that.

4 Let's show the power of collective action for our future and planet!

5 If we are together, we can do more!

READING 15·16

PART 02 핵심 직독직해

글을 의미 단위로 끊어 읽고 주어와 동사 에 표시하며 해석하시오.

READING 15

1 The name is for the study cafe of our school.

2 This new space will open next year.

3 Any student in our school can take part in this contest.

4 We hope many of you will participate.

5 How: Post a name with its meaning through a QR code.

READING 16

1 The graph above shows the percentage of GDP spent on health care in 2018.

2 Which country spent the least among the countries shown?

3 The US spent the highest percentage of GDP on health care among the countries shown.

4 The UK and Greece spent the same percentage of their GDP on health care.

5 They also each spent more than 5 percent of their GDP on health care.

READING 17

1 Benjamin Franklin is one of the most important people in American history.

2 He got some formal education but he was mostly self-taught.

3 After he worked for four years, he began to write his own stories.

4 Instead of his real name, he wrote under a pen name, Mrs. Silence Dogood.

5 People never thought that she was a 16-year-old boy!

READING 18

1 We can see them in shallow water to the deep sea.

2 Most sharks live 20 to 30 years, but some species can live far longer.

3 While humans use their teeth to bite and chew food, sharks use their teeth to grab food and swallow it all at once.

4 The bodies of sharks have dark skin on top and light skin on the bottom.

5 It helps sharks to hide from threats.

글을 의미 단위로 끊어 읽고 주어와 동사 에 표시하며 해석하시오.

READING **19**

1 So she often heard the stories of slaves from her grandmother.

2 A mostly white college turned Catlett down just because she was black.

3 She became one of the first three students to earn an MFA at the university.

4 In her art, she showed the injustice or unfairness of society.

5 She also showed the people who suffered from it.

READING **20**

1 Their singing makes me open the window.

2 Flower buds are about to bloom outside the window.

3 Suddenly, I feel a strong wish to clean my own room and put a new blanket on the bed!

4 Surprisingly, I see myself humming and dancing while cleaning!

5 You see, Grouchy always complains, but not me now!

READING 21

1 They were very hungry for a month because there was little food to eat.

2 However, after starving for three days, Salva and the boys luckily got something to eat.

3 While hunting, one of them caught a squirrel.

4 It won't last long enough — we need more wood.

5 The air was filled with a delicious smell.

READING 22

1 I was waiting for my mom to come back from the mall with a special present for me.

2 I was thrilled/ because I would soon have a new cell phone to communicate with!

3 I was daydreaming about using all of the apps.

4 I thought that maybe she had hidden my new phone inside the book.

5 But I slowly realized that my present was not a new cell phone, just a little book.

READING 23

1 Some studies found that reading is a great way to reduce stress levels, lowering them by 68%.

2 And it is far more effective than playing video games (21%).

3 Another study showed that just 30 minutes of reading can lower blood pressure.

4 Then worries or tensions may go away.

5 Why not open the pages of a book instead?

READING 24

1 When I get into bed, I think that there is somebody under it.

2 I look under the bed, then I think there is somebody on top of it.

3 It costs fifty dollars for a visit.

4 My brother helped me with the problem for just ten dollars.

5 He told me to cut the legs of the bed.

READING **25**

1 Ball sports have some rules about the balls used.

2 They are rules about the characteristics of the balls, such as size or weight.

3 However, if it is made of steel, it will be too stiff.

4 Similarly, along with stiffness, a ball needs a proper amount of bounce.

5 And a solid clay ball would not bounce at all.

READING **26**

1 Alpacas live in South American countries like Chile or Peru.

2 They have bad habits, so they may spit at you.

3 First, they want to show that they feel angry or upset.

4 In addition, their spit has a very bad smell because it includes the food they recently ate.

5 So, when you see some alpacas, you need to be kind to them.

READING 27

1 Imagine that you have to stay alone on a desert island.

2 For this reason, you must find water that is safe to drink.

3 Here are some tips to help you find clean drinking water.

4 But you should remember that it may still have some diseases in it.

5 If you keep these tips in mind, you will be safer on a desert island.

READING 28

1 When children are upset, what is a good way to calm them down?

2 This helps them change their focus from being upset to something else.

3 If you give them snacks, such as candy or chocolate, children will feel happier.

4 In the short term, using food in this way is effective.

5 Then, when they feel bad, upset, or even bored, they will want some food to make themselves feel better.

READING 29

1 Can you see any window or clock in a department store?

2 Windows and clocks make you think about the time.

3 Also, department stores decorate or hang advertisements on their walls.

4 If there are some clocks or windows on the walls, it is hard to use the walls.

5 So, the next time you visit a department store, look around carefully.

READING 30

1 And even just 60mg of caffeine can make you react faster.

2 Caffeine is also effective for relieving headaches when it is used together with medicine.

3 One study showed that caffeine can increase the chances of people with little sleep making mistakes.

4 Also, they did not get higher scores on tests, even after having caffeine, than a group with enough sleep.

5 Therefore, using caffeine cannot fully make up for not having enough sleep.

READING

31·32

PART 02 핵심 직독직해

글을 의미 단위로 끊어 읽고 <u>주어</u>와 <u>동사</u>에 표시하며 해석하시오.

READING 31

1 Where does the trash go after you throw it away?

2 But, in the fashion field, trash can become new, fancy products thanks to creative thinking.

3 They need many pieces of cloth and belts to make their bags.

4 Also, all their bags in the world are different because each bag is made from many different types of cloth.

5 This trend in the fashion field is not only unique, but also good for the environment.

READING 32

1 One late evening in August of 1952, a man opened and closed the piano cover three times in a theater.

2 Cage thought people could feel the music without the artist, so he removed the artist from the music.

3 Even Cage himself had no way to control the sounds in the theater.

4 There was still real-life noise and people also had some feelings and thoughts.

5 He wanted to show that all the things we feel can be music.

글을 의미 단위로 끊어 읽고 주어와 동사 에 표시하며 해석하시오.

READING **33**

1 Short-form media has content which is under 10 minutes or under 1,000 words.

2 With the rise of short-form media, people are turning away from long-form media like books and movies.

3 They lose their focus quickly and don't want to know the full content.

4 A study by Microsoft shows that short-form media decreased the attention time of teenagers.

5 They provide quick information but also decrease students' attention time.

READING **34**

1 When children become four years old, they start to understand other people's thinking.

2 You open the package and show her what's inside.

3 Her mom is waiting outside the room, so she cannot see what's inside.

4 They do not know someone needs to see inside to know what is in there.

5 So, they think everyone thinks the same way as they do.

READING 35

1 But all the traffic lights you meet are red.

2 They say that the reason for the way we think is selective memory.

3 Only strong memories remain in the brain, so we remember a failure or bad things much more than positive things.

4 This small difference makes us think we meet more red lights than green lights.

5 If this thinking is repeated often, we mostly remember the bad things and finally think that we always fail.

READING 36

1 When we talk to people, we also use our body language.

2 With this dictionary approach, they cannot find the many sides of social understanding.

3 But when people communicate by just memorizing certain signals, they cannot see the bigger picture.

4 Trying to use body language by reading a body language dictionary is like trying to speak French by reading a French dictionary.

5 Our body language might be thought of as robotic and confusing if we don't use it naturally.

READING 37

1   To find your own learning style, there is a simple question.

2   Third, you can watch others play and try it yourself.

3   For them, drawing a diagram or pictures is helpful for learning.

4   So, reading the text aloud can be a good way for them to learn something.

5   Knowing one's own learning style helps the student learn more effectively.

READING 38

1   The name "white hat" hacker is from old American movies about the country's "Wild West" days.

2   Heroes in those movies wore white hats, and the bad guys wore black hats.

3   Because of this problem, black hat hackers could get into the software and steal its data.

4   He made a new program to protect the software.

5   Since we use the Internet a lot, a white hat hacker like Maiffret plays an important role in protecting our personal information.

READING **39**

1 He was proud of his strength and wanted to show it off.

2 One day, when the ant family was going to work, the elephant sprayed a lot of water on them.

3 The ant slowly crawled into the elephant's body and started biting him.

4 The elephant was a big animal, but he couldn't do anything against the tiny ant.

5 From that day on, he didn't hurt other small animals anymore.

READING **40**

1 One day a poor man gave a bunch of grapes to a prince as a gift.

2 Slowly the prince finished the whole bunch of grapes by himself.

3 One of the friends asked, "Prince! Why did you eat all the grapes by yourself and not share them with us?"

4 The prince said, "I thought that if I shared the grapes with you, you would make funny faces and say the grapes were bad."

5 So I thought it would be better if I ate all the grapes happily by myself to please him.

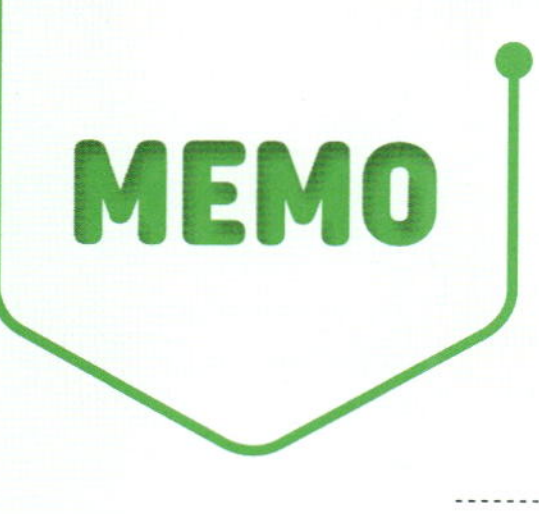

MEMO

기본 독해부터 수능 독해까지
한번에 완성

ANSWERS

Reading∞ master 중등

수능 plus 내신

Level 1

이투스북

Reading master 중등 ∞

수능 plus 내신

Level 1

ANSWERS

Chapter 01

중심 내용 파악하기

Unit 01 주제 파악하기

Reading Key 영어 지문 구조 이해하기 pp.10~13

정답

A 주제문 소음, 부정적인
예시 향상됨, 시끄러운, 조용한

B 예시 지루하고
주제문 갈등, 이야기

C 일반적인 이야기 행동
반론(주제문) 판단

D 주제문 조건
예시 (테니스를) 치는 즐거움, 배우고, 훈련(연마)해야
주제문 키워 가야

해석

A 교실 안의 소음은 아이들의 학업에 부정적인 영향을 미친다. 몇몇 연구에서, 아이들은 더 조용한 교실에서 더 잘 의사소통할 수 있었고 그들의 시험 결과는 향상되었다. 초등과 고등학교 학생을 대상으로 한 연구는 비슷한 결과를 보여 준다. 읽기와 수학 시험에서 시끄러운 교실에 있는 학생들은 더 조용한 환경에 있는 학생들보다 성적이 더 낮았다.

B Kryptonite가 없는 '슈퍼맨'을 상상해 보라. Voldemort가 없는 해리 포터 시리즈는 어떠한가? 그 영화들은 지루하고 예측 가능할 것이다. 지나친 조화는 따분한 이야기를 만든다. 갈등은 좋은 이야기에 필수적이다. 갈등이 없으면 이야기도 없다.

C 행동으로 사람들을 판단하는 것은 쉽다. 사람들은 보통 우리가 말보다 행동에 더 많은 가치를 두어야 한다고 말한다. 그러나 여러분은 누군가를 정의하기 전에 그들에게 다시 한 번 기회를 줘야 한다. 그들 중 몇몇은 여러분의 절친한 친구가 될 수도 있다. 그러니 사람들을 성급하게 판단하지 마라.

D 여러분은 행복의 조건을 살 수 있지만, 행복은 살 수 없다. 그것은 테니스를 치는 것과 같다. 여러분은 가게에서 공과 라켓을 살 수 있지만, (테니스를) 치는 즐거움을 살 수는 없다. 테니스의 즐거움을 경험하기 위해, 여러분은 (테니스를) 치는 법을 배우고, 스스로 훈련해야 한다. 행복도 이와 같다. 여러분은 행복을 키워 가야 한다. 여러분은 그것을 가게에서 살 수 없다.

READING 01 · 정답 ⑤ pp. 14~15

Mini Quiz 모범답안 they don't feel cold in the freezing Arctic temperatures

1 ④ **2** 모범 답안 북극곰들이 수영 후에 몸을 흔들면 물이 몸에서 바로 떨어지는 것 **3** (1) colorless (2) oily (3) black (4) fat (5) warm

해석

북극곰은 온혈 동물이지만, 영하의 북극 기온에서 추위를 느끼지 않는다. 그들은 특별한 털과 검은 피부 덕분에 북극에서 따뜻하게 지낸다. 첫째, 그들의 털은 빈 튜브처럼 대부분 투명하고 무색이다. 털은 공기로 채워져 있고 태양열을 가둔다. 북극곰의 털은 또한 기름지다. 북극곰들이 수영 후에 몸을 흔들면 물이 몸에서 바로 떨어진다. 이것은 그들이 젖는 것을 막는다. 둘째로, 북극곰은 털 아래에 검은 피부가 있다. 그것이 햇빛을 흡수해서 북극곰들은 쉽게 추워지지 않는다. 게다가, 검은 피부 아래에는 두꺼운 체지방층이 있다. 그것은 (북극곰들이) 수영하는 동안 그들을 따뜻하게 유지해 준다.

해설

p. 14

본문은 북극곰이 추운 북극에서 따뜻하게 지낼 수 있는 방법에 관해 설명한 글이므로 주제는 ⑤ '북극곰이 따뜻함을 유지하는 방법'이다.
① 북극의 동물들
② 위험에 처한 북극곰
③ 북극의 기온
④ 북극곰이 물에서 수영하는 방법

p. 15

1 북극곰은 검은 피부와 투명하고 무색인 털을 가지고 있다. 따라서 투명하고 무색의 피부를 가지고 있다는 ④의 내용은 본문과 일치하지 않는다.
① 그들은 온혈 동물이다.
② 그들의 비어있는 털은 태양열을 가둔다.
③ 그들은 수영 후에 몸을 흔든다.
⑤ 수영을 할 때, 그들은 추위를 느끼지 않는다.

2 밑줄 친 This는 바로 직전 문장을 의미한다. 즉, 북극곰들이 수영 후에 몸을 흔들면 물이 몸에서 바로 떨어지는 것을 의미한다.

3 **해석**
· 털: 그들의 투명하고 무색인 털은 태양열을 가둔다. / 그들의 기름진 털은 그들이 수영으로 젖지 않도록 도와준다.
· 피부: 그들은 검은 피부를 갖고 있으며, 그것은 햇빛을 흡수한다. / 그들은 피부 아래 두꺼운 체지방층을 갖고 있다.
→ 북극곰들은 북극에서 따뜻하게 지낼 수 있다.

- They **keep warm** in the Arctic **thanks to** their special hair and black skin.

  「keep + 형용사」는 '~한 상태를 유지하다'의 뜻이며, thanks to는 '~ 덕분에'의 뜻으로 명사를 이끈다.

- **When** they shake their body after swimming, the water comes off their body right away.

  when은 접속사로 '~할 때, ~하면'의 의미를 나타낸다.

- This **stops** them **from getting** wet.

  stop A from B는 'A가 B하는 것을 막다'의 뜻으로 전치사 from 다음에 동명사(동사 -ing)를 쓴다.

- It **keeps them warm** while swimming.

  keep A B는 'A(명사)가 B(형용사)한 상태를 유지하다'라는 뜻이며, while 다음에 주어인 they와 동사인 are가 생략되었다.

Reading Skill

모범 답안

주제문	• 북극곰은 영하의 기온에도 추위를 느끼지 않는다.
근거문	• 북극곰은 특별한 털과 검은 피부 덕분에 북극에서 따뜻하게 지낼/유지할 수 있다.

직독직해 Skill

- First, / their hair (S) is (V) / mostly clear and colorless, / like an empty tube.

  첫째 / 그들의 털은 ~이다 / 대부분 투명하고 무색인 / 빈 튜브처럼

READING **02** 정답 ⑤

pp. 16~17

Mini Quiz 주제문: You can enjoy many types of activities there.

근거문: 1. First, you can see the Iguazú Falls.
2. You can also see wild animals in the park.
3. Last, you can go hiking to different places.

1 ② 2 ⓐ Iguazú National Park ⓑ the Iguazú Falls
3 (1) biggest (2) animals (3) hiking

해석

이구아수 국립공원은 아르헨티나에서 매우 큰 국립공원이다. 그곳에서 다양한 종류의 활동을 즐길 수 있다. 먼저, 여러분은 이구아수 폭포를 볼 수 있다. 그것은 약 275개의 다양한 폭포로 이루어진 세계 최대의 폭포이다. 가장 높은 지점인 '악마의 목구멍'은 보트 투어를 하거나 헬리콥터를 타거나 산책로를 걷는 것만으로 경험할 수 있다. 공원에서는 야생동물도 볼 수 있다. 재규어, 물고기, 거북, 원숭이와 같은 많은 종류의 동물들이 있다. 마지막으로, 여러분은 여러 곳으로 하이킹을 갈 수 있다. 열대 우림 주변, 폭포 아래, 심지어 폭포 위에서도 하이킹을 할 수 있다. 비옷을 가져가는 것만 기억해라, 그렇지 않으면 젖을 수 있다.

해설

p. 16

본문은 아르헨티나의 이구아수 국립공원에서 즐길 거리에 관한 내용이므로 주제는 ⑤ '이구아수 국립공원에서 할 활동들'이다.

① 이구아수 폭포의 크기
② 아르헨티나의 국립공원들
③ 이구아수 폭포의 하이킹 코스
④ 이구아수 국립공원의 위치

p. 17

1 ② 이구아수 폭포의 높이에 관해서는 본문에서 언급되지 않았다.

  ① 이구아수 국립공원은 어디에 위치하는가? – 아르헨티나
  ③ 이구아수 폭포의 가장 높은 지점은 어디인가? – 악마의 목구멍
  ④ '악마의 목구멍'에 어떻게 갈 수 있는가? – 보트 투어나 헬리콥터 등을 이용
  ⑤ 이구아수 국립공원을 방문할 때 왜 비옷이 필요한가? – 젖을 수 있어서

2 ⓐ 그곳에서 다양한 종류의 활동을 즐길 수 있다.
  ⓑ 그것들은 약 275개의 다양한 폭포로 이루어진 세계 최대의 폭포이다.

3 **해석** 1. 세계 최대의 폭포인 이구아수 폭포를 보러 오세요.
  2. 재규어, 물고기, 거북, 원숭이와 같은 많은 종류의 동물들을 보세요.
  3. 열대 우림 주변, 폭포 아래, 폭포 위에 있는 다양한 하이킹 코스를 방문하세요.

구문 설명

- They're **the** world's **biggest** waterfalls with about 275 different waterfalls.

  「the + 형용사의 -est」는 최상급 표현으로 '가장 ~한'을 뜻하므로, the biggest waterfalls는 가장 큰 폭포를 의미한다.

- You can experience **the highest** point, the Devil's Throat, **by taking** a boat tour, helicopter ride, or just **by walking** on the trails.

  최상급 표현인 the highest가 쓰여, '가장 높은'의 의미로 해석된다. by -ing는 '~함으로써, ~해서'의 뜻으로 by 다음에 수단이나 방법의 내용을 쓴다.

- **There are** many kinds of animals such as jaguars, fish, turtles, and monkeys.

There are 구문은 '~가 있다'를 뜻하며 「there+동사+주어」의 어순으로 쓴다. 주어가 복수인 many kinds of animals이므로 복수형 동사 are를 쓴다.

· Just **remember to** bring your raincoat, **or** you **may** get wet.
「remember+to부정사」는 '(미래에) ~할 것을 기억하다'라는 뜻이며 「remember+동명사(동사+-ing)」는 '(과거에) ~한 것을 기억하다'의 의미임을 유의해야 한다.
「명령문+or」는 '~해라, 그렇지 않으면 …할 것이다'로 해석한다. 종속절에 may가 쓰여 뒷부분이 '…할지도 모른다'로 해석된다.

모범 답안

주제문	·이구아수 국립공원에서 다양한 활동(들)을 즐길 수 있다.
근거문	1. 이구아수 폭포를 볼 수 있다. 2. 야생동물을 볼 수 있다. 3. 열대 우림 주변, 폭포 아래, 폭포 위에서 하이킹을 할 수 있다.

· There are (V) / many kinds of animals (S) / such as jaguars, fish, turtles, and monkeys.
~가 있다 / 많은 종류의 동물들이 / 재규어, 물고기, 거북, 원숭이와 같은

READING **03** 정답 ④ pp. 18~19

(Mini Quiz) Sometimes a different view pleases us.

1 ⑤ **2** please **3** differently

해석

때때로 다른 관점은 우리를 즐겁게 한다. 예를 들어, 유명한 예술가인 파블로 피카소는 세상을 다르게 보려고 노력했다. 그의 유명한 작품 '세 명의 악사들'에서, 그는 세 명의 연주자들을 그렸다. 하지만 그는 세 사람을 그리지 않았다. 대신, 그는 추상적인 형태를 사용하였다. 여러분이 이 작품을 처음 볼 때는 그 연주자들을 알아차리지 못할 수도 있다. 아무것도 이해되지 않을 것이다. 하지만 계속해서 그 그림을 보면, 여러분은 그 그림 속에서 그들을 볼 수 있다! 그것은 마치 퍼즐과 같다. 피카소의 작

품은 특별한 그림의 방식을 보여 준다. 그의 작품은 형태, 사물, 그리고 색깔을 실제 세상과 매우 다르게 사용했다. 그의 그림들은 매우 독특해 보인다. 작품을 이해하기 위해서 여러분은 사물을 완전히 다르게 보아야 한다. 이것은 완전히 새로운 기쁨이 될 수 있다. 그것은 세상을 다르게 보는 기쁨이다.

해설

p. 18
본문은 유명한 화가인 파블로 피카소처럼 세상을 다른 시각으로 보는 즐거움에 대한 글이므로 주제는 ④ '다르게 보는 즐거움'이다.
① 파블로 피카소의 삶
② 예술과 함께 사는 이점
③ 색을 사용하는 다른 방법들
⑤ 다른 관점을 나누는 것의 중요성

p. 19
1 피카소는 실제 세상과 완전히 다르게 작품을 그렸다. 따라서 실제 세상의 모습과 비슷하게 그렸다는 ⑤의 내용은 본문과 일치하지 않는다.

2 amuse와 please는 '(사람을) 즐겁게 하다, 기쁘게 하다'라는 의미를 가지고 있다.

3 해석 파블로 피카소의 작품으로, 여러분은 세상을 다르게 보는 즐거움을 발견할 수 있습니다. 우리가 사물을 다르게 볼 때, 우리는 피카소처럼 완전히 새로운 기쁨을 경험할 수 있습니다.

구문 설명

· For example, Pablo Picasso, a famous artist, tried to see the world differently.
Pablo Picasso와 a famous artist(유명한 예술가)는 동격의 comma(콤마)로 연결되어 있다.

· **Nothing makes sense** to you.
Nothing은 단수 취급을 하므로 단수 동사를 사용해야 하고, make sense는 '이해가 되다'라는 뜻이다.

· But when you **keep looking** at the painting, you can see them in it!
「keep -ing」는 '계속 ~하는 중이다'의 뜻으로 어떤 행동을 계속해서 하는 경우에 쓰인다.

· His paintings **look** very **unique**.
「look+형용사」는 '~하게 보이다'라는 뜻이며, '~하게'라고 해석되더라도 '형용사'가 쓰인다는 점에 유의해야 한다.

· **To understand** the work, you should view things completely differently.
To understand는 목적을 나타내는 to부정사의 부사적 용법으로 '~하기 위하여'로 해석된다.

모범 답안

주제문	· 때때로 <u>다른 관점</u>은 우리를 즐겁게 한다.
근거문	· 작가: 파블로 피카소 · 작품명: <u>세 명의 악사들</u> · 특징: 세 명의 연주자들을 그리기 위해 추상적인 형태를 사용했다.

· To understand the work, / you (S) should view (V) / things / completely differently.
작품을 이해하기 위해서 / 여러분은 보아야 한다 / 사물들을 / 완전히 다르게

Unit 02 제목 파악하기

READING **04**  정답 ③   pp. 20~21

Mini Quiz   ancient Egyptians, cats

1 ③   2 ancient Egyptians
3 (1) (i)mportant (2) (m)agical (3) (j)ewelry

고대 이집트인들에게 고양이는 가장 특별한 동물이었다. 그들은 처음으로 고양이를 반려동물로 키웠다. 이집트인들은 고양이가 마법의 동물이라고 믿었다. 그들은 고양이가 행운을 가져다준다고 생각했다. 고양이들에게 경의를 표하기 위해, 부유한 가정은 그들에게 보석을 걸어 주었다. 자신들은 또한 고양이들에게 고품질의 음식을 주었다. 고양이는 고대 이집트 생활의 중요한 부분이었다. 고양이들이 죽었을 때, 그들의 주인들은 그들의 눈썹을 밀곤 했다. 그들은 눈썹이 다시 자랄 때까지 슬픔을 드러냈다. 고대 이집트인들은 심지어 법으로 고양이를 보호했다. 사람이 고양이를 죽였을 때, 그 사람 또한 죽임을 당했다. 그들에게 고양이들은 분명히 반려동물 그 이상이었다.

p. 20

고양이라는 동물이 고대 이집트인들에게 가지는 의미와 중요성에 대해 설명하는 글이므로 이 글의 제목으로 가장 적절한 것은 ③ '고대 이집트인들에게 있어서 고양이의 중요성'이다.
① 동물 보호법의 필요성

② 눈썹의 특별한 기능
④ 다른 나라들에서 가장 좋아하는 동물들
⑤ 고양이와 개의 차이점

p. 21

1 고대 이집트인들이 눈썹을 미는 것은 고양이의 죽음에 대한 슬픔을 표현하기 위한 것이므로 글의 내용과 일치하지 않는 것은 ③이다.
① 고양이는 고대 이집트인들에게 특별한 반려동물이었다.
② 일부 고양이는 고대 이집트에서 보석을 착용했다.
④ 고대 이집트인들은 고양이에 대한 법이 있었다.
⑤ 고양이는 고대 이집트인들에게 그저 동물이 아니었다.

2 밑줄 친 They는 앞 문장의 '고대 이집트인들'을 지칭하므로 이를 두 단어인 ancient Egyptians로 써야 한다.

3 **해석** 고양이는 고대 이집트인들에게 중요했다. 고대 이집트인들은 고양이가 마법의 동물이라고 생각했다. 고대 이집트의 고양이들은 심지어 보석과 고품질의 음식을 가졌다. 사람들은 고양이를 매우 잘 돌보았다.

· They first kept cats **as** pets.
as는 '~로서'라는 뜻이다.

· **To honor** the cats, rich families put jewelry on them.
To honor는 목적을 나타내는 to부정사의 부사적 용법으로 '~하기 위하여'로 해석된다.

· **When** cats died, their owners **would** shave their eyebrows.
When은 접속사로 '~할 때, ~하면'의 뜻이며 would는 조동사로 '~하곤 했다'의 의미이다.

· They showed their sadness **until** their eyebrows **grew back**.
until은 '~할 때까지'라는 뜻의 접속사로, 뒤에 주어와 동사를 갖춘 문장이 왔다. grow back은 '다시 자라다'의 뜻이다.

· The ancient Egyptians protected cats **even by law**.
by law는 '법률적으로, 법에 의해'라는 뜻이며, even은 '심지어, ~조차'라는 뜻으로 무언가를 강조할 때 쓰인다.

모범 답안

주제문	· <u>고양이</u>는 고대 이집트인들에게 가장 <u>특별한</u> 동물이었다.
근거문	· 고양이에게 <u>보석</u>을 걸어 주거나 <u>고품질의 음식</u>을 주었다. · 고양이가 죽으면 <u>눈썹</u>을 밀었다.

· They (S) showed (V) / their sadness / until / their eyebrows / grew back.
그들은 드러냈다 / 그들의 슬픔을 / ~할 때까지 / 그들의 눈썹이 / 다시 자랐다

READING **05** → 정답 ②   pp. 22~23

(Mini Quiz) There are many different foods for astronauts in space.

1 ④   2 모범답안 It's because there is no refrigerator in a spacecraft. / It's because a spacecraft doesn't have a refrigerator.   3 (1) dried (2) canned (3) tubes

해석

캠핑을 갈 때, 여러분은 반드시 충분한 음식을 가지고 가야 한다. 우주비행사들이 우주에 갈 때도 같은 일을 한다. 그들은 음식을 준비한다. 지구에서와 마찬가지로, 우주비행사들은 하루에 세 끼를 먹는다. 우주에는 우주비행사들을 위한 많은 다양한 음식들이 있다. 건조된 음식은 매우 흔하다. 통조림으로 된 감자와 고기가 있다. 우주선은 신선한 과일과 채소를 저장할 수 있다. 우주선 안에는 오븐도 있고 그것은 음식을 따뜻하게 만들 수 있다. 하지만 냉장고가 없다. 그래서 모든 음식은 쉽게 보관할 수 있도록 포장되어 있다. 소금은 액체로 나온다. 보통의 소금은 그냥 떠다니고 말 것이다. 케첩, 머스타드, 마요네즈 같은 소스도 튜브에 넣어져 이용할 수 있다. 이러한 다양한 우주 음식들로, 우주비행사들은 우주에서 건강하게 지낼 수 있다.

해설

p. 22
우주비행사들이 우주에서 먹을 수 있는 다양한 음식에 대해 설명하고 있는 글이므로 이 글의 제목으로 가장 적절한 것은 ② '우주비행사들을 위한 우주 음식'이다.
① 다양한 종류의 소금
③ 캠핑을 위해 필요한 것
④ 우주비행사가 되는 방법
⑤ 다른 문화에서 온 음식들

p. 23
1 우주에서 소금이 필요하지 않은 것이 아니라 소금이 액체 형태라고 설명하고 있으므로 글의 내용을 바르게 이해하지 못한 학생은 ④이다.

2 글의 내용에 따르면 우주에서의 음식이 쉽게 보관할 수 있도록 포장되어 나오는 이유는 우주선에 냉장고가 없기 때문이므로 It's because there is no refrigerator in a spacecraft.의 내용으로 답을 써야 한다.

3 **해석** 우주비행사들은 우주에서 많은 다양한 음식들을 먹을 수 있다. 모든 음식은 쉽게 보관할 수 있도록 포장되어 있다. 비록 몇몇 신선한 음식들을 이용할 수 있지만, 다른 음식들은 건조되거나 통조림으로 만들어진다. 소스는 튜브로 나온다.

(구문 설명)

· When you go camping, you **make sure to** bring enough food.
「make sure to+동사원형」은 '반드시(꼭) ~하다'라는 뜻이다.

· Like on Earth, astronauts eat three meals **a day**.
a day는 '하루에'라는 뜻이고 a month, a year는 각각 '한 달에, 일 년에'라는 뜻이다.

· There is also an oven in a spacecraft and it can **make food warm**.
make A(명사) B(형용사)는 'A를 B하게 만들다'는 뜻이다.

· Salt comes **as** liquid.
as는 '~로'라는 뜻으로 소금이 액체 상태임을 설명한다.

· Sauces **like** ketchup, mustard, and mayonnaise are also available in tubes.
like는 '~와 같은'이란 뜻을 가지며 예시를 들 때 사용한다.

모범 답안

주제문	· 우주비행사들을 위한 다양한 음식(들)이 있다.
근거문	· 건조된 음식과 감자와 고기 통조림이 있으며, 신선한 과일과 채소를 보관할 수도 있다. · 소금은 액체 형태이고, 소스들은 튜브에 넣어져 있다.

· With these various space foods, / astronauts (S) can stay (V) / healthy / in space.
이러한 다양한 우주 음식들로 / 우주비행사들은 유지할 수 있다 / 건강하게 / 우주에서

READING **06** → 정답 ④   pp. 24~25

(Mini Quiz) 모범답안 failure, success

1 ②   2 success   3 (1) failure (2) winning (3) failure

여러분은 전혀 실패한 적 없는 사람을 알고 있나요? 아니면 스포츠 역사 상 우승 기록만 있는 사람을 생각할 수 있나요? 아마 아닐 겁니다. 예를 들어, Roger Federer는 20개의 그랜드 슬램 타이틀을 보유한 세계 최고의 테니스 선수입니다. 그러나 그는 실제로 60개 이상의 그랜드 슬 램 토너먼트에서 경기를 했습니다. 다시 말해서, 그는 토너먼트의 2/3 이상에서 패했습니다. 그는 이긴 것보다 더욱 많은 토너먼트에서 졌습니 다. 여전히, 우리는 그를 실패자가 아니라 챔피언으로 생각합니다. 실패 는 성공을 만듭니다. 그러니 실패를 두려워하지 마세요. 경기에서 지거나 시험을 통과하지 못하는 것은 괜찮습니다. 그 누구도 완벽하지는 않습니 다. 여러분의 실패를 받아들이고 그것으로부터 나아가려고 노력하세요.

해설

p. 24

본문은 성공은 실패를 기반으로 한다는 내용을 주제로 하므로, ④ '성공 은 실패 없이 오지 않는다'가 제목으로 가장 적절하다.

① 완벽해져라

② 여러분만의 경기를 만들어라

③ 이기는 것이 가장 중요하다

⑤ 목표를 세우고, 경기를 위해 연습해라

p. 25

1 Roger Federer가 우승 기록만 가지고 있다는 ②는 본문의 내용 과 일치하지 않는다.

　① 그는 매우 훌륭한 테니스 선수이다.

　③ 그는 20개의 그랜드 슬램 타이틀을 획득하였다.

　④ 그는 60개 이상의 그랜드 슬램 토너먼트에서 경기를 했다.

　⑤ 사람들은 그를 실패자가 아닌 성공한 사람으로 여긴다.

2 Ann: 나 어제 영어시험 통과하지 못했어.

　Jiho: 너무 걱정하지 마. 실패는 성공의 디딤돌이야.

3 해석 글쓴이의 조언

　사람들은 그들의 실패로부터 배우고, 그것(실패)은 성공을 이끕니 다. 그것(실패)은 경기에서 이기는 것보다 더 중요합니다. 따라서 당 신의 실패를 두려워하지 마세요.

구문 설명

- Roger Federer, for example, is **the world's greatest** tennis player **with** twenty Grand Slam titles.
　최상급 표현인 the greatest가 쓰여, '최고의, 가장 훌륭한'의 의미 로 해석된다. 「with + 명사」는 '~을 가진, ~을 보유한'의 뜻이다.

- But he actually played in **more than** sixty Grand Slam tournaments.
　more than은 비교급 표현으로 '~ 이상의, ~보다 더 많은'을 뜻한 다. 형용사 many의 비교급 형태인 more가 사용되었다.

- In other words, he lost in more than **two-thirds** of the tournaments.

영어에서 분수를 나타낼 때에는 '분자–분모' 순으로 읽으며 분자는 기수, 분모는 서수로 쓴다. 분자가 2 이상일 때는 분모에 복수의 -s를 붙이므로 $\frac{2}{3}$는 two-thirds가 된다.

- Still, we **think of him as a champion**, not as a failure.
　think of A as B는 'A를 B로 생각하다(여기다)'를 뜻하며 뒤에 not as a failure가 이어져 '그(A)를 실패자가 아닌 챔피언(B)으 로 생각한다'로 해석된다.

- Losing a game or **not passing** a test is okay.
　동명사(동사원형 -ing) 형태가 문장의 주어로 쓰였으며, 동명사 주어 에 A or B 구문이 사용되어 '경기에서 지거나 시험을 통과하지 못하 는 것'의 의미로 해석된다. 동명사의 부정은 동명사 앞에 not을 쓴다.

Reading Skill

모범 답안

주제문	· 실패는 성공을 만든다.
예시	· Roger Federer는 경기에서 이긴 횟수보다 진 횟수 가 훨씬 더 많다.

직독직해 Skill

- Losing a game or not passing a test (S) / is (V) okay.
　경기에서 지는 것 또는 시험을 통과하지 못하는 것은 / 괜찮다

Unit 03 목적·주장 파악하기

READING **07** 　정답 ④

pp. 26~27

Mini Quiz　모범 답안 Before your visit, please advise your students not to throw waste in the zoo.

1 ⑤　**2** 쓰레기를 삼키는 것　**3** (1) Trash　(2) harmful　(3) eat (4) sick

해석

강 선생님께

저는 Fun & Joy 동물원의 관광 안내원입니다. 현장 학습으로 저희 동물 원을 방문해 주셔서 감사합니다! 이곳에서 멋진 하루를 보내시기 바랍니

다. 선생님께 부탁드리고 싶은 게 있습니다. 방문하시기 전에 학생들에게 동물원에 쓰레기를 버리지 않도록 지도해 주십시오. 쓰레기통은 동물원 곳곳에 있습니다. 비닐봉지와 기타 쓰레기들은 우리 동물들에게 매우 해로울 수 있습니다. 어린아이들처럼 동물들은 입으로 사물을 시험하는 것을 아주 좋아합니다. 동물들은 이 쓰레기를 음식으로 착각하여 삼킬 수도 있습니다. 그것이 그들을 매우 아프게 할 수 있습니다. 그러므로 우리의 사랑스러운 동물들의 건강을 위해 학생들이 동물원에 쓰레기를 버리면 안 됩니다. 협조해 주셔서 감사합니다.

Danna Smith 드림

p. 26

동물원으로 현장 학습을 오는 학생들에게 동물원에 쓰레기를 버리지 않도록 지도해 달라고 부탁하는 내용의 글이므로 이 글의 목적은 ④가 가장 적절하다.

p. 27

1 ① 누가 이 메일을 썼는가? – Danna Smith
   ② Danna Smith의 직업은 무엇인가? – (Fun&Joy 동물원의) 관광 안내원
   ③ 필자는 누구에게 이 메일을 보낼 것인가? – 강 선생님
   ④ 강 선생님과 그의 학생들은 어디로 현장 학습을 갈 예정인가?
      – Fun&Joy 동물원
   ⑤ 동물원에서 학생들이 제일 좋아하는 활동은 무엇인가?
      – (알 수 없음)

2 밑줄 친 It은 쓰레기를 음식으로 착각해서 삼키는 행동을 가리킨다.

3 원인: 쓰레기는 동물원에서 해로울 수 있다.
   결과: 동물원의 동물들이 쓰레기를 먹을 수도 있고 동물들이 아프게 될 수 있다.

- I would like to **ask you a favor**.
  「ask+사람+a favor」는 '~에게 부탁을 하다'라는 의미이다.

- Before your visit, please **advise** your students **not to throw** waste in the zoo.
  advise ~ not to...는 '~에게 …하지 말라고 지도(조언)하다'의 의미이다.

- They may **mistake** this trash for food **and swallow** it.
  mistake와 swallow는 may 뒤에 이어지는 동사로, and로 병렬 연결되어 있으므로 형태가 같아야 한다.

- It can **make them** very **sick**.
  「make+목적어+형용사」는 '~을 …하게 하다'라는 의미이다.

모범 답안

주제문	• 학생들은 <u>동물원</u>에 <u>쓰레기</u>를 <u>버리면</u> 안 된다.
근거문	• <u>동물들</u>은 <u>쓰레기</u>를 <u>삼켜서</u> <u>아플</u> 수 있다.

- For the health of our lovely animals, / students (S) should not throw (V) / waste / in the zoo.
  사랑스러운 동물들의 건강을 위해 / 학생들은 버려서는 안 된다 / 쓰레기를 / 동물원에

READING 08 • 정답 ④　　　　pp.28~29

Mini Quiz　So, don't forget to ~ the Send button.

1 ②, ④　　**2** (f)ix, (a)fter
3 (B) Write your email. → (C) Read your writing carefully.
→ (D) Correct any mistakes in your writing.
→ (A) Click the Send button.

이메일을 보낼 때 보내기 버튼을 바로 누르지 마십시오. 보내기 버튼을 누르기 전에는 끔찍한 일이 일어나지 않을 것입니다. 여러분의 글에는 잘못된 철자나 사실의 오류가 있을 수 있습니다. 그러나 보내기 버튼을 누르지 않으면 상관없습니다. 왜일까요? 시간을 내서 실수를 수정할 수 있으니까요. 그리고 아무도 그 차이를 알 수 없을 것입니다. 그러니 보내기 버튼을 절대로 급하게 누르지 마십시오. 다시 보고 수정하는 것이 우선이고 보내는 것이 나중에 와야 합니다. 이메일을 보낸 후에 실수를 발견하면 큰 문제가 될 수 있습니다. 따라서 보내기 버튼을 누르기 전에 글을 주의 깊게 읽는 것을 잊지 마십시오. 이메일로 학교 과제나 업무 서신을 보내는 경우에도 마찬가지입니다.

p. 28

이메일을 보내고 난 후 실수를 알게 되면 문제가 될 수 있기 때문에 이메일을 보내기 전에 자신이 쓴 글을 주의 깊게 읽어야 한다는 내용이므로, 필자가 주장하는 바는 ④가 가장 적절하다.

p. 29

1 There can be misspellings or errors of fact in your writing.에서 <u>실수</u>의 구체적인 예를 알 수 있다.

2 질문: 이메일을 보내기 전에 무엇을 기억해야 하나요?
대답: 보내기 버튼을 누른 <u>후에는</u> 실수를 <u>수정할</u> 수 없기 때문에 글을 주의 깊게 읽어야 합니다.

3 (B) 이메일을 쓴다. → (C) 글을 주의 깊게 읽는다. → (D) 글에 있는
실수를 수정한다. → (A) 보내기 버튼을 누른다.

구문 설명

- **Nothing terrible** will happen before you click the Send button.
  -thing으로 끝나는 명사는 형용사가 뒤에서 수식한다.

- However, it doesn't matter **if** you **don't** click the Send button.
  if ~ not은 '만약 ~하지 않으면'이라는 의미이다.

- And nobody will **be able to** know the difference.
  be able to는 '~할 수 있다'의 의미로 can으로 바꾸어 쓸 수 있다.

- If you see any mistakes **after sending** an email, it can be a big problem.
  after -ing는 「after+주어+동사」로 바꿔 쓸 수 있으므로, after sending은 after you send의 의미로 이해한다.

- **The same goes for** sending school assignments or business letters by email.
  the same goes for는 '~인 경우도 마찬가지다'라는 의미이다.

Reading Skill

모범 답안

주제문	• 보내기 버튼을 누르기 전에 글을 주의 깊게 읽어야 〔검토해야〕 한다.
근거문	• 이메일을 보낸 후에 실수를 발견하면 큰 문제가 될 수 있다.

직독직해 Skill

- Nothing terrible (S) will happen (V)/ before you click the Send button.
  끔찍한 어떤 일도 일어나지 않을 것이다 / 보내기 버튼을 누르기 전에는

Unit 04 요지 파악하기

READING **09** 정답 ②

pp. 30~31

Mini Quiz I realized that I could learn more by teaching others.

---

1 ③ 2 at first, helped, teaching
3 (1) spend (2) time (3) understand (4) clearly

해석

우리는 지난달 과학 수업 시간에 새로운 tutor-tutee 프로젝트를 시작했다. 그것은 일종의 또래 지도였다. 과학 선생님은 "이 프로젝트는 배우는 사람들에게 도움이 될 거예요. 또한 가르치는 사람들에게도 좋을 거예요!"라고 말씀하셨다. 나는 과학을 제일 좋아했다. 나는 과학을 잘해서 학생 교사로 자원했다. 나는 친구를 가르쳤다. 그 애는 과학을 잘 못했다. 처음에 나는 배우는 사람과 너무 많은 시간을 보내고 있다고 생각했다. 시간 낭비라는 생각도 들었다. 그러나 나중에 나는 내가 틀렸다는 것을 알았다. 나는 가르치는 사람으로서 자료를 더 잘 그리고 더 명확하게 이해하기 시작했다. 또한 프로젝트 덕분에 기말시험에서 더 좋은 점수를 받았다. 나는 다른 사람들을 가르치면서 더 많은 것을 배울 수 있다는 것을 깨달았다.

해설

p. 30

tutor-tutee 프로젝트를 통해 친구에게 과학 과목을 가르치면서 시간 낭비같다고 생각했던 처음과는 달리 자료를 더 잘 그리고 더 명확하게 이해하게 되었고 성적도 더 좋아졌다는 내용이므로, ② '가르치는 것은 두 번 배우는 것이다.'가 글의 요지로 가장 적절하다.
① 시간이 돈이다.
③ 배움에 늦은 것은 없다.
④ 첫 시작이 항상 제일 어렵다.
⑤ 어려울 때 돕는 친구가 진정한 친구이다.

p. 31

1 또래 지도를 통해 깨달은 좋은 점들에 대해 말하고 있으므로 답할 수 있는 질문은 ③ '또래 지도의 이점은 무엇이었나?'이다.
① 학생들은 어떻게 시간을 절약할 수 있을까?
② 또래 지도는 언제 끝났나?
④ 새로운 친구들을 사귀는 제일 좋은 방법은 무엇인가?
⑤ 왜 어떤 학생들은 과학을 못했고 또 어떤 학생들은 과학을 잘했는가?

2 A: 과학 수업 시간의 새로운 프로젝트는 어땠니?
  B: 아주 좋았어. 사실, 처음에는 별로였어.
     하지만, 결국에는 나에게 도움이 되었어.
  A: 어째서?
  B: 나는 다른 사람들을 가르침으로써 더 많이 배울 수 있었어.

3  해석 tutor-tutee의 단점: 나는 시간을 너무 많이 소비해.
  tutor-tutee의 장점: 나는 자료를 더 잘 그리고 더 명확하게 이해하기 시작해.

구문 설명

- It was **a kind of** peer teaching.
  a kind of ~는 '일종의 ~'라는 의미이다.

• I **was good at** science, **so** I volunteered as a student teacher.
be good at ~은 '~을 잘하다'의 의미로 be poor at ~과 반대 의미이다. so는 '그래서'의 의미로 이어지는 내용은 결과를 나타낸다.

• I also got a better grade on the final exam **thanks to** the project.
thanks to는 '~ 덕분에'라는 의미이다.

• I realized that I could learn more **by teaching** others.
by -ing는 '~함으로써'라는 의미이다.

Reading Skill

모범 답안

상황	• 과학 시간에 나는 <u>tutor(student teacher)</u>를 자원했다.
Tutor-tutee에 대한 나의 생각	• 생각 1: 시간 낭비라고 생각했다. ↓ • 생각 2: 자료를 더 <u>명확하게 이해하기</u> 시작했다.
결론	• 다른 사람을 <u>가르치는</u> 것은 더 많이 <u>배울</u> 수 있는 것임을 깨달았다.

직독직해 Skill

• I (S) realized (V) / that I could learn more by teaching others.
나는 깨달았다 / 다른 사람을 가르침으로써 더 많이 배울 수 있다는 것을

(Mini Quiz) Always try to observe nature closely!

1 ④   **2** soft → rough
3 (1) discovery (2) rough (3) dust (4) paint

해석

자연은 발견의 원천이다. 자연을 관찰하면 인간의 삶이 더 나아질 수 있다. 그것은 우리의 삶이 더 쉽고 편안해질 수 있다는 것을 의미한다. 예를 들어, 특수 페인트를 사용하면 여러분의 집을 깨끗하게 유지할 수 있다. 페인트의 거친 표면이 먼지를 밀어낸다. 이 페인트를 쓰고 난 후에는 집의 외부를 덜 청소할 수 있다. 이 발견은 연잎을 관찰하는 것에서 나왔다. 사람들이 알다시피 연꽃은 진흙 연못에 산다. 그러나 연잎은 항상 깨

끗해 보인다. 이것이 가능한 이유는 무엇일까? 현미경으로 연꽃잎을 보라. 그러면 답을 알 수 있다. 그것 위에는 많은 작은 돌기들이 있다. 그것들은 작은 못처럼 보이고 표면을 거칠게 만든다. 따라서 먼지를 차단할 수 있다. 항상 자연을 면밀히 관찰하도록 애쓰라!

해설

p. 32

먼지를 차단해 주는 페인트의 발견은 연꽃잎을 관찰하는 것에서 비롯되었고 이는 인간의 삶을 편리하게 해 주고 있다. 이처럼 자연은 발견의 원천이므로 자연을 면밀히 관찰해야 한다는 ⑤가 이 글의 요지로 가장 적절하다.

p. 33

1 ④ nail은 글에서 '못'이라는 의미로 쓰였다.

2 연꽃잎처럼 특수 페인트의 부드러운(→ 거친) 표면이 먼지를 밀어낸다.

3 **해석** 자연은 인간의 삶을 위한 발견의 원천이다. 예를 들어, 연꽃잎의 거친 표면은 먼지를 차단한다. 인류는 연꽃잎을 관찰하여 이를 발견해서 특수 페인트에 적용했다.

구문 설명

• **Observing** nature can **make human life better.**
Observing은 주어 역할을 하는 동명사이다. 「make+목적어+목적격보어」는 '~을 …하게 만들다'라는 의미이다.

• **For example**, special paint can **keep your house clean.**
for example은 구체적인 예를 들 때 사용한다. 「keep+목적어+형용사」는 '~을 …하게 유지하다'라는 의미이다.

• However, its leaves always **look clean.**
「look+형용사」는 '~하게 보이다'의 의미로 look의 보어로 부사가 아닌 형용사가 오는 것에 주의한다.

Reading Skill

모범 답안

주제문	• <u>자연</u>은 <u>발견</u>의 원천이므로 자연을 면밀히 <u>관찰</u>해라.
근거문	• 연꽃잎의 <u>거친</u> <u>표면</u>은 먼지를 <u>차단</u>하게 한다. ↓ 활용 • 특수한 <u>페인트</u>는 먼지를 <u>차단</u>하게 한다.

직독직해 Skill

• For example, / special paint (S) can keep (V) / your house / clean.
예를 들어 / 특수한 페인트가 유지하게 할 수 있다 / 여러분의 집을 / 깨끗하게

READING **11** 정답 ④ pp. 34~35

Mini Quiz hand gestures

1 ③, ⑤ **2** emoji **3** (1) hand (2) communication
(3) same (4) careful

해석

우리는 언어를 통해 다른 사람들과 소통한다. 그러나 우리는 의사소통을 위해서 손동작도 사용한다. 우리는 그것들을 일상생활에서 자주 사용한다. 우리는 또한 해외여행을 할 때 그것들을 사용하기도 한다. 그러나, 모든 손동작이 모든 문화에서 동일한 의미를 갖는 것은 아니다! 그러므로 우리는 그것들을 언제 그리고 어떻게 사용할지 주의해야 한다. 엄지척이 좋은 예이다. 이 제스처는 매우 인기 있고 잘 알려져 있다. 전세계 사람들이 흔히 그것을 사용한다. 그것은 사랑받는 이모지이기도 하다. 일반적으로 그것은 한국, 일본과 같은 많은 국가에서 동의 또는 '좋다'를 의미한다. 그러나 태국에서는 모욕일 수 있다. 그리고 그것은 호주에서 '아니요'를 의미하거나 무례함을 보이는 것일 수 있다. 엄지척과 같은 제스처는 많은 문화나 국가에서 다른 의미를 지닌다. 그러니 오해를 피하기 위해서는 그것들을 어떻게 사용할지 주의해라!

해설

p. 34

같은 제스처라도 문화나 나라마다 다른 의미를 나타낼 수 있다는 내용이므로, 요약문은 The various meanings of hand gestures in different cultures may lead to misunderstandings. (다른 문화권에서 손동작의 다양한 의미는 오해로 이어질 수 있다.)로 쓰는 것이 가장 적절하다.

p. 35

1 엄지척(thumbs up) 제스처는 나라마다 agreement, okay, insult, no, rudeness의 의미가 될 수 있다고 했다. 미안함이나 사과의 의미는 언급되지 않았다.

2 이모지(emotion+image)는 이메일이나 문자 메시지와 같은 전자 통신에서 감정이나 생각을 표현하는 데 사용되는 디지털 이미지를 의미한다.

3 **해석** 사람들은 일상생활에서 의사소통을 위해 손동작을 사용한다. 사람들은 해외여행을 할 때 그것을 사용하기도 한다. 하나의 손동작이 모든 문화에서 똑같은 의미를 갖는 것은 아니다! 이러한 이유로 사람들은 그것들을 사용할 때 주의해야 한다.

구문 설명

· We **often** use them in daily life.
often과 같이 빈도를 나타내는 부사는 일반동사 앞에 위치한다.

· However, **not all** hand gestures have the same meaning in every culture!
not all은 '모든 ~가 …인 것은 아니다'라는 부분 부정의 의미이다.

· It usually means agreement or "okay" in many countries **like** Korea and Japan.
like는 '~와 같은'의 의미로 such as와 바꾸어 쓸 수 있다.

Reading Skill

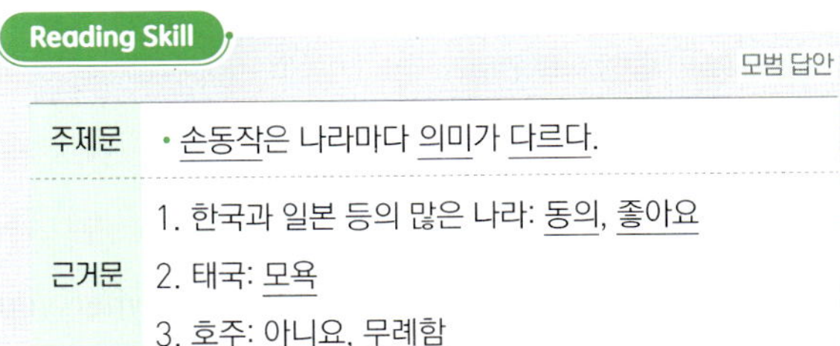

	모범 답안
주제문	· 손동작은 나라마다 의미가 다르다.
근거문	1. 한국과 일본 등의 많은 나라: 동의, 좋아요 2. 태국: 모욕 3. 호주: 아니요, 무례함

직독직해 Skill

· Not all hand gestures (S) have (V) / the same meaning / in every culture!
모든 손동작이 갖는 것은 아니다 / 같은 의미를 / 모든 문화에서

READING **12** 정답 ③ pp. 36~37

Mini Quiz To save time, make a to-do list.
Also, use time-saving services.

1 ⑤ **2** to-do list, focus
3 (1) upset (2) Save (3) create (4) use

해석

시간이 충분하지 않다고 자주 느끼는가? 그것은 시간이 충분하지 않을 때 할 일이 너무 많다고 느끼는 감정이다. 그것이 바로 '시간 기근'이다. 그것은 여러분을 긴장하게 한다. 짜증 나게도 한다. 시험공부를 할 때 이런 경험을 할 수도 있다. 한 연구에 따르면 시간 기근으로 인해 학생들은 낮은 점수를 받았을 때보다 더 많은 스트레스를 받을 수 있다고 한다. 하지만 걱정하지 마라. 이를 극복하는 방법이 있다. 시간을 절약함으로써 더 편안해질 수 있다. 시간을 절약하려면 할 일 목록을 만들라. 더 긴급한 일에 집중할 수 있도록 도와준다. 또한 시간 절약 서비스를 이용하라. 예를 들어, 외식이나 요리 대신 음식 배달 서비스를 이용할 수 있다.

해설

p. 36

할 일은 너무 많지만 시간이 충분하지 않을 때 느끼는 시간 기근은 시간을 절약함으로써 극복할 수 있다는 내용이므로, 요약문은 Saving time can help you avoid time famine.(시간 절약은 여러분이 시간 기근을 피하는 데 도움을 줄 수 있다.)으로 쓰는 것이 가장 적절하다.

p. 37

1 ⑤는 할 일 목록을 만들었을 때 받을 수 있는 도움이다.

2 할 일 목록 만들기는 여러분이 더 중요한 일들에 집중할 수 있도록 도와준다.

3 **해석** 문제점: 시간 기근 때문에 근심스럽다.
해결책: 시간을 절약하라.
해결책 예시: 할 일 목록 만들기
　　　　　　　시간 절약 서비스 이용하기

구문 설명

- It is the **feeling of** having too much to do when you do not have enough time.
feeling of -ing는 '~라는 감정'이라는 의미로, 전치사 of 뒤에 동사가 올 때는 -ing 형태의 동명사가 온다.

- One study shows that time famine can make students **feel more stressed** than when they get a low score.
feel 다음에는 형용사나 형용사의 비교급 표현이 보어로 온다. stressed는 '스트레스가 쌓인'이라는 형용사 표현으로 쓰였다.

- For instance, you can use a food delivery service **instead of eating** out **or cooking** meals.
instead of -ing는 '~하는 대신에'라는 의미이다. eating과 cooking이 or에 의해 병렬로 연결되어 있다.

Reading Skill

모범 답안

의미 정의	· 시간 기근: 　할 일은 많은데 충분한 시간이 없다고 느끼는 것
대응 방안	1. 할 일 목록 만들기 2. 시간 절약 서비스 이용하기 　→ 시간을 절약하기

직독직해 Skill

- It (S) helps (V) / you / to focus/ on the more urgent things.
그것이 돕는다 / 여러분이 / 집중하도록 / 더 긴급한 일들에

Mini Quiz However

1 ④　2 fair　3 (1) note　(2) bathroom

해석

Rhonda는 셰어 하우스에 살고 있었다. 청소부들은 주말마다 와서 두 곳의 화장실에 화장지를 약간 남겨 두었다. 그러나, 모든 화장지가 월요일쯤 다 떨어졌다. 화장지는 모든 사람을 위한 것이었지만 일부는 공평한 몫보다 더 많이 가져갔다. 그녀는 그 문제에 대해 화가 났다. 그래서 그녀는 화장실 중 한 곳에 메모를 붙여 놓기로 결심했다. "화장지를 모두 가져가지 마세요. 공유 물품입니다. 모두를 위한 것입니다." 그러자 놀라운 변화가 일어났다. 그녀는 화장지 한 통이 몇 시간 후에, 그리고 또 다른 화장지 한 통이 다음 날에 돌아오는 것을 보고 기뻤다. 하지만, 메모가 없는 다른 화장실에는 청소부들이 더 가져올 때까지 화장지가 돌아오지 않았다.

해설

p. 38

셰어 하우스에서 공용으로 쓰는 화장지가 낭비되는 일이 생기자 Rhonda가 화장지는 공유 물품이고 모두를 위한 것이니 가져가지 말라는 메모를 화장실에 붙여 두었더니 사람들이 화장지를 다시 가져다 놓는 변화가 일어났다는 이야기이므로, Rhonda's small action made a change in people's behavior.(Rhonda의 작은 행동이 사람들의 행동에 변화를 만들어 냈다.)로 쓴 요약문이 가장 적절하다.

p. 39

1 Rhonda는 처음에 화났다가(upset) 나중에 기뻤다(glad)고 했으므로, ④ angry → pleased가 가장 적절하다.

2 '그 중개인은 우리에게 그 집에 대해 합리적인 가격을 제시했다'라는 문장으로 reasonable은 글에서 fair와 바꿔 쓸 수 있다.

3 **해석** Rhonda는 화장지 두 통이 돌아온 것에 기뻤다. 그러나, 메모가 없는 다른 화장실에서는 청소부들이 화장지를 더 가져올 때까지 화장지가 하나도 돌아오지 않았다. 아마도, Rhonda는 셰어 하우스의 다른 화장실에도 똑같은 메모를 둘 것이다.

구문 설명

- However, all the toilet paper **was gone** by Monday.
be gone은 '없어지다'의 의미이다.

- So, she **decided to put** a note in one of the bathrooms.
「decide to + 동사원형」은 '~하기로 결심하다'의 의미이다.

- However, in **the other** bathroom with no note, no toilet paper came back until the cleaners brought more.
두 개 중 하나는 one, 나머지 하나는 the other로 나타낸다.

모범 답안

상황	1. 장소: 셰어 하우스의 화장실 2. 상황: 일부 사람들이 공유 물품을 가져감
해결 방법	• Rhonda의 쪽지 내용: "화장지는 모두를 위한 공유 물품입니다. 화장지를 가져가지 마세요."

직독직해 Skill

• She (S) felt (V) / upset / about the matter.
그녀는 (기분을) 느꼈다 / 화나는 / 그 문제에 관해

Chapter 02 정보 파악하기

Reading Key 필요한 정보 중심으로 빠르게 독해하기 pp. 42~43

정답

A 여름 캠프, 날짜, 비용, 활동

B 사하라 사막, 짧은, 약 500마리, 150~170cm, 야행성

해석

A 여름 캠프
제주도에서 만나요. 모든 중학생을 환영합니다!
• 날짜: 7월 23~25일
• 참가비: 1인당 150달러
• 활동: 하이킹, 수영, 그리고 서핑
• 모든 (참가) 학생은 배낭을 받게 됩니다.
더 많은 정보를 원하시면, www.jejusummercamp.com
을 방문하세요.

B addax는 영양의 일종이다. 그것은 사하라 사막의 일부 지역
에 산다. 그것은 나선형 뿔과 짧은 다리를 갖고 있다. 야생에
는 대략 500마리만 남아 있다. addax의 길이는 150~170
센티미터이다. 수컷은 암컷보다 약간 더 크다. addax는 사
막의 더위 때문에 주로 밤에 활동한다.

Unit 06 안내문·도표 파악하기

pp. 44~45

READING 14 · 정답 ③

(Mini Quiz) Switch off and give an hour for Earth!

1 ④   **2** once a month → once a year (또는 every year /
yearly)   **3** 모범 답안 (1) Saturday, March 25
(2) Turn lights off from 8:30 p.m. to 9:30 p.m. / Switch
off the lights for an hour. (3) For our future and planet

해석

Earth Hour
여러분의 작은 행동이 우리 지구를 구할 수 있습니다!
'불이 꺼지는' 순간은 2007년에 시작되었습니다.
불을 끄고 지구를 위해 한 시간만 투자하세요!

3월 25일 토요일

오후 8시 30분부터 오후 9시 30분까지 불을 <u>끄세요</u>.

단지 60분이요? 네, 한 시간만요.

매년 우리는 Earth Hour를 기념하기 위해 전 세계에서 함께 <u>모여서</u>
한 가지 상징적인 행동을 취합니다: 한 시간 동안만 불을 <u>끄는</u> 것입니다.

그러나 그것은 훨씬 그 이상입니다.

그것은 화합의 상징입니다. 희망의 상징입니다.

우리의 미래와 지구를 위한 집단행동의 힘을 보여 줍시다!

우리가 함께라면 더 많은 것을 할 수 있습니다!

가족, 친구, 이웃과 함께 이 행사에 참여하세요!

p. 44

지구와 우리의 미래를 위해 3월 25일 토요일 오후 8시 30분에서 9시
30분까지 한 시간 동안 불을 끄는 연례 행사에 관한 안내문이다.

p. 45

1 ⓓ는 모이는 것이고 나머지는 모두 불을 끄는 행동을 의미한다.

2 every year는 '매년'이라는 의미로 once a year, yearly로 바
꾸어 쓸 수 있다.

3 해석 언제?: <u>3월 25일 토요일</u>
무엇을 하는가?: <u>저녁 8시 30분에서 9시 30분 사이에 불을 끈다</u>
무엇을 위해?: <u>우리의 미래와 지구를 위해</u>

구문 설명

· **Switch** off and **give** an hour for Earth!
동사원형으로 시작하는 명령문으로 '~하라'는 의미이다.

· Turn lights off **from** 8:30 p.m. **to** 9:30 p.m.
「from ~ to ....」는 '~에서 …까지'라는 의미로 기간이나 범위를 나타
낸다.

· **If we are together**, we can do more!
「if+주어+동사」는 '~한다면'의 의미로 조건을 나타낸다.

· **Join** this event with your family, friends, and neighbors!
join은 '~에 참가하다, 합류하다'의 의미이고 뒤에 전치사 없이 바로
명사가 나온다.

Reading Skill

모범 답안

주요 내용	· <u>Earth Hour</u> 행사에 관한 안내와 홍보 · 행사 활동: <u>1시간 동안 소등하기</u>

READING **15** 정답 ⑤   pp. 46~47

Mini Quiz ① Please create ~ for the study cafe of our
school.
② Any student in our school can take part in this contest.
③ Students can study alone or in groups.
④ How: Post a name with its meaning through a QR code.
⑤ Prize: 1st Place (1 person) ~3rd Place (3 people)

1 ①, ③   **2** (1) 이름: 놀멍쉬멍공멍 (2) 이유: 이름의 의미를 함께
게시하지 않았기 때문에   **3** (1) naming (2) making(creating)
(3) study (4) QR (5) meaning (6) November

해석

이름 짓기 대회

여러분의 열정과 창의성을 보여 주세요.

최고의 이름을 만들어 주세요.

우리 학교 스터디 카페 이름입니다.

이 새로운 공간은 내년에 문을 열 것입니다.

학생들만 이 공간을 사용할 수 있습니다.

학생들은 혼자 또는 그룹으로 공부할 수 있습니다.

때때로 학생들은 여기서 놀 수 있습니다.

우리 학교 학생이라면 누구나 이 대회에 참가할 수 있습니다.

많은 참여 바랍니다.

수상자들에게는 멋진 선물을 드립니다.

10월 1일부터 11월 30일까지 이름을 제출할 수 있습니다.

방법: QR 코드로 이름과 의미를 함께 게시하세요.

상품: 1등 (1명) – 태블릿 PC
     2등 (2명) – 이어폰
     3등 (3명) – 영화 티켓

수상자 발표: 12월 7일

해설

p. 46

수상자는 총 6명이므로 ⑤는 내용과 일치하지 않는다.

1 ① 오픈 시기: '내년'이라고 글에 언급되어 있다.
③ 이용 대상: '학생들만' 해당된다.

2 제출 방법을 보면 QR 코드로 이름과 의미를 함께 게시하라고 했는데 이름의 의미를 게시하지 않은 것을 알 수 있다.

3 해석 A: 안녕, 이름 짓기 대회에 대해 들었니?
B: 그게 뭔데?
A: 우리 학교의 새로운 스터디 카페 이름을 짓는 거야.
B: 와, 재미있겠다! 어떻게 제출할 수 있니?
A: 새 이름을 의미와 함께 QR 코드를 통해 제출해야 해. 11월 마지막 날까지 제출하는 것을 잊지 마.
B: 정말 고마워!

구문 설명

- **Only students** can use this space.
「only+명사」는 '오직 ~만'이라는 의미이다.

- Any student in our school can **take part in** this contest.
take part in ~은 '~에 참가하다'의 의미로 participate in으로 바꿔 쓸 수 있다.

- We will **give** great gifts **to** the winners.
give A to B는 'B에게 A를 주다'의 의미이다.

- Post a name **with** its meaning through a QR code.
with는 '~와 함께'라는 의미이다.

Reading Skill

모범 답안

주요 내용	• 이름 짓기 대회 안내 및 홍보 • 행사 활동: 우리 학교의 스터디 카페의 이름 짓기 활동

직독직해 Skill

- We (S) will give (V) / great gifts / to the winners.
우리는 줄 것이다 / 멋진 선물을 / 수상자들에게

READING **16** 정답 ⑤　　　　pp. 48~49

Mini Quiz　The graph above shows the percentage of GDP spent on health care in 2018.

---

1 ①　**2** (1) lower → higher 또는 Belgium → Türkiye
(2) less → more　(3) highest → lowest 또는 Türkiye → The US　**3** (1) US, Switzerland, France, Belgium　(2) UK, Greece　(3) Türkiye

---

해석

2018년 GDP 대비 의료비 지출 비율

위 그래프는 2018년 GDP 대비 의료비 지출 비율을 보여 줍니다. 표시된 국가 중 가장 많이 지출한 국가는 어디인가요? 표시된 국가 중 가장 적게 지출한 국가는 어디인가요? 국가간에 큰 차이가 있나요? 보고 비교해 봅시다. ① 미국은 표시된 국가들 중에서 의료비에 GDP 대비 가장 높은 비율을 지출했습니다. ② 스위스는 GDP의 12.2퍼센트를 의료비에 지출했습니다. 그것은 미국보다 적습니다. ③ 프랑스는 벨기에보다 의료비에 GDP 대비 더 높은 비율을 지출했습니다. ④ 튀르키예는 GDP의 5퍼센트 미만을 의료비에 지출했습니다. ⑤ 영국과 그리스는 GDP의 같은 비율을 의료비에 지출했습니다. 그들은 또한 각각 GDP의 5퍼센트 이상을 의료비에 지출했습니다.

해설

⑤ 영국은 9.8퍼센트, 그리스는 7.8퍼센트로 의료비에 각각 다른 비율을 지출했으므로 도표의 내용과 일치하지 않는다.

1 일반적으로 도표의 제목과 도표 설명글의 첫 문장에서 도표가 무엇을 보여 주는지 알 수 있다.

2 (1) 벨기에는(→튀르키예는) 그리스보다 GDP의 더 낮은(→ 더 높은) 비율을 의료비에 지출했다.
(2) 스위스는 프랑스보다 GDP의 1퍼센트 더 적게(→ 더 많이) 의료비에 지출했다.
(3) 튀르키예는(→미국은) 2018년에 7개 국가들 중 GDP 대비 가장 높은(→ 낮은) 비율을 의료비에 지출했다.

3 해석 (1) 미국, 스위스, 프랑스, 벨기에는 2018년에 각각 GDP의 10퍼센트 이상을 의료비에 지출했다.
(2) 영국과 그리스는 2018년에 각각 GDP의 5퍼센트 이상, 10퍼센트 미만을 의료비로 지출했다.
(3) 튀르키예는 2018년에 GDP의 5퍼센트 미만을 의료비에 지출했다.

구문 설명

- Which country spent **the most** among the countries shown?
the most는 much의 최상급으로 '가장 많이'의 의미이다.

- Which country spent **the least** among the countries shown?
the least는 little의 최상급으로 '가장 적게'의 의미이다.

- That's **less than** the US.

  '…보다 적은'이라고 할 때는 「less than …」으로 표현한다.

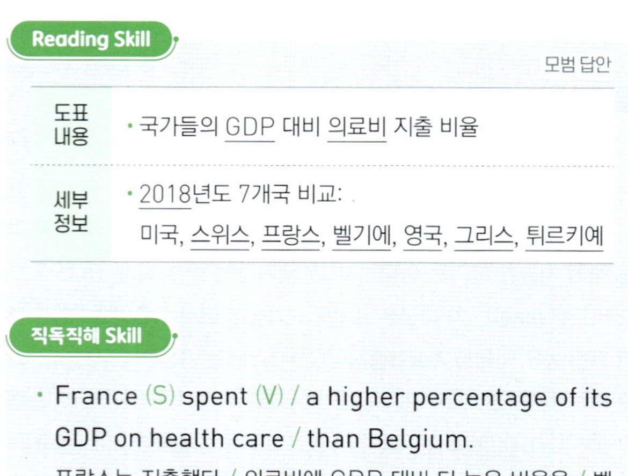

모범 답안

도표 내용	·국가들의 GDP 대비 의료비 지출 비율
세부 정보	·2018년도 7개국 비교: 　미국, 스위스, 프랑스, 벨기에, 영국, 그리스, 튀르키예

- France (S) spent (V) / a higher percentage of its GDP on health care / than Belgium.

  프랑스는 지출했다 / 의료비에 GDP 대비 더 높은 비율을 / 벨기에보다

Unit 07 내용 일치 파악하기

READING **17** 정답 ④　　　　　　　pp. 50~51

Mini Quiz ① Benjamin Franklin is one of ~ in American history.

② He was born in Boston on January 17, 1706.

③ He ~ mostly self-taught.

④ After he worked for four years, ~ his own stories.

⑤ Instead of his real name, ~ Mrs. Silence Dogood.

1 ②　**2** pen, name, own, stories　**3** (1) January, 17
(2) 1706　(3) Boston　(4) Mrs. Silence Dogood　(5) write
(6) stories

해석

Benjamin Franklin은 미국 역사상 가장 중요한 인물 중 한 명이다. 그는 출판업자, 작가, 발명가, 과학자였다. 그는 1706년 1월 17일 보스턴에서 태어났다. 그는 17명의 자녀 중 15번째였다. 그의 아버지는 비누와 양초를 만들었다. 그는 학교 교육을 받았지만 대부분 스스로 공부했다. 12세에 그는 형의 신문사에서 일하기 시작했다. 그는 4년 동안 일한 후, 자신의 이야기를 쓰기 시작했다. 진짜 이름 대신 Mrs. Silence Dogood이라는 필명으로 썼다. 사람들은 그의 이야기를 좋아했다. 그리고 그들은 작가가 유부녀일지도 모른다고 생각했다. 사람들은 결코 그녀가 16세 소년이라고는 생각하지 않았다!

해설

p. 50

형의 신문사에서 4년 동안 일한 후에, 자신의 이야기를 썼다.

p. 51

1 ⓑ는 Benjamin Franklin의 형을 가리키고 나머지는 모두 Benjamin Franklin을 가리킨다.

2 Mrs. Silence Dogood은 Benjamin Franklin이 자신의 이야기를 썼을 때의 필명이었다.

3 **해석** Benjamin Franklin에 관한 모든 것
출생일: 1706년 1월 17일　　　출생지: 미국 보스턴
필명: Mrs. Silence Dogood
Q: 16세에 그는 무엇을 했습니까?
A: 그는 자신의 이야기를 쓰기 시작했다.

구문 설명

- Benjamin Franklin is **one of the most important people** in American history.

  「one of the+최상급+복수명사」는 '가장 ~한 사람(것)들 중 한 명(하나)'이라고 해석한다.

- He was **a publisher, author, inventor, and scientist**.

  관사 a 다음에 직업을 나타내는 명사가 반복되어 나오면 한 사람이 동시에 여러 가지 직업을 가지고 있음을 표현한다.

- **At the age of 12,** he started to work for his brother's newspaper.

  at the age of는 '~세의 나이에'라는 의미로 When he was 12로 바꿔 쓸 수 있다.

- People never thought that she was a **16-year-old boy!**

  「숫자+단위명사(year)+형용사(old)」가 명사를 수식하는 형용사로 쓰이는데, 이때 단위명사는 항상 단수형을 써야 한다.

모범 답안

대상	·이름: Benjamin Franklin
정보	·출생일: 1706년 1월 17일 ·출생지: 보스턴 ·가족 관계: 17명의 자녀 중 15번째 ·(모든) 직업: 출판업자, 작가, 발명가, 과학자

- At the age of 12, / he (S) started (V) / to work for his brother's newspaper.

  12세에 / 그는 시작했다 / 형의 신문사에서 일하기

Mini Quiz　Sharks live in all areas of the seas.
Most sharks live 20 to ~ longer.
Sharks have big, sharp teeth.
They eat animals like fish or seals.
Most sharks have good eyesight.
They have fantastic ~, too.
The bodies of sharks ~ bottom.

1 ③　**2** 상어는 몸의 윗부분은 어두운 피부색이고 아랫부분은 밝은 피부색을 띤다.　**3** (1)Shark (2)20 (3)30 (4)shallow (5)deep (6)food (7)colors (8)prey

---

해석

상어는 바다의 모든 지역에 산다. 얕은 물에서 깊은 바다까지 그들을 볼 수 있다. 대부분의 상어는 20에서 30년을 살지만 일부 종은 훨씬 더 오래 살 수 있다. 상어는 크고 날카로운 이빨을 가지고 있다. 인간은 치아를 사용하여 음식을 물고 씹는 반면에, 상어는 이빨을 사용하여 먹이를 잡고 한 번에 삼킨다. 그들은 다른 먹이뿐만 아니라 물고기나 물개와 같은 동물을 먹는다. 예를 들어, 뱀상어는 거북이를 먹는 것을 좋아한다. 그리고 청상아리는 오징어를 좋아한다. 대부분의 상어는 시력이 좋다. 그들은 환상적인 야간 시력을 가지고 있고 색상도 구별할 수 있다. 상어는 몸의 윗부분은 어두운 피부색이고 아랫부분은 밝은 피부색을 띤다. 그것은 상어가 위협으로부터 숨도록 돕는다. 그것은 또한 먹이 사냥을 더 쉽게 만들어 준다.

해설

p. 52

They have ~ and can see colors, too.라는 문장에서 상어는 색상도 구별할 수 있다는 것을 알 수 있다.

p. 53

1 ⓐ While은 '반면에'라는 의미로 쓰였다.

2 대명사 It은 앞에 나온 문장 The bodies of sharks have dark skin on top and light skin on the bottom.을 가리킨다.

3 **해석** 나는 상어
- 나는 평균 20~30년을 산다.
- 나는 얕은 물에서 깊은 바다까지 여기저기서 산다.
- 나는 이빨로 물고기나 물개와 같은 먹이를 잡는다.
- 나는 위아래 다른 피부 색깔 덕분에 위협으로부터 숨고 쉽게 먹이를 사냥할 수 있다.

구문 설명

- **Most sharks live 20 to 30 years, but some species can live far longer.**

---

far는 비교급 longer를 수식하면서 '훨씬 더'라는 의미를 갖는다.

- **While** humans use their teeth to bite and chew food, sharks use their teeth to grab food and swallow it all at once.
  while은 '반면에'라는 의미로 서로 상반된 내용을 연결할 때 사용한다.

- It **helps sharks to hide** from threats.
  「help+목적어+to부정사」는 '~가 …하도록 돕다'라는 의미이다.

- It can **make hunting prey easier**, too.
  「make+목적어+보어(형용사)」는 '~을 …하게 만들다'라는 의미이다.

Reading Skill

모범 답안

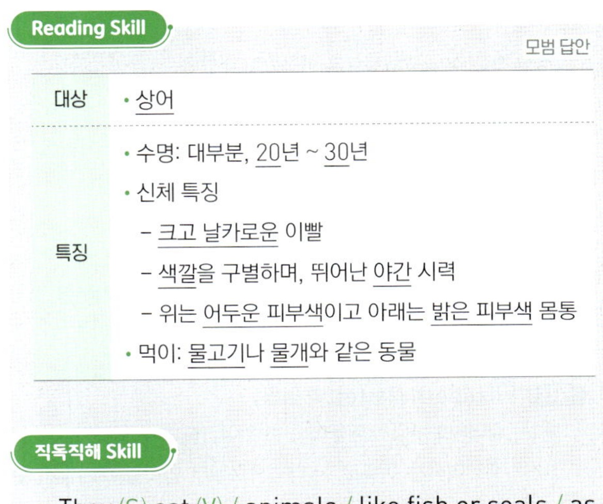

대상	·상어
특징	· 수명: 대부분, 20년 ~ 30년 · 신체 특징 　－ 크고 날카로운 이빨 　－ 색깔을 구별하며, 뛰어난 야간 시력 　－ 위는 어두운 피부색이고 아래는 밝은 피부색 몸통 · 먹이: 물고기나 물개와 같은 동물

직독직해 Skill

- They (S) eat (V) / animals / like fish or seals / as well as other prey.
  그들은 먹는다 / 동물들을 / 물고기나 물개와 같은 / 다른 먹이뿐만 아니라

Mini Quiz　Throughout her life, she created art.

1 ④　**2** (u)nfair　**3** (1)slaves (2)black (3)suffered (4)injustice (5)unfairness

해석

Elizabeth Catlett은 1915년 워싱턴 D.C.에서 태어났다. 그녀의 조부모는 노예였다. 그래서 그녀는 할머니에게서 노예 이야기를 자주

들었다. 대부분이 백인 학생들인 한 대학은 그녀가 흑인이라는 이유만으로 Catlett을 거부했다. 대신에 Catlett은 흑인 학생들을 위한 대학교인 Howard 대학교에서 디자인과 그림을 공부했다. 그녀는 Iowa 대학교에서 미술 석사 학위를 받았다. 그녀는 그 대학교에서 미술 석사 학위를 취득한 최초의 세 명의 학생들 중 한 명이 되었다. 평생 동안 그녀는 예술 창작 활동을 했다. 예술에서 그녀는 사회의 부당함이나 불공평을 보여 주었다. 그녀는 또한 그로 인해 고통받는 사람들도 보여 주었다. 그녀는 미국과 멕시코에서 많은 상을 받았다. 그녀는 멕시코에서 60년 이상을 보냈다. 그녀는 1962년에 멕시코 시민이 되었다. Catlett은 2012년 멕시코에 있는 그녀의 집에서 사망했다.

모범 답안

대상	• Elizabeth Catlett
정보	• 출생 연도와 출생지: 1915년, 워싱턴 D.C. • 두각을 나타낸 분야: 미술 • 여생을 보낸 곳: 멕시코 • 업적: 사회의 부당함이나 불공평을 다루는 예술 활동

직독직해 Skill

• Instead, / Catlett (S) studied (V) / design and drawing / at Howard University, a university for black students.
대신에 / Catlett은 공부했다 / 디자인과 그림을 / 흑인 학생들을 위한 대학인 Howard 대학에서

해설

p. 54

'사회의 부당함이나 불공평으로 인해 고통받는 사람들을 보여 주었다'는 내용이 있으므로 ⑤의 내용은 맞지 않다.

p. 55

1 ④ 수상 작품 수는 구체적으로 언급되지 않았다.
　① 출생지: 워싱턴 D.C.
　② 인종: 흑인
　③ 전공 분야: 디자인과 그림
　⑤ 사망 연도: 2012년

2 Catlett이 흑인이라는 이유만으로 한 대학이 그녀를 거부한 것에 대해서 아마도 그녀는 그것이 불공평하다고 느꼈을 것이다.

3 **해석** Elizabeth Catlett의 경험
　• 그녀는 할머니로부터 노예들에 관한 이야기를 자주 들었다.
　• 그녀는 흑인이라는 이유로 한 대학으로부터 입학을 허가받지 못했다.

　예술가로서의 Elizabeth Catlett
　• 그녀는 사회적 부당함이나 불공평으로부터 고통받는 사람들을 보여 주는 많은 작품을 창조해 냈다.

구문 설명

• Elizabeth Catlett **was born** in Washington, D.C., in 1915.
be born은 '태어나다'라는 의미로 항상 수동태로 쓴다.

• A mostly white college turned Catlett down just **because** she was black.
because 뒤에는 원인이 되는 내용이 나온다.

• **Instead**, Catlett studied design and drawing at Howard University, a university for black students.
instead는 '대신에'라는 의미이다.

• She also showed the people who **suffered from** it.
suffer from은 '~로부터 고통받다'의 의미이다.

Chapter 03 묘사된 분위기나 심경 파악하기

Reading Key 인물과 사건 중심으로 빠르게 읽기 pp. 58~59

정답

A
상황 묘사 1	결혼
상황 묘사 2	축하 행사, 음악, 춤추고, 즐거운, 손뼉
글 전반의 분위기	joyful

B
단서 (1)	이웃
단서 (2)	기쁘게
단서 (3)	미소
Shirley의 심경	excited

해석

A 족장이 Jane과 Sam에게 말했다. "너희는 이제 결혼했다." 결혼식이 끝나자마자, 축하 행사가 시작되었다. 젊은 청년들과 아가씨들이 음악에 맞춰 춤을 추기 시작했다. 그들은 원을 그리며 춤추고 즐거운 소리를 냈다. Jane은 그들과 함께했다. 사람들은 손뼉을 치고 노래를 부르기 시작했다. Jane과 Sam은 행복한 두 사람이었다.

B 집에 오는 길에, Shirley는 길 건너편에 있는 낯선 트럭을 보았다. 새 이웃이었다! Shirley는 그들에 대해 알고 싶었다. 그녀는 아빠에게 달려가 기쁘게 물었다. "새 이웃에 대해 뭔가 알고 계셔요?" 그는 "그럼. 그들에게는 딱 네 나이의 여자아이가 한 명 있어."라고 말했다. 정말 멋진 일이었다! 그녀는 미소가 멈추지 않았다. 그녀와 새로 온 여자아이는 제일 친한 친구가 될 것이다.

Unit 08 분위기·심경 파악하기

READING 20 정답 ② pp. 60~61

Mini Quiz A new season is coming.
There are no more biting winds all around.
No more chilly air.
All the snow is melting away.
Flower buds ~ the window.

1 spring **2** ③

3 (1) winter (2) hated (3) Grouchy (4) spring (5) enjoy
(6) hum

해석

새로운 계절이 다가오고 있다. 사방에 더 이상 살을 에는 듯한 바람은 없다. 더 이상 차가운 공기도 없다. 모든 눈이 녹고 있다. 새들이 행복하게 노래하고 있다. 그들의 노래는 나로 하여금 창문을 열게 만든다. 나는 창문을 열고 신선한 공기를 마신다. 모든 것이 새롭게 느껴지고 새롭게 보인다. 창밖에 꽃봉오리가 피려고 한다. 그것은 나를 계속 미소 짓게 만든다. 갑자기 내 방을 청소하고 침대에 새 이불을 깔고 싶은 강한 욕구를 느낀다! 내 입에서 콧노래가 나온다. 놀랍게도 청소를 하면서 흥얼거리고 춤추는 내 모습을 본다! 나는 전에는 청소하는 것을 좋아하지 않았다! 그러나 지금은? 나는 더 이상 만화 '개구쟁이 스머프'의 Grouchy(투덜이)가 아니다! 여러분도 알다시피, Grouchy는 항상 불평하지만, 지금 나는 아니다! 나는 청소를 즐기고 있다.

해설

p. 60
봄이 오고 노래를 흥얼거리고 춤추며 청소하는 '나'를 보여 주므로 ② '명랑하고 활기찬'이 글의 분위기로 가장 적절하다.
① 지루하고 따분한 ③ 낭만적이고 감동적인
④ 외롭고 우울한 ⑤ 긴장되고 무서운

p. 61
1 살을 에는 듯한 바람과 차가운 공기, 녹고 있는 눈, 꽃봉오리가 피어나는 새로운 계절은 봄이라고 볼 수 있다.

2 biting은 극도로 추운 날씨, 특히 신체적 고통을 유발하는 날씨를 묘사할 때 사용된다. 따라서 ③ 'freezing(몹시 추운)'의 의미와 같다.
① 온화한, 포근한 ② 먹을 수 있는
④ 배고픈 ⑤ 뜨거운

3 **해석**

	이전	지금
계절	겨울	봄
내 태도의 변화	나는 청소를 싫어했다. ⇨ 나는 청소를 즐긴다. 나는 만화 '개구쟁이 스머프'의 Grouchy였다.	나는 청소를 하면서 흥얼거리고 춤춘다.

구문 설명

- There are **no more** biting winds all around.
  no more는 '더 이상 ~이 아니다'의 의미이다.

- Their singing **makes me open** the window.
  「make+사람+동사원형」은 '~에게 …하도록 만들다'라는 의미이다.

- I **open** the window **and get** some fresh air.
  open과 get은 and로 병렬 연결되어 있기 때문에 형태가 같아야 한다.

- **Everything** feels and seems new.

every-의 의미는 '모두'이지만 형태는 단수이기 때문에 뒤에 단수 동사가 이어진다.

- Flower buds **are about to** bloom outside the window.
be about to는 '막 ~하려고 하다'의 의미이다.

- I am **enjoying cleaning**.
enjoy -ing는 '~하는 것을 즐기다'의 의미이다.

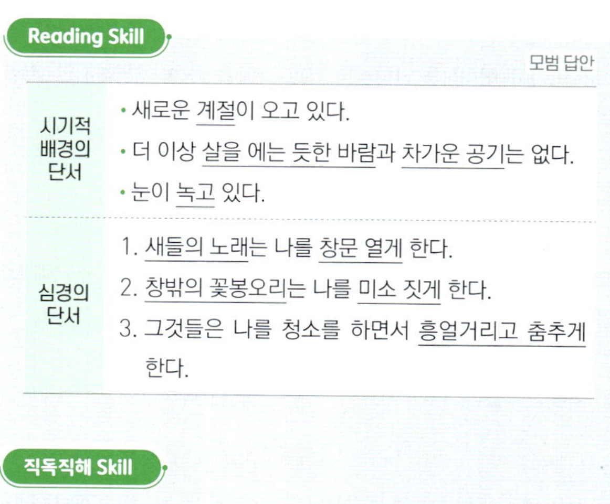

직독직해 Skill

- It (S) makes (V) / me / keep smiling.
그것이 ~하게 만든다 / 나를 / 계속해서 미소 짓게

READING 21 → 정답 ④   pp. 62~63

(Mini Quiz) 모범 답안 They couldn't hide the joy in their voices. It seemed that it was the best day!

1 ③   **2** joyful   **3** (1) built (2) happy (3) delicious

해석

먹을 것이 거의 없었기 때문에 그들은 한 달 동안 매우 배가 고팠다. 그들은 먹을 것을 위해 동물을 사냥하려고 했다. 그러나 그들은 사냥에 너무 서툴렀다. 하지만 3일 동안 굶은 끝에 Salva와 소년들은 운좋게 먹을 것을 얻었다. 사냥하는 동안, 그들 중 한 명이 다람쥐를 잡았다. 그들은 불을 피울 나무를 모았다. 그런 다음 그것을 불에 구웠다. 이것 중 아무것도 조용히 일어나지 않았다. 그들은 목소리에 기쁨을 숨길 수 없었다. 최고의 날인 것 같았다!
"불이 더 커야 해."
"충분히 오래가지 않을 거야. 더 많은 나무가 필요해."
"빨리, 그것을 뒤집어, 타고 있어!"
그것의 육즙이 떨어지고 지글지글 끓었다. 공기는 맛있는 냄새로 가득 찼다.

해설

p. 62
3일 동안 굶다가 먹을 것을 사냥해서 잡고 그것을 불에 구우면서 소년들이 신이 나 있는 상황이다.
① 슬픈   ② 화가 난   ③ 의심하는   ④ 신이 난   ⑤ 실망한

p. 63
1 ③은 소년들이 불을 피울 나무를 모으고 불에 다람쥐를 굽는 상황을 나타내고 나머지는 모두 다람쥐를 나타낸다.

2 '목소리에 기쁨을 숨길 수 없었다.'는 것은 '그들이 매우 즐거웠다'의 의미이다.

3 해석 사냥하는 동안 한 소년이 다람쥐를 잡았다. 그들은 그것을 요리하기 위해 불을 피웠다. 그들은 매우 배가 고팠지만 행복했다. 맛있는 냄새가 공기를 통해 퍼졌다.

구문 설명

- They were very hungry for a month because there was **little** food to eat.
little은 '거의 없다'라는 부정의 의미를 가진다. (cf. a little은 '약간은, 조금은 있는'이라는 긍정의 의미를 가진다.)

- But they **were** too **poor at** hunting.
be poor at -ing는 '~에 서툴다, ~을 못하다'의 의미로 be good at -ing와 반대 의미이다.

- **While hunting**, one of them caught a squirrel.
while 뒤의 주어와 be동사는 흔히 생략된다.(= While they were hunting)

- The fire **needs to** be bigger.
need to는 '~할 필요가 있다'의 의미이다.

- The air **was filled with** a delicious smell.
be filled with는 '~로 가득 차다'의 의미이다.

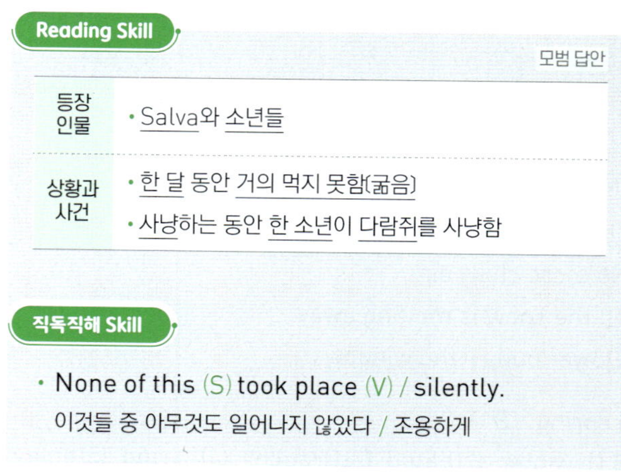

READING **22** · 정답 ⑤

(Mini Quiz) 모범 답안 But I slowly realized that my present was not a new cell phone, just a little book.

1 ②, ④   **2** Because he or she thought that maybe mom had hidden a new phone inside the book.
3 (1) ⓓ new cell phone (2) ⓕ communicate (3) ⓑ mom
(4) ⓐ me (5) ⓔ present (6) ⓒ little book

해석

나는 엄마가 나를 위한 특별한 선물을 가지고 쇼핑몰에서 돌아오시길 기다리고 있었다. 나는 그것이 무엇인지 알고 있다고 꽤 확신했다. 곧 새 휴대폰으로 소통할 수 있게 되어서 매우 신이 났다! 멋진 앱을 다운로드하고 싶었다. 나는 모든 앱을 사용하는 꿈을 꾸고 있었다. 친구들과 게임을 하는 상상도 하고 있었다! 그런데 엄마가 웃으시며 한 권의 책을 건네주셨다. 나는 페이지를 획획 넘겼다. 나는 그녀가 내 새 휴대폰을 책 안에 숨겼을지도 모른다고 생각했다. 하지만 내 선물이 새 휴대폰이 아니라 그저 작은 책 한 권이라는 걸 천천히 깨달았다. 책 안에는 새 휴대폰이 없었다!

해설

p. 64

엄마가 선물로 휴대폰을 사 주실 거라고 기대하고 신이 났었는데(excited) 결국 선물이 작은 책 한 권임을 깨닫고 실망하는(disappointed) 상황이다.
① 걱정하는 → 화가 난   ② 놀란 → 기쁜
③ 부끄러운 → 자랑스러운   ④ 화가 난 → 만족한
⑤ 신이 난 → 실망한

p. 65

1 it은 a new cell phone을 가리키고 있고 글쓴이는 새 휴대폰으로 멋진 앱을 다운받고 그것을 이용해 친구들과 소통하고 게임하는 것을 기대하고 있다. '휴대폰으로 산책하는 것'과 '책 읽기'는 글에서 언급되지 않았다.

2 I thought that maybe she had hidden my new phone inside the book.이라는 문장에서 이유를 알 수 있다.

3 해석 나는 엄마가 집으로 돌아오시기를 기다리고 있었다.
⇩
나는 엄마에게 받는 특별한 선물로 새 휴대폰을 기대했다.
⇩
나는 곧 그것으로 소통할 수 있을 것이기 때문에 매우 신이 났다!
⇩
드디어, 엄마가 내게 선물을 주셨다.
⇩
나는 내 선물이 작은 책 한 권임을 깨달았다.

구문 설명

· I **was** pretty **sure that** I knew what it was.
be sure that은 '~을 확신하다'의 의미이다.

· I really **wanted to** download cool apps.
want to는 '~하기를 원하다'의 의미이다.

· I **was daydreaming about** using all of the apps.
was -ing는 과거의 상태나 동작이 진행 중인 것을 의미하며, daydream about은 '~에 대한 헛된 공상에 잠기다'라는 의미이다.

· But I slowly realized **that** my present was **not a new cell phone**, **just a little book**.
that은 realized의 목적어 역할을 하는 절을 이끄는 접속사이다.
not a new cell phone, just a little book은 '새 휴대폰이 아닌, 단지 작은 책 한 권'이라는 의미이다.

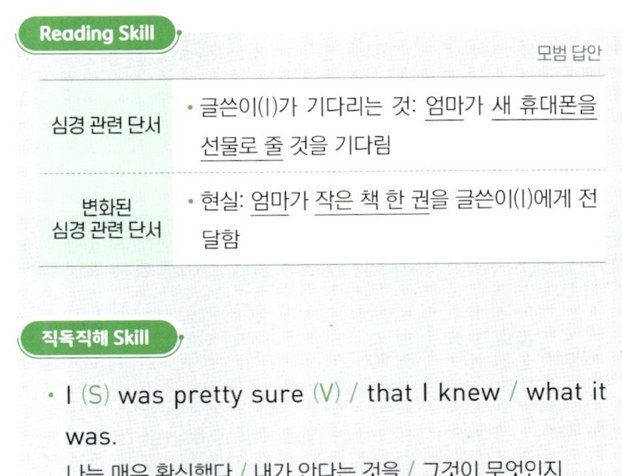

Reading Skill

모범 답안

심경 관련 단서	· 글쓴이(I)가 기다리는 것: 엄마가 새 휴대폰을 선물로 줄 것을 기다림
변화된 심경 관련 단서	· 현실: 엄마가 작은 책 한 권을 글쓴이(I)에게 전달함

직독직해 Skill

· I (S) was pretty sure (V) / that I knew / what it was.
나는 매우 확신했다 / 내가 안다는 것을 / 그것이 무엇인지

Chapter 04 글의 흐름 파악하기

정답

A　b. 물고기가 수영을 잘하는 이유

B　경계, 이상적
　　흐름상 어색한 이유: 주어진 글은 강이 경계로 이상적이라 했고, (A)는 그렇지 않은 예를 들었으므로 자연스럽게 이어질 수 없다.
　　(A) 예를 들어　(B) 그러나, 바뀔 수 있다

해석

A　물고기는 어떻게 부드럽게 위아래로 헤엄칠 수 있을까? 수면 위로 떠오르기 위해, 대부분의 물고기들은 부레를 사용한다.

Unit 09 글의 순서 파악하기

READING **23** ・정답 ④　pp. 70~71

Mini Quiz　Reading books has many benefits.

1 ⑤　**2** much(still/a lot/even)　**3** (1) Reduce, Stress (2) Reading books (3) Going for a walk

해석

독서에는 많은 이점이 있다. 흥미롭게도 그중 하나는 스트레스를 줄여 준다는 것이다.

(C) 몇몇 연구들은 독서가 스트레스 수준을 68퍼센트까지 줄이는 좋은 방법이라는 것을 알아냈다. 그것은 음악을 듣는 것(61퍼센트)보다 더 효과적이다. 그것은 또한 차를 마시는 것(54퍼센트)이나 산책하는 것(42퍼센트)보다 더 효과적이다. 그리고 그것은 비디오 게임을 하는 것(21퍼센트)보다 훨씬 더 효과적이다.

(A) 또 다른 연구는 30분의 독서만으로도 혈압을 낮출 수 있음을 보여 주었다. 그리고 그것은 심장 박동 수를 낮출 수 있다. 그러면 걱정이나 긴장이 사라질 수 있다. 마침내 여러분은 마음이 편안해진다.

(B) 게다가 여러분은 집에서, 공원에서, 도서관에서, 어디에서나 독서를 즐길 수 있다. 또한, 책은 그렇게 비싸지 않다. 그러니 휴대폰에서 멀어지도록 하자. 대신에 책장을 펼쳐 보는 게 어떨까?

해설

p. 70

독서의 많은 이점 중 스트레스를 줄여 주는 것에 대해 여러 연구의 예를 들어 준 후에, 추가로 어디에서나 즐길 수 있고 비용도 많이 들지 않으니 책을 읽자고 권유하는 흐름이 자연스럽다.

(A) Another는 '또 다른'이라는 의미로 (C) Some studies로 언급된 단락 뒤에 와야 하고, (B) Besides는 '게다가'라는 의미로, 주로 앞에서 언급된 것 외에 추가로 언급할 때 사용되므로 연결어 등을 통해서도 순서를 예측할 수 있다.

p. 71

1 ① 혈압을 낮추는 방법
　② 건강을 위한 가장 효과적인 운동
　③ 독서에 대한 비용 줄이기
　④ 긴장을 푸는 데 도움이 되는 많은 다양한 활동들
　⑤ 독서: 스트레스를 줄여 주는 좋은 방법

2 비교급 앞의 far는 '훨씬 더'라는 의미로 비교급을 강조하는 말이다.

3 **해석** 다양한 활동이 스트레스를 얼마나 많이 줄일 수 있나요?

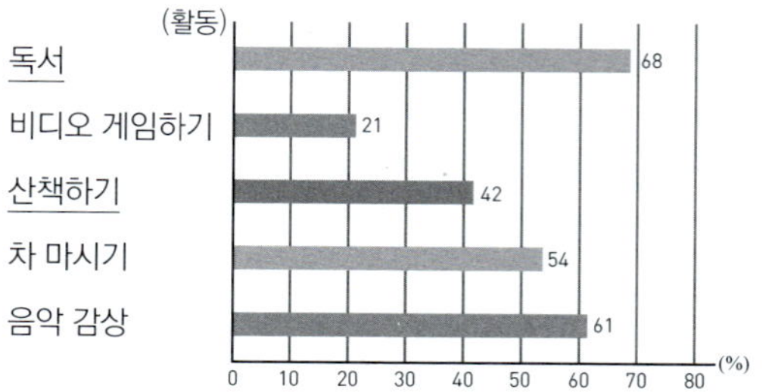

구문 설명

- Interestingly, **one of them is** to reduce stress.
　「one of+복수명사」가 주어로 쓰일 때는 뒤에 단수 동사가 이어진다.

- **Why not** open the pages of a book instead?
　Why not ~?은 '~하는 게 어때?', '~하지 그러니?'라고 권유하는 표현이다.

- Some studies found that reading is a great way to reduce stress levels, lowering them **by 68%**.
　by 뒤에 숫자가 오면 '~까지'라는 의미로 변화 등의 차이를 나타낸다.

- And it is **far more effective than** playing video games (21%).
　비교급 앞의 far는 '훨씬'이라는 의미로 비교급을 강조하는 말로 still, even, much, a lot 등으로 바꿔 쓸 수 있다.

모범 답안

주제문	· 이점이 많은 독서
근거문	· 근거 1: 스트레스 지수 – 68퍼센트까지 줄여 줌 · 근거 2: 30분 독서 – 혈압과 심장 박동 수를 낮춰 줌 · 근거 3: 장소 – 어디에서나 가능 · 근거 4: 비용 – 저렴

· Besides, / you (S) can enjoy (V) / reading anywhere.
게다가 / 여러분은 즐길 수 있다 / 어디에서나 독서를

READING **24** · 정답 ⑤　　　　　　pp. 72~73

Mini Quiz 모범 답안 A woman: she, I, you / A doctor: I /
My brother: he / They: a woman and a doctor

1 ①　2 침대의 다리를 자르는 것
3 (1) Come, here　(2) week　(3) legs　(4) bed
Her Choice: ✔ Her brother

해석

한 여자가 진료를 받으러 갔다. 그녀는 "저는 문제가 있어요. 제가 침대에
들어갈 때, 그 밑에 누군가가 있다고 생각돼요. 침대 밑을 보면 그 위에
누군가가 있는 것 같아요. 위, 아래, 위, 아래. 미칠 것 같아요!"
(C) 의사가 말했다. "3개월 동안 제게 오세요. 일주일에 한 번 여기로 오시
면 문제 해결을 도와드리겠습니다. 한 번 방문하는 데 50달러가 듭니다."
(B) 며칠 후, 그들은 거리에서 만났다. "왜 다시는 저를 찾아오지 않으셨
습니까?" 의사가 물었다. 그 여자가 말했다. "다행히, 제 문제가 사라졌
어요. 제 동생이 단돈 10달러로 문제 해결을 도와주었어요."
(A) 의사는 충격을 받았다. "그가 당신에게 무엇을 해 줬죠?" 여자가 말
했다. "정말 간단해요. 그는 제게 침대 다리를 자르라고 말했어요. 선생
님의 제안보다 훨씬 더 저렴했지요."

해설

p. 72
등장인물들을 지칭하는 대명사가 누구를 지칭하는지 살피면서 읽으면
글의 흐름을 파악하는 데 도움이 된다.

p. 73
1 의사를 방문하면 3개월 동안 일주일에 한 번씩 한 번 갈 때마다 50
달러를 내야 했지만 여자의 동생의 말대로 침대 다리를 잘랐고 문제
가 해결되었다. 침대 다리를 자르는 데는 단돈 10달러밖에 들지 않
았다.

2 It은 바로 앞에 나온 to cut the legs of the bed를 가리킨다.

3 **해석**

		그녀의 선택
의사의 제안	3개월 동안 일주일에 한 번씩 제게 오세요.	☐
동생의 제안	침대의 다리를 자르세요.	✔

구문 설명

· I think I'm going **go crazy**!
go crazy는 go mad의 뜻이고 go 뒤에 형용사가 오면 '어떤 상
태로 변하다'의 의미이다.

· He **told me to cut** the legs of the bed.
「tell+A+to 동사원형(B)」은 'A에게 B하라고 말하다'의 의미이다.

· It was much **cheaper than** your suggestion.
cheaper than은 '~보다 더 저렴한'이라는 의미의 비교급 표현이다.

· My brother **helped me with the problem** for just
ten dollars.
「help A with B」는 'A가 B를 (해결하는 것을) 돕다'의 의미이며
for just ten dollars는 '단지 10달러로'라는 의미이다.

· It **costs** fifty dollars for a visit.
cost는 '(비용이) ~ 들다'의 의미이며 for a visit은 '1회 방문에 대
해'라는 의미이다.

모범 답안

문제	· 여자는 침대 위와 아래에 누군가가 있다고 생각함
해결 방법	· 해결한 사람: 그녀의 동생 · 방법: 침대의 다리 자르기

· I (S) will help (V) / you / with your problem.
내가 도울 것이다 / 당신을 / 그 문제에 대해

READING **25** · 정답 ②　　　　　　pp. 74~75

Mini Quiz Ball sports have some rules about the
balls used.

1 ④　　2 bounce too high → not bounce at all
3 ⓐ size ⓑ weight ⓒ stiffness ⓓ hard ⓔ soft
ⓕ bounce ⓖ bouncy

우리는 공을 가지고 대부분의 주요 스포츠 활동을 한다. 따라서 공은 스포츠에서 매우 중요하다.
(B) 구기 종목에는 사용되는 공에 대한 몇 가지 규칙이 있다. 규칙은 크기나 무게와 같은 공의 특성에 관한 것이다. 공은 또한 일정한 단단함이 있어야 한다.
(A) 공은 크기가 정확해야 한다. 또한, 적절한 무게를 가져야 한다. 그러나 강철로 만들어지면 너무 단단할 것이다. 또는, 발포 고무로 만들어지면 너무 부드러울 것이다.
(C) 마찬가지로, 단단함과 함께 공은 적절하게 튕겨야 한다. 고무로만 만들어진 공은 대부분의 스포츠에서 너무 잘 튈 수 있다. 그리고 점토로만 만들어진 공은 전혀 튀지 않을 것이다.

p. 74

공의 특성에 대한 규칙이 있고 그 규칙은 크기, 무게, 단단함에 관한 것이다. 단단함 외에 튕기는 정도도 중요하다는 내용이다.

p. 75

1　size, weight, stiffness, bounce를 공의 특성에 대한 규칙들로 소개했지만, 공의 색상에 대한 언급은 없었다.

2　공이 점토로만 만들어지면 너무 높이 튈 것이다.
　→ 전혀 튕기지 않을 것이다

3　 스포츠에서 공에 대한 규칙
　☐ 크기: 크기가 정확해야 한다.
　☐ 무게: 적당히 무겁거나 가벼워야 한다.
　☐ 단단함: 일정한 단단함이 있어야 한다.
　　ex 강철공은 너무 단단할 것이다.
　　　　발포 고무공은 너무 부드러울 것이다.
　☐ 튕김: 적절한 정도의 튕김이 있어야 한다.
　　ex 고무로만 만들어진 공은 너무 잘 튈 것이다.

· **So**, balls are very important in sports.
　So는 '그러므로'의 의미로 결론을 나타내고, Therefore로 바꿔 쓸 수 있다.

· However, if it **is made of** steel, it will be too stiff.
　be made of는 '~로 만들어지다'의 의미이다.

· They are rules about the characteristics of the balls, **such as** size or weight.
　such as ~는 '~와 같은'이라는 의미로 구체적 예를 들 때 쓰고, like 로 바꿔 쓸 수 있다.

· **Similarly, along with** stiffness, a ball needs a proper amount of bounce.
　Similarly는 '마찬가지로'라는 의미이고 along with는 '~에 덧붙여, ~와 함께'라는 의미이다.

· And a solid clay ball would **not** bounce **at all**.
　not ~ at all은 '전혀 ~하지 않다'라는 강한 부정의 의미이다.

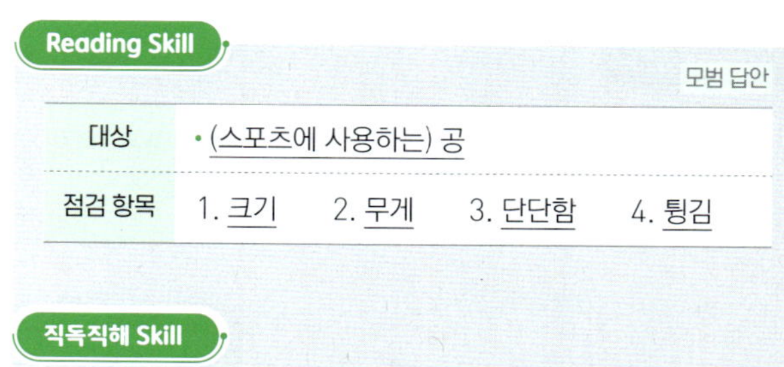

모범 답안

대상	· (스포츠에 사용하는) 공		
점검 항목	1. 크기	2. 무게	3. 단단함　　4. 튕김

· And / a solid clay ball (S) / would not bounce (V) at all.
　그리고 / 점토로만 만들어진 공은 / 튀어오르지 않을 것이다 / 전혀

Unit 10 주어진 문장 넣기

READING **26** ― 정답 ④　　　　　　pp. 76~77

Mini Quiz　긍정: cute, peaceful　부정: spit

1 ③　　2 it(the spit) includes the food they recently ate
3 (1) habits　(2) spitting　(3) feeling　(4) protect　(5) danger

여러분은 알파카를 좋아하는가? 알파카는 칠레나 페루와 같은 남아메리카 나라들에 산다. 그들은 매우 부드러운 털을 가지고 있다. 그리고 알파카는 귀여운 얼굴과 큰 몸으로 유명하다. 하지만 이 동물을 만날 때 여러분은 항상 조심해야 한다! 그들은 나쁜 습관을 가지고 있어서 여러분에게 침을 뱉을 수도 있다. 그들은 왜 침을 뱉을까? 첫째, 그들은 화가 났거나 기분이 좋지 않다는 것을 보여 주고 싶어 한다. 둘째, 그들은 위험으로부터 그들 자신을 보호하기를 원한다. 게다가 그들의 침에는 그들이 최근에 먹은 음식이 포함되어 있기 때문에 매우 고약한 냄새가 난다. 그러나 그렇게 걱정할 필요는 없다. 알파카는 안전하다고 느낄 때는 평화로운 동물이다. 그래서 알파카를 보면 친절하게 대해야 한다.

p. 76

주어진 문장은 'However(그러나)'가 포함되었고 '걱정할 필요가 없다'

는 내용이므로 앞뒤 내용이 반전을 이루는 곳에 들어가야 한다. 따라서 앞부분은 침을 뱉는 알파카의 습관과 그 이유에 대해 말하고 있으나 뒷부분에서는 평화로운 동물이라는 내용이 나오는 ④에 들어가는 것이 가장 적절하다.

p. 77

1 they are famous for their cute faces and big bodies 로 보아, 알파카는 '작은 몸'이 아니라 '큰 몸'을 가진 동물이다.

2 In addition, their spit has a very bad smell because it includes the food they recently ate.으로 보아, 고약한 냄새가 나는 이유는 최근에 먹은 음식이 침에 포함되어 있기 때문이라는 것을 알 수 있다.

3 **해석** 알파카는 침을 뱉는 것과 같은 나쁜 습관이 있다.
이유 1: 기분이 좋지 않음을 보여 주고 싶어 한다.
이유 2: 위험으로부터 그들 자신을 보호하기를 원한다.

구문 설명

- However, you **don't have to** worry about that much.
  have to는 '~해야 한다'라는 의미이고 don't have to는 '~할 필요는 없다'의 의미로 해석된다.

- And they **are famous for** their cute faces and big bodies.
  be famous for는 '~로 유명하다'라는 의미이다.

- But **when** you meet these animals, you **should** always be careful!
  when절은 '~할 때'의 의미로 해석되며, should는 '~해야 한다'는 의미의 조동사로 뒤에 동사원형이 온다.

- **In addition**, their spit has a very bad smell because it includes **the food they recently ate**.
  In addition은 '게다가'의 의미를 가진 접속사이며 the food 뒤에 나오는 they recently ate는 the food를 꾸며 '그들이 최근에 먹은 음식'의 의미로 해석된다.

Reading Skill

모범 답안

대상	· 알파카
부정적인 면	· 나쁜 습관: 침을 뱉음
긍정적인 면	· 평소 성향: 대체로 평화로움

직독직해 Skill

- Second, / they (S) want (V) / to protect themselves from danger.
  둘째, / 그들은 원한다 / 그들 자신을 위험으로부터 보호하기를

Mini Quiz 모범 답안 desert island, find some water, safe to drink, streams, rivers, rainwater, foods 등

1 ③   **2** (1) T (2) F (Rainwater → Water in streams or rivers)   **3** (1) streams (2) rainwater (3) foods (4) coconuts

해석

무인도에 혼자 머물러야 한다고 상상해 보라. 여러분은 가장 먼저 무엇을 하겠는가? 여러분은 'SOS 사인 만들기' 또는 '음식 찾기'라고 대답할지도 모른다. 그러나 나는 여러분이 가장 먼저 마실 물을 찾는 것을 추천한다. 물은 여러분이 생존하도록 돕는 가장 중요한 것이다. 만약에 몸에 충분한 물이 없다면, 여러분은 심지어 3일 만에도 죽을 것이다. 이러한 이유 때문에, 여러분은 마시기에 안전한 물을 찾아야 한다. 여기에 깨끗한 마실 물을 찾는 데 도움이 되는 몇 가지 조언이 있다. 첫째, 시냇물이나 강물은 대부분 안전하다. 그러나 여기에도 질병이 있을 수 있다는 것을 기억해야 한다. 둘째, 빗물은 마실 수 있으므로 빗물을 저장해라. 셋째, 코코넛이나 과일과 같은 많은 음식에는 물이 들어 있다. 이러한 조언을 명심한다면 여러분은 무인도에서 더욱 안전해질 것이다.

해설

p. 78

'무인도에서 혼자 지내야 한다면 가장 먼저 무엇을 하겠는가?'라는 질문에 대한 독자들의 답변을 예상하는 부분 뒤에 바로 물이 필요한 이유에 대한 뒷받침 문장들이 나오고 있다. 따라서 ①에 '물을 가장 먼저 찾아야 한다'는 필자의 주장이 들어가는 것이 가장 적절하다.

p. 79

1 전체적으로 무인도에서 물을 찾는 것의 필요성과 찾는 요령에 대해 언급하고 있으므로, 필자의 주장으로 가장 적절한 것은 ③이다. ④도 물에 관한 내용이기는 하지만 글 내용 전체를 포괄하지는 못한다.

2 (1) 본문의 내용 중 If you don't have enough water in your body, you will die, even in just three days. 문장으로 미루어 보아 (1) 문장은 글의 내용과 일치한다.
(2) 빗물은 마실 수 있으므로 보관해야 한다고 했고, 질병이 있을 수 있는 것은 시냇물이나 강물이다.

3 **해석** 무인도에서 깨끗한 물을 어떻게 찾을 수 있는가?
조언 1: 시냇물이나 강물을 찾아라.
조언 2: 빗물을 보관해라.
조언 3: 코코넛이나 과일과 같은 음식을 먹어라.

구문 설명

- **Imagine** that you **have to** stay alone on a desert island.
  동사원형으로 시작하는 명령문 문장으로 Imagine that은 '~을

상상해 보라'라고 해석한다. have to는 '~해야 한다'는 뜻의 조동사이다.

· **Water is the most important thing** to help you survive.
the most important thing은 '가장 중요한 것'이라는 최상급 표현이다.

· For this reason, you **must** find water **that is safe to drink**.
must는 '~해야 한다'는 강력한 주장을 나타내는 조동사이며, water 뒤에 나오는 that is safe to drink 부분이 앞의 water를 수식해 '마실 수 있는 안전한 물'이라는 의미가 된다.

· **Here are** some tips **to help you find clean drinking water**.
Here are ~는 '여기에 ~가 있다'라는 의미로 다음에 나올 내용을 예상하게 해 준다. to부정사는 some tips를 수식하고 「help+목적어+(to)동사원형」의 형태로 '~가 …하는 것을 돕다'라는 의미이므로, '깨끗한 마실 물을 찾는 것을 돕는'으로 해석된다.

Reading Skill

모범 답안

상황	· 무인도에서 혼자 머물러야 하는 상황
주장	· 가장 먼저 물을 찾아라.

직독직해 Skill

· If you don't have enough water in your body, / you (S) will die (V), / even in just three days.
만약에 몸에 충분한 물이 없다면, / 여러분은 죽을 것이다 / 심지어 3일 만에도

READING **28** 정답 ③ pp. 80~81

Mini Quiz So, But, Then

1 ② 2 아이들이 화가 났을 때 음식을 주는 것 / 아이들을 달래기 위해 음식을 주는(사용하는) 것
3 (1) food (2) upset (3) mouth (4) harmful

해석

아이들이 화가 났을 때, 그들을 진정시키는 좋은 방법은 무엇일까? 쉽고 빠른 하나의 방법은 그들에게 음식을 주는 것이다. 이것은 그들의 초점을 화난 것에서 다른 곳으로 돌리는 데 도움이 된다. 그들은 다른 일을

하기 위해 손과 입을 사용할 것이다. 그래서 그들은 화난 일을 잊을 수 있다. 그들에게 사탕이나 초콜릿과 같은 간식을 준다면, 아이들은 더 행복할 것이다. 단기적으로는, 이렇게 음식을 이용하는 것이 효과적이다. 하지만 장기적으로 이것은 해로울 수 있다. 아이들은 자신들이 어떤 부정적인 감정을 보이면 간식을 받을 것이라고 생각할지도 모른다. 그러면 그들은 기분이 나쁘거나, 화나거나, 심지어 지루할 때도 자신의 기분이 더 좋아지게 하기 위해 음식을 원하게 될 것이다.

해설

p. 80
주어진 문장은 '음식을 사용하는 것의 단기적인 효과'에 대한 내용이므로, 다음에 But(하지만)으로 이어지며 '장기적으로 해로울 수 있다'는 내용이 나오는 ③에 들어가는 것이 가장 적절하다.

p. 81
1 전체적으로 아이가 화가 났을 때 아이를 진정시키기 위해 사용하는 방법에 대한 글이므로, ② '아이들을 진정시키는 한 가지 방법'이 적절한 제목이다.
① 아이들이 화가 난 이유
③ 아이들이 가장 좋아하는 간식
④ 아이들을 행복하게 만드는 좋은 음식
⑤ 아이들의 감정을 조절하는 것의 어려움

2 아이들이 화가 났을 때 음식을 주는 것이 단기적으로는 효과가 있지만 장기적으로 해로울 수 있다고 말하고 있다.

3 **해석** 아이들이 화가 났을 때, 그들에게 음식을 주는 것은 그들을 진정시키는 효과적인 방법이다. 아이들이 음식을 받으면 그들의 초점이 화난 것에서 다른 것으로 바뀐다. 그들의 손과 입을 사용할 것이기 때문이다. 하지만 장기적으로는 그들이 자신의 감정을 조절하기 위해 음식을 먹고 싶어질지도 모르기 때문에 해로울 수 있다.

구문 설명

· **One easy and quick way is to give** them some food.
주어가 One easy and quick way이기 때문에 단수동사 is가 쓰였다. is 뒤의 to부정사는 '~하는 것'이라는 의미이다.

· **This** helps them **change** their focus **from** being upset **to** something else.
This는 앞 문장의 '화가 났을 때 음식을 주는 것'을 지칭한다. change from A to B는 'A에서 B로 바꾸다'라는 의미이다.

· So, they can forget **the things they are angry about**.
the things에 이어지는 they are angry about은 the things를 꾸며 '그들이 화가 난 것(대상)'이라는 의미이다. be angry about은 '~에 대해 화가 나다'라는 의미이다.

· If you give them snacks, **such as** candy or chocolate, children will **feel happier**.
such as는 예시를 나타내기 위해 사용되었다. feel 뒤에는 happier라는 비교급이 사용되어 '더 행복하게 느끼다'라는 의미가 된다.

모범 답안

중심 소재	• 아이가 화가 났을 때 음식을 주는 것
단기적 효과	• 아이가 진정함
장기적 효과	• 아이가 부정적 감정을 보이면 간식(음식)을 받는다고 생각함

직독직해 Skill

• The children (S) might think (V) / that they will get a snack / if they show any negative emotions.
아이들은 생각할지도 모른다 / 그들이 간식을 받을 것이라고 / 그들이 어떤 부정적인 감정을 보이면

Unit 11 무관한 문장 찾기

READING 29 · 정답 ②

pp. 82~83

Mini Quiz Actually, there are no windows or clocks in most department stores.

1 ② 2 hang 3 (1) prices → time (2) (마지막 문장) windows → walls

해석

백화점에서 창문이나 시계를 볼 수 있는가? 여러분은 이것에 대해 생각조차 하지 않을 수도 있다. 실제로 대부분의 백화점에는 창문이나 시계가 없다. 왜 이럴까? 이것은 백화점의 비밀스러운 마케팅 기술이다. 창문과 시계는 여러분에게 시간을 생각하도록 만든다. 백화점은 사람들이 시간을 생각하지 않고 쇼핑을 즐기기를 원한다. 그래서 그들은 이 방법으로 사람들이 쇼핑에 집중하도록 만든다. 또한 백화점은 벽을 장식하거나 벽에 광고들을 건다. (공간이 넓기 때문에 벽을 꾸미는 것은 어렵다.) 벽에 시계나 창문이 있으면 벽을 사용하기가 어렵다. 이것이 백화점의 비밀이다. 그러니 다음번에 백화점을 방문하면, 주변을 잘 둘러보라. 백화점 벽에 창문, 시계, 또는 광고가 있는가?

해설

p. 82

전체적으로 백화점에서 창문이나 시계를 볼 수 없는 이유에 대해 설명하고 있다. ①에 장식이나 광고를 위해 벽을 사용한다는 내용이 나오고 있지만 이 부분은 백화점에 창문이나 시계가 없는 추가적인 이유일 뿐이다. 따라서 ②의 '공간이 넓기 때문에 벽을 꾸미는 것이 어렵다'는 내용은 앞뒤 문장과도 어울리지 않고 전체 흐름과도 관련이 없다.

p. 83

1 ② 백화점에 시계가 없는 이유를 '시간을 알 수 없도록, 벽을 꾸밀 수 있도록'이라는 두 가지 이유를 들어 설명했다.

2 공통으로 들어갈 단어는 '(물건을) 걸다, 어슬렁거리다, (전화를) 끊다'라는 표현에 쓰이는 hang이다.
  • 너의 재킷을 옷장에 걸어라.
  • 전화를 끊어도 될까요?
  • 그 십 대들은 잠시 동안 밖에서 어슬렁거린다.

3 **해석** 많은 백화점에는 창문이나 시계가 없다. 마케팅 비밀로 백화점은 우리가 쇼핑을 하는 동안 우리의 주의를 끌고 싶어한다. 우리는 가격(→ 시간)을 생각하지 않고 쇼핑을 즐길 것이다. 그들은 장식을 하거나 광고를 걸기 위해 창문(→ 벽)을 사용할 필요가 있다.

구문 설명

• Can you see **any** window or clock in a department store?
any는 '어떤'의 의미로 주로 의문문이나 부정문에서 쓰인다. 긍정문에서는 some이 쓰인다.

• Windows and clocks **make you think** about the time.
「make+목적어(A)+동사원형(B)」은 'A가 B하도록 만들다'라는 의미로 사용된다.

• If there are some clocks or windows on the walls, **it** is hard **to use the walls**.
it은 가주어로 진주어인 to use the walls를 대신해서 사용된다.

• So, **the next time you visit a department store, look** around carefully.
you visit a department store가 the next time을 꾸며 '여러분이 백화점을 방문하는 다음번에'라는 의미로 해석되며, 뒷부분은 명령문이 제시되어 '~하라'라는 의미이다.

Reading Skill

모범 답안

중심 소재	• 백화점에서 창문과 시계를 볼 수 없는 이유
목적	• 사람들이 시간을 알지 못하게 하여 쇼핑에 집중하도록 함 • 벽을 꾸미거나 광고를 전시하는 용도

직독직해 Skill

• The department store (S) / wants (V) / people to enjoy shopping / without thinking about the time.
백화점은 / 원한다 / 사람들이 쇼핑을 즐기기를 / 시간을 생각하지 않고

Mini Quiz To do your work better, you need sleep more than coffee.

1 ④   **2** ⓐ caffeine, ⓑ with little sleep
3 (1) same (2) more (3) lower

해석

커피 한 잔이 여러분을 깨우는 데 도움이 될 수 있다고 생각하는가? 대부분의 연구에서는 카페인이 여러분을 하루 종일 깨어 있도록 돕는다고 한다. 그리고 심지어 60mg의 카페인도 여러분이 더 빠르게 반응하도록 만든다. 카페인은 약과 함께 사용되면 두통을 완화하는 데에도 효과적이다. 그러나 카페인은 숙면을 대신할 수 없다. (걱정이 많으면 숙면을 하기가 어렵다.) 한 연구는 카페인이 수면을 거의 취하지 않은 사람들이 실수할 가능성을 증가시킨다는 것을 보여 준다. 또한 그 사람들은 카페인을 섭취한 후에도 수면을 충분히 취한 그룹보다 높은 점수를 받지 못했다. 따라서 카페인을 이용하는 것은 충분한 수면을 취하지 못한 것을 완전히 보충할 수는 없다. 일을 더 잘하기 위해서, 여러분은 커피보다는 더 많은 수면이 필요하다.

해설

p. 84

전체적으로 카페인의 효과에 대해 언급하는 글인데, ① '걱정이 많으면 숙면하기 어렵다'는 내용은 전체의 흐름에서 벗어난다.

p. 85

1 '카페인 섭취가 잠을 대신할 수는 없다'는 내용이므로 ④가 가장 적절한 반응이다.
   ① 커피가 건강에 좋다는 내용은 언급되지 않았다.
   ② 카페인을 섭취했음에도 잠을 적게 잔 사람이 시험에서 더 많은 실수를 했다는 내용이므로 적절하지 않다.
   ③ 약과 함께 카페인을 섭취하면 두통에 도움이 된다는 연구 결과가 있기는 하지만, 두통약 대신 커피를 마시라는 내용은 아니다.
   ⑤ 불면증에 대한 내용은 없다.

2 ⓐ it은 '그것이 약과 함께 사용되면 두통에 효과가 있다'는 내용으로 앞서 언급한 caffeine을 가리킨다. ⓑ they는 앞 문장의 the people with little sleep을 가리킨다.

3 **해석** 카페인을 이용하는 것은 충분한 수면을 갖는 것과 같지 않다. 충분한 수면 없이 카페인을 섭취한 사람들은 더 많은 실수를 하고 더 낮은 점수를 받는다.

구문 설명

· Do you **think** a cup of coffee can help you wake up?
think 뒤에 접속사 that이 생략되어 있고 또 다른 절이 이어져 해석에 유의해야 한다.

· Caffeine is also effective for relieving headaches when it **is used** together **with** medicine.
be used with는 동사 use가 수동태로 사용된 것으로 '~와 함께 사용되다'라는 뜻이다.

· However, caffeine cannot **take the place of** a good night's sleep.
take the place of는 '~을(~의 자리를) 대신하다'라는 의미이다. 즉, '카페인이 숙면을 대신할 수 없다'라는 의미를 나타낸다.

· **To do your work better**, you need sleep more than coffee.
To do your work better는 '~하기 위해서는'이라는 의미이다.

Reading Skill   모범 답안

중심 내용	· 카페인의 효과
부작용	· 연구 내용 1: 실수할 가능성이/가 증가함 · 연구 내용 2: 충분한 수면을 취한 그룹보다 점수가 낮음

직독직해 Skill

· Most studies (S) show (V) / that caffeine helps you stay awake all day long.
대부분의 연구는 보여 준다 / 카페인이 여러분을 하루 종일 깨어 있도록 돕는 것을

내용 추론하기

정답

A b. the identity of the group

주제문   정체성

세부적 내용   느리게, 빠르게, 함께

B 본보기, 행동

해석

A 많은 공동체들은 그들 자신만의 춤을 가지고 있다. 그들은 집단의 정체성을 표현한다. 예를 들어, 아프리카 사람들은 춤을 느리게 춘다. 스페인 사람들은 춤을 빠르게 춘다. 스코틀랜드 사람들은 함께 춤을 춘다.

B 아이들은 대부분 본보기에 의해 배운다. 그들은 부모와 그들보다 나이가 많은 형제자매들을 본받아 자신의 행동을 형성한다. 따라서 당신의 아이들에게 훌륭한 역할 모델이 되어라. 말보다 행동이 중요한 법이다.

Unit 12 빈칸 완성하기 1(단어)

READING 31   정답 ③   pp. 90~91

Mini Quiz   모범 답안 But, in the fashion field, trash can become new, fancy products thanks to creative thinking.

1 ④   **2** upcycling

3 (1) trash   (2) creative   (3) eco-friendly(good)

해석

쓰레기는 여러분이 버린 후에 어디로 갈까? 여러분은 그것이 지구를 해칠 것이라고 생각할지도 모른다. 그러나 패션 분야에서는 쓰레기가 창의적인 사고 덕분에 새롭고 멋진 제품이 될 수 있다. 그것은 '업사이클링'이라고 불리는 새로운 종류의 패션이다. 독일의 회사 'Freitag'은 많은 방수천과 안전벨트로 가방을 만든다. 그들의 가방을 만들기 위해서는 많은 천과 벨트가 필요하다. 자연스럽게 아주 많은 쓰레기가 사용된

다. 그들의 가방은 튼튼하고 방수가 되며 친환경적이기 때문에 곧 유명해졌다. 또한, 각각의 가방이 많은 다른 종류의 천으로 만들어지기 때문에 세상의 모든 그들의 가방은 다르다. 패션 분야의 이러한 경향은 독특할 뿐만 아니라 환경에도 좋다.

해설

p. 90

많은 쓰레기를 수거해서 새롭고 멋진 제품을 만들기 때문에 그 제품들은 독특하기도 하고, 환경에도 좋을 것이다. 그러므로 빈칸에는 ③ environment가 적절하다.

p. 91

1 독일의 Freitag이 만든 가방은 '각각 다른 천으로 만들어지기 때문에 세계에 같은 가방이 없다'고 했으므로 ④는 글의 내용과 일치하지 않는다.

2 This trend는 앞의 It is a new kind of fashion, called 'upcycling'.에서 언급한 upcycling (fashion)을 의미한다.

3 **해석** 질문: 업사이클링은 무엇인가요?

대답: 그건 쓰레기로 새로운 제품을 만드는 거예요. 창의적인 생각으로 독특하고 친환경적인(좋은) 제품이 만들어집니다.

구문 설명

- It is a new kind of fashion, **called** 'upcycling'.
  fashion 뒤에 있는 comma(,)는 앞의 명사와 뒤의 명사가 동격임을 나타내며, called는 '~라고 불리는'의 뜻으로 쓰인 과거분사이다.

- The German company 'Freitag' makes bags **from many pieces of waterproof cloth and safety belts.**
  from은 '~을 사용하여'라는 의미로, 도구나 수단을 나타낸다.

- This trend in the fashion field is **not only** unique, **but also** good for the environment.
  not only A but (also) B는 'A뿐만 아니라 B도'라는 뜻으로 B as well as A로 바꿔 쓸 수 있다.

Reading Skill   모범 답안

중심 내용	· 업사이클링의 장점
근거 문장	1. 창의적 2. 친환경적

직독직해 Skill

- You (S) may think (V) / it will harm the earth.
  당신은 생각할지도 모른다 / 그것이 지구를 해칠 거라고

READING 32 ● 정답 ①

Mini Quiz 주제문: Cage thought people could feel the music without the artist, so he removed the artist from the music.
모범 답안 핵심 단어: not press, 4'33'', feel, without the artist, removed, could not make an impact 등

1 ① **2** (1) composer (2) remove
3 (1) silence (2) artist (3) noise (4) No(no)

해석

1952년 8월 어느 늦은 저녁, 한 남자가 극장에서 피아노 덮개를 세 번 열었다가 닫았다. 그는 피아노 위에 있는 타이머를 눌렀다. 그리고 그는 4분 33초 동안 어떤 건반도 누르지 않았다. 이상하게 보이겠지만 이것은 John Cage의 4분 33초라는 작품이었다. 침묵만이 흐르는 유명한 곡이었다. Cage는 사람들이 연주자 없이도 음악을 느낄 수 있다고 생각해서 음악에서 연주자를 제거했다. 공연하는 동안, 연주자와 작곡가는 음악에 영향을 줄 수 없었다. 심지어 Cage 본인조차도 극장의 소리를 제어할 방법이 없었다. 여전히 실생활 소음이 있었고 사람들은 느낌과 생각도 가질 수 있었다. 그는 우리가 느끼는 모든 것이 음악이 될 수 있다는 것을 보여 주고 싶었다.

해설

p. 92

John Cage의 4'33″라는 작품에 대한 내용이다. 4분 33초 동안 피아노의 어떤 건반도 치지 않았다는 것, 연주자 없이도 음악을 느낄 수 있다고 생각해서 연주자를 제거했다는 내용으로 미루어 볼 때 빈칸에는 ① '침묵'이 들어가야 적절하다.
② 합창 ③ 가사 ④ 웃음 ⑤ 콧노래

p. 93

1 연주 없이 침묵으로 이루어진 4'33″라는 음악 작품에 대한 글이므로 제목은 ① '연주자가 없는 음악'이 가장 적절하다.
  ② 타이머를 효율적으로 사용하는 법
  ③ 극장에서의 좋은 예절
  ④ 인간에게 고통을 주는 소음
  ⑤ 음악을 느끼는 법

2 (1) 대부분의 경우, 클래식 음악을 작곡하는 사람: composer(작곡가)
  (2) 사물이나 사람을 한 장소에서 빼다: remove(제거하다)

3 **해석**
  Q: John Cage의 4분 33초는 무엇인가요?
  A: 침묵만 있고 연주자는 없는 음악입니다.
  Q: 음악에서 연주자를 제거한 결과는 어떻게 되었나요?
  A: 사람들이 실생활 소음 속에서 느낌과 생각을 가질 수 있었습니다.
  Q: John Cage가 4분 33초 동안 극장의 소리를 제어할 수 있었나요?
  A: 아니요, 그는 소리를 제어할 방법이 없었습니다.

구문 설명

- One late evening in August of 1952, a man opened and closed the piano cover **three times** in a theater.
  three times는 '세 번'이라는 의미로 배수를 나타내는 표현이다.

- It **seems strange**, but **it** was John Cage's 4'33''.
  seem은 '~하게 보이다'라는 의미를 가진 동사로, 뒤에는 부사가 아닌 형용사 보어가 온다. it은 앞에서 계속 언급되고 있는 '침묵으로 이루어진 음악 작품'을 일컫는다.

- **Even** Cage **himself** had no way **to control** the sounds in the theater.
  even은 '~조차도'라는 의미의 부사이다. himself는 Cage를 강조하는 재귀대명사이고, to control은 '~을 제어할'의 의미로 no way를 수식한다.

- He wanted to show **that all the things we feel** can be music.
  that절은 show의 목적어이다. we feel은 all the things를 수식하여 '우리가 느끼는 모든 것들'의 의미로 that절의 주어이고 can be가 동사이다.

Reading Skill

모범 답안

주제문	• Cage는 사람들이 연주자 없이도 음악을 느낄 수 있다고 생각했다.
근거 문장	• 연주자는 4분 33초 동안 어떤 건반도 치지 않았다. • Cage의 4'33″에서는 누구도 음악에 영향을 줄 수 없었다.

직독직해 Skill

- During the performance, / the artist and composer (S) / could not make (V) an impact / on the music.
  공연을 하는 동안 / 연주자와 작곡가는 영향을 줄 수 없었다 / 음악에

Unit 13 빈칸 완성하기 2 (어구·문장)

READING 33 ▸ 정답 ⑤   pp. 94~95

Mini Quiz 주제문: Short videos have both ~ attention time.
근거 문장: People become familiar with ~ quickly.
A study by Microsoft shows ~ of teenagers.

1 ③   **2** 집중(하는) 시간   **3** (1) 10 (2) 1,000 (3) books
(4) movies (5) information (6) content (7) attention

해석

유튜브 쇼츠, 틱톡, 인스타그램 릴스. 여러분은 이런 종류의 영상을 봤을지도 모른다. 그것들은 모두 '쇼트폼 미디어'이다. 쇼트폼 미디어는 10분 미만 또는 1,000단어 미만의 콘텐츠를 가진다. 사람들은 쉽고 빠르게 정보를 얻을 수 있기 때문에 이 짧은 영상에 익숙해진다. 쇼트폼 미디어의 등장으로 사람들은 책과 영화와 같은 롱폼 미디어를 외면하고 있다. 그들은 빠르게 집중력을 잃고 전체적인 내용을 알고 싶어 하지 않는다. Microsoft의 연구에 따르면 쇼트폼 미디어가 십 대들의 집중 시간을 감소시켰다고 한다. 단 몇 년 만에, 그것은 10초 이상에서 8초가 되었다. 8초는 금붕어의 그것보다도 더 짧기 때문에 이는 심각한 문제이다. 학교에서 학생들은 또한 그들의 수업에 집중하는 데 어려움을 겪는다. 짧은 영상에는 좋은 점과 나쁜 점이 모두 있다: 그것들은 빠른 정보를 제공하지만, 또한 학생들의 집중 시간도 감소시킨다.

해설

p. 94

쇼트폼 미디어의 영향으로 롱폼 미디어를 외면하게 되는 이유에 해당되는 내용이므로, 빈칸에는 ⑤ '집중력을 빨리 잃는다'라는 내용이 적절하다.
① 관심을 받고 싶어 한다
② 책을 많이 읽는 것을 좋아한다
③ 이미 내용을 안다
④ 롱폼 미디어에 집중한다

p. 95

1 이 글은 '쇼트폼 미디어'의 장단점에 대한 글이다. ③ 롱폼(long-form) 미디어의 문제점에 대해서는 언급되지 않았다.
 ① 유튜브 쇼츠, 틱톡, 인스타그램 릴스 등이 제시되었다.
 ② 빠르고 쉽게 정보를 얻을 수 있기 때문이다.
 ④ 최근 연구에 따르면 8초이다.
 ⑤ 수업에 집중하는 데 어려움을 겪는다.

2 8초는 '금붕어의 그것'보다 짧다는 내용이므로 that이 가리키는 것은 앞서 제시된 the attention time, 즉 집중(하는) 시간이다.

3 **해석**
쇼트폼 미디어

정의: 10분 미만 또는 1,000단어 미만의 콘텐츠
예시: 유튜브 쇼츠, 틱톡, 인스타그램 릴스
　　　cf. 롱폼 미디어의 예시: 책과 영화
좋은 점: 우리는 쉽고 빠르게 정보를 얻을 수 있다.
나쁜 점: 사람들은 전체적인 내용을 알고 싶어 하지 않는다.
　　　학생들이 짧은 집중 시간을 보인다.

구문 설명

· You **might** watch these kinds of videos.
might는 '~일지도 모른다'라는 뜻의 조동사로 뒤에는 동사원형이 온다.

· **With the rise of** short-form media, people are **turning away from** long-form media like books and movies.
with the rise of는 '~의 등장으로'라는 뜻이며, turn away from은 '~을 외면하다, 관심이 줄어들다'라는 뜻의 표현이다.

· Short videos have **both** good **and** bad points: They provide quick information but also decrease students' attention time.
both A and B는 'A와 B 둘 다'라는 뜻이다. :(colon) 뒤에 나오는 문장은 앞의 내용을 부연 설명한다.

Reading Skill

모범 답안

주제문	· 쇼트폼 미디어의 장단점: 빠른(신속한) 정보와 짧은 집중 시간
근거문	· 장점: 쉽고 빠르게 얻을 수 있는 정보 · 단점: 십 대(들)의 줄어든 집중 시간 / 학생들의 (학교 수업에) 짧은 집중 시간

직독직해 Skill

· In school, / students (S) also have (V) difficulty focusing / on their classes.
학교에서 / 학생들은 또한 집중하는 것에 어려움을 겪는다 / 자신들의 수업에

READING 34 ▸ 정답 ④   pp. 96~97

Mini Quiz They do not know ~ the same way as they do.

1 ③　2 모범 답안 ⓐ 4세 소녀 ⓑ 4세 소녀의 엄마
3 (1) package　(2) Gum　(3) mom　(4) Pencil　(5) thinking

아이들은 4세가 되면 다른 사람의 생각을 이해하기 시작한다. 예를 들어, 네 살짜리 소녀에게 "껌 통 안에 무엇이 들어있니?"라고 물을 수 있다. 그 아이는 "껌"이라고 말할 것이다. 당신은 껌 통을 열어 그녀에게 안에 무엇이 있는지를 보여 준다. 그 안에는 연필이 있다. 그런 다음 당신은 그녀에게 "너희 엄마는 안에 무엇이 있다고 생각하실 것 같아?"라고 물어본다. 그녀의 엄마는 방 밖에서 기다리고 있어서 안에 무엇이 들어 있는지 볼 수 없다. 여전히 그 아이는 "껌"이라고 말할 것이다. 그 아이는 엄마가 안에 들어있는 연필을 보지 못했다는 것을 알기 때문이다. 그러나 4세 미만의 어린이의 경우 같은 예시에서 "연필"이라고 말할 것이다. 그들은 그들의 엄마가 안을 보지 못했다는 사실을 상상할 수 없다. 그들은 누군가가 무엇이 거기 있는지를 알기 위해 내부를 볼 필요가 있다는 것을 모른다. 그래서 그들은 모두가 그들과 같은 방식으로 이해한다고 생각한다.

해설

p. 96

4세가 되면 이전과 달리 다른 사람의 생각을 이해할 수 있다는 내용으로 ④ '다른 사람들의 생각을 이해한다'가 들어가는 것이 적절하다.
① 그들의 필요를 표현한다
② 그들의 물건을 다른 사람들과 공유한다
③ 각각의 물건에 이름을 지어 준다
⑤ 배움의 기쁨을 이해한다

p. 97

1 4세 미만의 아이들은 엄마가 안을 보지 못했다는 사실을 상상할 수 없다는 내용으로 미루어볼 때, 4세 미만의 어린이들은 자신의 현실 너머를 상상할 수 없다는 내용이므로, 빈칸에는 under와 imagine 이 들어가야 적절하다.

2 ⓐ의 앞 문장에 a four-year-old girl이라는 내용이 있으므로 ⓐ는 '4세 소녀'를 의미한다. ⓑ의 앞에는 Her mom is ~라는 표현이 있으므로 여기의 she는 '(4세) 소녀의 엄마'를 의미한다.

3 **해석**

조건

1. 안에 연필이 들어 있는 껌 통의 내부를 보여 준다.
2. 두 집단의 아이들에게 "너희 엄마는 안에 무엇이 있다고 생각하실까?"라고 묻는다.

결과

4살 아이들: 그들은 엄마가 통 안을 보지 못했다는 사실을 알고 있기 때문에 "껌"이라고 대답했다.

4살 미만의 아이들: 그들은 다른 사람의 생각을 이해하지 못하기 때문에 "연필"이라고 대답했다.

구문 설명

· You **open** the package **and show her what's inside.**
open과 show가 접속사 and에 의해 병렬 연결되어 있다. show A B는 'A에게 B를 보여 주다'라는 뜻으로, show B to A로 쓸 수도 있다.

· Then, you ask her, "What will **your mom think** is inside?"
your mom think가 삽입된 형태로 '너희 엄마는 안에 무엇이 있다고 생각하실까?'라는 의미이다.

· They cannot **imagine** their mom did not see inside.
imagine 뒤에 접속사 that이 생략된 형태이다.

· They do not **know** someone **needs to** see inside **to know** what is in there.
know 뒤에 접속사 that이 생략되어 있고, need to는 '~해야 한다'의 의미로 have to와 같은 표현이다. to know는 목적을 나타내는 to부정사로 '알기 위해서'라고 해석한다.

Reading Skill

모범 답안

껌 통 안에 무엇이 있을지에 대한 질문	
4세 이상 어린이	1번째 대답(아이의 생각) : 껌
	2번째 대답(엄마의 생각 추론) : 껌
4세 미만 어린이	1번째 대답(아이의 생각) : 껌
	2번째 대답(엄마의 생각 추론) : 연필

직독직해 Skill

· It (S) is (V) / because she knows / her mother did not see the pencil inside.
그것은 ~이다 / 그녀가 알기 때문에 / 엄마가 안에 있는 연필을 보지 못했다는 것을

Unit 14 밑줄 친 부분 파악하기

READING **35**　정답 ⑤　　pp. 98~99

Mini Quiz　주제문: Only strong memories ~ positive things.
예시문: For example, our brain does not focus on ~ than green lights.

1 ②　2 **모범 답안** remember, bad(negative), things
3 ⓐ focus　ⓑ green　ⓒ bad　ⓓ failure　ⓔ remember
ⓕ red

해석

학교에 늦었다고 상상해 보라. 그러나 여러분이 만나는 모든 신호등이 적색이다. 당신은 "잘못될 수 있는 모든 것은 잘못될 것이다"라고 생각할지도 모른다. 이런 생각을 머피의 법칙이라고 한다. 그러나 몇몇 과학자들은 우리가 그렇게 부정적으로 생각할 필요가 없다고 말한다. 그들은 우리가 생각하는 방식의 이유를 선택적 기억이라고 말한다. 우리의 뇌는 우리가 한 모든 것을 기억하지는 못한다. 오직 강렬한 기억들만이 뇌에 남아서 우리는 긍정적인 것들보다는 실패나 안 좋은 일을 훨씬 많이 기억한다. 예를 들어, 우리의 뇌는 녹색 신호일 때 길을 쉽게 건너는 것에는 초점을 맞추지 않는다. 그러나 적색 신호에서 우리는 멈춰서 몇 분 동안 기다려야 한다. 이런 작은 차이가 녹색 신호보다 적색 신호를 더 많이 만났다고 생각하게 만든다. 만약 이런 생각들이 자주 반복되면, 우리는 대부분 안 좋은 것들만 기억해서 결론적으로 항상 실패한다고 생각한다.

해설

p. 98

실패나 안 좋은 일과 같은 강렬한 기억만이 뇌에서 더 많이 기억된다고 했으므로, 몇 분씩 서서 기다리게 하는 적색 신호(a red light)는 ⑤ '우리가 강하게 기억하는 안 좋은 일'에 해당한다고 볼 수 있다.
① 작은 차이
② 부정적 사고
③ 안전을 유지하기 위한 긍정적인 신호
④ 선택적으로 일들을 기억하는 것

p. 99

1 머피의 법칙이 일어나는 이유를 설명하는 글이므로 핵심어인 Murphy's Law와 그 이유에 해당하는 Selective Memory를 모두 포함하는 ② '머피의 법칙: 선택적 기억의 결과'가 글의 제목으로 가장 적절하다.
① 신호등: 길을 안전하게 건너는 방법
③ 부정적인 생각이 우리를 실패하게 한다
④ 기억의 비밀: 모든 것을 기억하려고 노력하기
⑤ 지각: 나쁜 습관

2 마지막 문장에서 알 수 있듯이, 사람들은 '안 좋은 것들만 대부분 기억하기 때문에' 결론적으로 항상 실패한다고 생각한다. 따라서 이와 관련된 내용이 들어가는 게 적절하다.

3 **해석**
〈좋은 기억에 대한 예시〉
우리의 뇌는 녹색 신호에서 길을 쉽게 건너는 것에 초점을 맞추지 않는다.
〈안 좋은 기억에 대한 예시〉
우리의 뇌는 적색 신호에서 멈춰야 할 때 안 좋은 일을 더 오래 기억한다.

〈선택적 기억〉
우리는 안 좋은 일이나 실패를 주로 기억한다.

구문 설명

· **Imagine** that you are late for school.
'~하라'라는 의미의 명령문에서는 주어가 생략되고 동사원형으로 시작한다.

· But all the traffic lights **you meet** are red.
you meet이 the traffic lights를 꾸며 '당신이 만나는 모든 신호등들'이라는 뜻을 나타낸다. 그러므로 주어는 all the traffic lights, 동사는 are이다.

· However, some scientists say that we **don't have to** think so negatively.
don't have to는 '~할 필요 없다'라는 뜻으로, don't need to로 쓸 수도 있다.

· For example, our brain does not **focus on crossing** the street easily when there is a green light.
focus on은 '~에 초점을 맞추다, 집중하다'라는 뜻이며, 전치사 on 뒤의 crossing은 '건너는 것'이라는 뜻의 동명사로 쓰였다.

Reading Skill　　모범 답안

주제문	· 실패나 나쁜 일이 더 강력해서 뇌가 더 잘 기억하는 것을 선택적 기억이라고 한다.
예시문	· 뇌(우리)는 녹색 신호등에서 길을 건너는 것은 기억하지(신경쓰지) 않는다. · 뇌(우리)는 적색 신호등에서 몇 분 기다린(멈춘) 것을 더 기억한다.

직독직해 Skill

· Only strong memories (S) remain (V) / in the brain.
오직 강렬한 기억만이 남는다 / 뇌에

READING **36** 정답 ④ pp. 100~101

Mini Quiz 모범답안 a set of rules, by just memorizing 등

1 ③ **2** social, understanding
3 (1)communicate (2)memorizing (3)picture (4)robotic

해석

우리가 사람들에게 이야기를 할 때, 우리는 몸짓 언어도 사용한다. 몇몇 사람들은 몸짓 언어를 사전처럼 생각한다. 그들은 몸짓 언어를 한 세트의 규칙처럼 사용한다. 이러한 사전적인 접근으로는 사회적 이해의 많은 측면을 찾을 수 없다. 그들은 팔짱을 낀 사람을 보고 화가 났다고 생각하거나, 미소 짓고 있는 사람을 보고 행복하다고 생각할 수도 있다. 그러나 사람들이 단순히 어떤 신호들을 암기하는 것만으로 소통한다면 그들은 더 큰 그림을 보지 못할 것이다. 그것은 그것보다 더 복잡하기 때문이다. 몸짓 언어 사전을 읽어서 몸짓 언어를 사용하려고 하는 것은 프랑스어 사전을 읽어서 프랑스어를 말하려고 하는 것과 같다. 우리가 몸짓 언어를 자연스럽게 사용하지 않으면 우리의 몸짓 언어는 로봇 같고 혼란스럽다고 생각될 수 있다.

해설

p. 100

by reading a body language dictionary는 ④ '사회적 의미를 이해하지 않고' 몸짓 언어를 하나의 규칙처럼 생각해서 단순히 신호들을 외워서 사용하는 것을 말한다.
① 전문가의 도움으로
② 몸짓 언어와 프랑스어 배우는 것을 비교함으로써
③ 사회적 맥락에서 몸짓 언어를 배움으로써
⑤ 사람들이 모국어를 배우는 방식으로

p. 101

1 이 글은 단순히 몸짓 언어를 규칙처럼 외워서 파악하는 것이 아니라 사회적 의미를 이해해서 의사소통을 해야 한다는 내용이다. 따라서 필자가 주장하는 바는 ③이 가장 적절하다.

2 효과적인 몸짓 언어는 각 신호들의 총합 이상을 포함하고 우리가 그 속에서 다양한 측면의 '사회적 맥락'을 찾을 수 있어야 하므로 빈칸에는 social understanding이 들어가야 한다.

3 **해석**
 '사전적 접근'의 의미: 단순히 각각의 몸짓 언어 신호를 외움으로써
   의사소통하는 것
 '사전적 접근'의 결과들: 1. 우리는 더 큰 그림을 볼 수 없다.
       2. 우리의 몸짓 언어는 로봇처럼 생각되어
        사람들은 혼란스러울지도 모른다.

구문 설명

· **Some people think body language is like a dictionary.**
 like는 '~같이'라는 뜻의 전치사이다.

· **It's more complicated than that.**
 more complicated는 complicated의 비교급이다. 여기서 It은 communication을, that은 memorizing some signals를 나타낸다.

· **Trying to use body language by reading a body language dictionary is like trying to speak French by reading a French dictionary.**
 주어가 긴 문장으로 Trying to use body language by reading a body language dictionary 부분이 주어에 해당된다. ~ is like …는 '~는 …와 같다'라는 의미이다.

· **Our body language might be thought of as robotic and confusing if we don't use it naturally.**
 '추측'의 조동사 might 뒤에 be thought라는 수동태가 이어진 형태이다. it은 our body language를 가리킨다.

Reading Skill
모범 답안

중심 내용	몸짓 언어 사용시의 주의점
근거 문장	몸짓 언어를 암기하여 의사소통하는 것은 큰 그림을 보지 못하는 것

직독직해 Skill

· They (S) might see (V₁) / someone with their arms crossed / and / think (V₂) / they're angry.
 그들은 볼지도 모른다 / 팔짱을 낀 누군가를 / 그리고 / 생각할지도 모른다 / 그들이 화났다고

긴 글 독해하기

정답

A　세부 내용　통증(고통), 말, 부정적인, 고통스러운, 건강, 긍정
　　　　적인, 긍정적인
　　　주제문　현명하게, 긍정적으로

B　꿈, 입양, 포기, 가족
　　(B)-(A)-(C)

해석

A　독일의 과학자들은 흥미로운 실험을 했다. 그들은 주사를 맞기 전에 "이거 아플 거야"와 같은 무서운 경고를 들으면 바늘이 피부에 닿기도 전에 통증을 느낄 수 있다는 것을 발견했다! 과학자들은 사람들의 뇌를 관찰하기 위해 특별한 기계를 사용했고 사람들이 고통스러운 무언가가 오고 있다는 것을 의미하는 단어를 들으면, 고통을 느끼는 그들의 뇌의 부분이 매우 활성화된다는 것을 발견했다.

이것은 말이 정말로 중요하다는 것을 보여 준다. 우리가 부정적이거나 고통스러운 말을 듣거나 말할 때, 우리의 뇌는 그 고통을 느끼기 시작한다. 하지만 걱정하지 마라. 우리는 우리 자신에게 말하는 방식을 바꿈으로써 우리 자신의 건강을 통제할 수 있다! 만약 우리가 긍정적인 생각을 하고, 긍정적인 말을 하고, 긍정적인 사람들과 어울린다면, 우리의 몸은 더 나아질 것이다. 우리는 심지어 더 낮은 혈압과 스트레스 호르몬을 갖게 될지도 모른다! 그러니 우리의 말을 현명하게 선택하고 항상 긍정적으로 생각하도록 노력하자!

B　Tim Burke는 어렸을 때부터 직업적으로 경기하는 것을 꿈꿨던 재능 있는 야구 선수였다. 그는 그의 꿈을 이루기 위해 열심히 노력했고 Montreal Expos에서 뛰었다. Tim은 야구하는 것을 아주 좋아했지만, 그는 그의 가족을 훨씬 더 사랑했다. Tim과 그의 아내는 아이를 갖기를 원했지만 가질 수 없다는 것을 알게 되었다. 그래서 그들은 가정이 필요한 아이들을 입양하기로 결정했다. 그들은 다른 나라에서 온 특수 교육이 필요한 네 명의 아이들을 입양했다. Tim은 그의 아이들에게 가능한 최고의 삶을 주기를 원했던 자상한 아버지였다.

(A) 그래서 Tim은 프로 선수가 되기 위해 너무나 열심히 노력했음에도 불구하고 야구를 그만둔다는 어려운 결정을 내렸다. 그는 그의 가족과 더 많은 시간을 보내고 싶었고 그가 될 수 있는 최고의 아버지와 남편이 되고 싶었다. Tim은 그에게 가족이 가장 중요하다는 것을 알았고, 그는 이 결정을 내리는 것에 행복했다.

(B) 하지만 야구 선수로서의 Tim의 직업은 그가 많은 여행을 해야 한다는 것을 의미했다. 그는 경기를 하기 위해 다른 도시와 나라들로 여행해야 했고, 때때로 집을 떠나 긴 시간을 보내야 했다. 이것은 그가 원하는 만큼의 시간을 가족들과 보내는 것을 어렵게 만들었다.

(C) 어느날 한 기자가 Tim에게 왜 야구를 그만두느냐고 물었다. Tim은 비록 그가 야구를 하는 것을 좋아했지만, 그의 가족은 그가 더 필요하다고 대답했다. 그는 그의 아이들과 그의 아내를 위해 그곳에 있고 싶었고, 그가 야구를 계속한다면 그렇게 할 수 없다는 것을 알고 있었다.

Unit 15 장문 독해하기

Mini Quiz　모범답안　But a learning style gives you an answer to how you can learn best. / Knowing one's own learning style helps the student learn more ineffectively. So, understand how you learn and use it as much as possible!

1 ⑤　**2** ⑤　**3** learning, style　**4** (1) a, e, g　(2) c, d, f　(3) b, h

해석

무언가를 배우는 데 있어 중요한 것은 무엇인가? 높은 IQ? 좋은 선생님? 충분한 공부 시간? 그것들 모두 관련이 있다. 그러나 학습 스타일은 여러분이 가장 잘 배울 수 있는 방법에 대한 정답을 제공한다. 여러분 자신의 학습 스타일을 파악하기 위한 간단한 질문이 있다. 새로운 보드게임을 하는 법을 배우고 싶다면, 어떻게 하겠는가? 첫째, 설명서를 잘 읽고 메모할 수 있다. 둘째, 다른 사람의 설명을 듣고 질문할 수 있다. 셋째, 다른 사람들이 놀이하는 것을 보고 직접 해 볼 수 있다. 여러분만의 행동은 여러분의 학습 스타일을 보여 줄 수 있다.

학습 스타일에는 세 가지 유형이 있다. 첫 번째 유형은 시각적 학습이다. 시각적 학습 스타일을 가진 사람들은 읽고 필기하면서 학습한다. 그들에게는 도표나 그림을 그리는 것이 학습에 도움이 된다. 두 번째 종류의 사람은 소리에 집중한다. 그들은 무언가를 듣고 말하는 것을 통해 배운다. 따라서 글을 큰 소리로 읽는 것이 그들이 무언가를 학습하는 좋은 방법이 될 수 있다. 마지막 유형의 사람은 몸을 사용한다. 그들은 몸을 움직여서 배운다. 그들은 무언가를 배우기 위해 역할극을 사용할 수 있다. 모든 학생은 배우기 위한 자신만의 학습 스타일을 사용한다. 자신의 학습 스타일을 아는 것은 학생이 더 비효율적으로(→ 효율적으로) 배우는 데 도움이 된다. 따라서 여러분이 어떻게 배우는지를 이해해서 그것을 가능한 한 많이 활용하라!

p. 108

1 학습을 효과적으로 하기 위해 자신의 학습 스타일을 알 수 있도록 세 가지 학습 유형을 소개하는 글이므로 ⑤ '학습 방법에 대한 좋은 답: 자신의 학습 스타일을 아는 것'이 제목으로 가장 적절하다.
① 살을 빼기 위해 몸을 움직이기
② 좋은 선생님이 좋은 학생을 만든다.
③ 학습 전략으로 도표 그리기
④ 간단한 질문: 여러분은 공부를 잘하나요?

p. 109

2 학습 스타일을 아는 것은 더 효과적으로 배우는 방법을 제시하는 것이므로 ⓔ ineffectively(비효율적으로)는 effectively(효율적으로)로 써야 한다.

3 뭔가를 배우는 여러분만의 행동은 여러분의 학습 스타일을 보여 준다는 내용이 적절하므로 빈칸에는 learning style이 적절하다.

4 해석 학습 스타일의 3가지 유형
(1) 시각적 학습자들
    a. 차트와 표를 사용하기
    e. 필기하기
    g. 사진을 사용하기
(2) 청각적 학습자들
    c. 듣기를 사용하기
    d. 소리내어 읽기
    f. 뭔가를 말하기
(3) 신체적 학습자들
    b. 역할극을 사용하기
    h. 스스로 해 보기

구문 설명

· If you want to learn **how to play** a new board game, what will you do?
if는 '~한다면'이라는 의미를 지닌 접속사로 조건의 부사절을 이끈다. 「how+to부정사」는 '~하는 방법'으로 해석한다.

· For **them**, **drawing** a diagram or pictures **is** helpful for learning.
them은 앞에서 언급된 people with visual learning style을 가리킨다. drawing은 주어 역할을 하는 동명사이며 단수 취급한다.

· They learn **through hearing and saying** something.
through는 '~을 통하여'라는 의미이고, hearing과 saying은 and에 의해 같은 형태로 병렬 연결되었다.

· **Knowing** one's own learning style **helps the student learn** more effectively.
Knowing은 주어 역할을 하는 동명사이다. 「help+목적어+목적격보어」는 '(목적어)가 ~하는 것을 돕다'라는 의미로 목적격보어로 동사원형이나 to부정사가 올 수 있다.

Reading Skill
모범 답안

주제문	· 여러분의 학습 스타일을 아는 것은 효과적인 학습에 중요하다.

직독직해 Skill

· But / a learning style (S) / gives (V) / you an answer / to how you can learn best.
그러나 / 학습 스타일은 / 준다 / 여러분에게 답을 / 어떻게 여러분이 가장 잘 배울 수 있는지에 대한

READING 38
pp. 110~111

Mini Quiz 모범 답안 white hat hackers
- They use ~ with security.
- They follow the law when they hack.
- The name ~ days.
- Since ~ our personal information.

1 ④ 2 ⑤
3 American, movies, movies, heroes, white, hats
4 (1) law (2) security (3) protect

해석

해킹은 항상 나쁠까? 선한 해커, 즉 화이트 햇 해커도 있다. 그들은 자신들의 해킹 기술을 사용하여 보안과 관련된 문제를 찾는다. 그들은 블랙 햇 해커들과 다르다. 그들은 해킹할 때 법을 준수한다. '하얀 모자' 해커의 이름은 미국 "거친 서부" 시대에 대한 오래된 미국 영화에서 따왔다. 이런 영화에서 영웅들은 흰 모자를 쓰고 나쁜 사람들은 검은 모자를 썼다. 그래서 오늘날의 선한 해커는 '하얀 모자' 해커가 되었다.
Marc Maiffret은 유명한 화이트 햇 해커 중 한 명이다. 그는 Microsoft 소프트웨어의 큰 약점을 발견했다. 이 문제 때문에 블랙 햇 해커가 그 소프트웨어에 침입하여 데이터를 훔칠 수도 있었다. 그러나 그는 Microsoft가 그 문제를 해결하도록 도왔다. 그는 소프트웨어를 공격할(→ 보호할) 수 있는 새로운 프로그램을 만들었다. 우리는 인터넷을 많이 사용하기 때문에 Maiffret과 같은 화이트 햇 해커는 우리의 개인 정보를 보호하는 데 중요한 역할을 한다.

p. 110

1 이 글은 선한 해커인 화이트 햇 해커에 관해 설명하고 있다. 그들이 하는 일, 이름의 유래, 유명한 화이트 햇 해커 등을 소개하고 있으므로 ④ '화이트 햇 해커: 소프트웨어 보호자'라는 제목이 적절하다.

① 해커가 되는 법

② Marc Maiffret, 우리의 영웅

③ 블랙 햇 해커는 왜 유명한가?

⑤ 미국 영화에서 흰색과 검은색 모자의 의미

p. 111

2 화이트 햇 해커는 소프트웨어를 침입해 정보를 빼내 가려는 블랙 햇 해커를 막기 때문에 ⓔ 소프트웨어를 '공격한다(attack)'가 아니라 '보호한다(protect)'는 내용이 자연스럽다.

3 첫 번째 단락 마지막 부분에서 화이트 햇 해커 이름의 유래를 파악할 수 있다. 오래된 미국 서부 영화에서 영웅들이 흰색 모자를 쓴 것에서 유래되었다.

4 [해석] 화이트 햇 해커는 ……

(1) 해킹을 할 때 법을 따라야 한다.

(2) 보안 문제들을 찾기 위해 그들의 해킹 기술을 사용해야 한다.

(3) 우리의 개인 정보를 보호하기 위해 해결책들을 제시해야 한다.

[구문 설명]

- **They are different from** black hat hackers.

  They는 white hat hackers를 가리키며, be different from 은 '~와 다르다'라는 의미이다.

- The name "white hat" hacker **is from** old American movies about the country's "Wild West" days.

  from은 '~로부터, ~에서'라는 의미의 전치사로, be동사와 함께 쓰여 '~에서 오다(유래하다)'라는 의미로 사용되었다.

- Marc Maiffret is **one of the famous white hat hackers**.

  one of는 '~ 중 하나'라는 의미로 of 뒤에 복수 명사가 온다.

- **Since** we use the Internet a lot, a white hat hacker like Maiffret **plays an important role in protecting** our personal information.

  Since는 '~ 때문에'라는 뜻의 접속사이다. play a role은 '역할을 하다'라는 뜻이며 role 앞에 important 등의 형용사를 넣어 다양한 의미를 나타낼 수 있다. 전치사 in 뒤의 protecting은 동명사이다.

[Reading Skill]

모범 답안

핵심어	· 화이트 햇 해커(선량한 해커)
부연 설명	· 유래: 오래된 미국 (서부) 영화의 영웅들이 흰색 모자를 쓰고 나옴 · 역할: 보안과 관련된 문제점 발견, 소프트웨어 보호, 개인 정보 보호

[직독직해 Skill]

- They (S) use (V) / their hacking skills / to find some problems with security.

  그들은 사용한다 / 그들의 해킹 기술을 / 보안과 관련된 문제들을 찾기 위해서

Unit 16 복합 문단 독해하기

READING **39**

pp. 112~114

(Mini Quiz) 모범 답안 (A) The elephant looked down on all the small animals.

(B) The ant slowly crawled into the elephant's body and started biting him.

(C) Finally, he apologized to the ant.

(D) One day, when the ant family was going to work, the elephant sprayed a lot of water on them.

1 ④ **2** ③ **3** ④ **4** ⑤

5 (1) elephant (2) ants (3) sprayed (4) pain

[해석]

(A) 울창하고 푸른 숲에 거대한 코끼리와 작은 개미 가족이 살고 있었다. 코끼리는 모든 작은 동물들을 무시했다. 그는 자신의 힘을 자랑스러워해서 과시하고 싶어 했다. 반면에 개미 가족은 항상 먹이를 구하느라 바빴다.

(D) 어느 날, 개미 가족이 일하러 갈 때 코끼리가 그들에게 많은 물을 뿌렸다. "아야! 남을 이렇게 다치게 하면 안 돼!" 개미들 중 한 마리가 소리쳤다. 코끼리가 말했다. "오, 어리석은 개미야! 조용히 하지 않으면 죽여버릴거야." 불쌍한 개미는 겁이 났지만 그에게 교훈을 주기로 결심했다.

(B) 개미는 천천히 코끼리의 몸으로 기어들어 가서 코끼리를 물기 시작했다. 곧, 코끼리는 움직일 수 없었다. 코끼리는 개미를 쫓아내려 했지만

<u>개미</u>는 계속해서 물었다. 코끼리는 큰 동물이었지만 작은 개미에 대항해서 아무것도 할 수 없었다.

(C) 그는 고통으로 소리를 지르며 울기 시작했다. 결국 그는 개미에게 사과했다. 개미는 "네가 우리를 다치게 했을 때 우리 기분이 이랬어!"라고 말했다. 개미가 무는 것을 멈추고 코끼리의 몸에서 나왔다. 그날부터 그는 더 이상 다른 작은 동물들을 해치지 않았다.

해설

p. 113

1 사건이 시작되는 (D)가 가장 먼저 와야 한다. 코끼리가 개미 가족에게 물을 뿌려서 개미 가족 중 한 마리가 코끼리의 몸 속으로 들어가 코끼리를 물고(B), 이를 못견딘 코끼리가 깨달음을 얻는(C) 흐름이 가장 적절하다.

2 ⓒ의 he는 코끼리를 물었던 개미 한 마리이고, 나머지는 모두 코끼리를 가리킨다.

3 (C)에서 코끼리는 개미에게 사과하고 더 이상 다른 동물들을 해치지 않았다는 내용이 나오므로 ④는 적절하지 않다.

4 코끼리에게 해를 입었던 개미가 코끼리에게도 자기가 겪었던 감정을 알게 해 주었기 때문에 가장 적절한 교훈은 ⑤ '역지사지'이다.
① 이열치열 ② 다다익선 ③ 고통 없이는 얻는 것도 없다.
④ 호랑이도 제 말 하면 온다.

p. 114

5 **해석** 거대한 <u>코끼리</u>와 작은 <u>개미</u> 가족이 살고 있었다. 개미 가족이 일하러 가는 길에 코끼리가 물을 <u>뿌려서</u> 그들을 다치게 했다. 그래서 개미 중 한 마리가 그의 몸으로 기어들어 가 그를 물어 버렸다. 그는 <u>고통</u>에 소리치고 결국 개미에게 미안하다고 말했다. 그날부터 그는 더 이상 남을 해치지 않았다.

구문 설명

· In a thick, green forest, **there lived** a huge elephant and a tiny family of ants.
there lived …는 '…가 살았다'라는 의미이다.

· He **was proud of** his strength **and wanted** to show it off.
be proud of는 '~을 자랑스러워 하다'라는 의미로 of 뒤에는 명사가 온다. 동사 was와 wanted가 and에 의해 병렬 구조를 이루고 있다.

· The elephant was a big animal, but he couldn't do anything **against the tiny ant**.
against는 '~에 대항하여'라는 의미로 사용되어 '그 작은 개미에 대항하여'라는 뜻이다.

· **This** is **how we feel** when you hurt us!
This는 코끼리가 느끼고 있는 고통을 가리킨다. 「how+주어+동사」는 '어떻게 (주어)가 ~하는지'라고 해석한다.

Reading Skill

모범 답안

단락 요약 (가급적 6하 원칙을 준수할 것)

(A) <u>거대한 코끼리와 작은 개미 가족이 있었는데, 코끼리는 자신의 힘을 과시하고 싶었다.</u>

(B) <u>개미가 코끼리를 물기 시작했다. 코끼리는 아무것도 할 수 없었다.</u>

(C) <u>코끼리가 울면서 개미에게 사과했다. 코끼리는 다른 동물들을 더 이상 해치지 않았다.</u>

(D) <u>코끼리가 개미 가족에게 물을 뿌려서 다치게 했다. 그중 한 개미는 무서웠지만 코끼리에게 교훈을 주기로 결심했다.</u>

직독직해 Skill

· Keep(V₁) / quiet, // or / I (S) will kill(V₂) / you.
유지해라 / 조용히 // 아니면 / 나는 죽일 것이다 / 너를

READING **40**

pp. 116~118

Mini Quiz 모범 답안 One day, a poor man → he, The close friends of the prince → they, you would ~ bad → That, Then, Usually, This time 등

1 ③ **2** ② **3** ③ **4** ④ **5** (1) prince (2) surprised (3) by, himself (4) sour (5) hurt

해석

(A) 어느 날 가난한 한 남자가 왕자에게 포도 한 송이를 선물로 주었다. 그는 너무 가난해서 다른 것을 살 수는 없었기 때문에 그에게 선물을 가져올 수 있어서 매우 신났다. 그는 포도를 왕자 가까이에 놓고 말했다. "오. 왕자님, 제가 드리는 이 작은 선물을 부디 받아 주세요." 그는 왕자에게 작은 선물을 줄 수 있어서 매우 행복했다.

(C) 왕자는 정중하게 그에게 감사를 표했다. 남자가 그를 바라보자, 왕자는 포도 한 개를 먹었다. 그러고 나서 <u>그</u>는 또 하나를 먹었다. 천천히 왕자는 혼자서 포도 한 송이를 다 먹었다. 그는 <u>자신</u>의 주변 누구에게도 포도를 주지 않았다. 가난한 남자는 매우 기뻐하며 떠났다. 왕자의 가까운 친구들은 매우 놀랐다.

(D) 보통 왕자는 자신이 가진 모든 것을 다른 사람들과 나누었다. 그는 자신이 받은 것은 무엇이든 다른 사람들에게 나눠 주었고, 그들은 그것을 함께 먹었다. 이번에는 달랐다. <u>그</u>는 혼자 포도 한 송이를 다 먹었다. 친구들 중 한 명이 물었다. "왕자님! 왜 우리와 함께 포도를 나눠 드시지

않고 혼자서 다 드셨나요?" 그는 웃으며 포도가 너무 시어서 그랬다고 말했다.

(B) 왕자는 "만약에 내가 여러분과 포도를 나눠 먹었다면 여러분은 우스꽝스러운 표정을 지으며 포도가 별로라고 말했을 것입니다. 그것은 가난한 남자의 감정을 상하게 했을 것입니다. 그래서 그를 기쁘게 해 주기 위해 나 혼자서 포도 전부를 행복하게 먹는 것이 더 낫겠다고 생각했습니다. 나는 그 가난한 남자의 기분을 상하게 하고 싶지 않았습니다." 라고 말했다. 왕자 주변의 모든 사람들이 감명을 받았다.

p. 117

1 가난한 남자가 왕자에게 포도 한 송이를 선물로 주었고(A), 왕자는 감사를 표하며 혼자서 포도를 다 먹었다(C). 무엇이든 항상 다른 사람들과 나누던 왕자여서 친구가 혼자만 먹은 이유를 묻자(D), 포도가 너무 시어서 나눠 먹으면 다른 사람들의 표정에 그것이 드러나 가난한 남자가 기분이 상했을 것 같아서 그랬다고 답해 모두가 감명을 받았다(B)는 흐름이 가장 적절하다.

2 ⓑ는 왕자가 기쁘게 하고 싶은 대상인 the poor man을 지칭한다. 나머지는 모두 prince를 가리킨다.

3 Slowly the prince finished the whole bunch of grapes by himself.라고 했으므로 ③은 적절하지 않다.

4 왕자가 가난한 남자의 기분을 상하게 하고 싶지 않았다고 했으므로, 이를 미루어볼 때 ④가 가장 적절하다.

p. 118

5

> 어느 날 가난한 한 남자가 왕자에게 한 송이의 포도를 선물로 주었다.
>
> ⇩
>
> 왕자는 그 가난한 남자에게 선물을 받고 정중히 감사를 표하고 포도를 먹기 시작했다. 왕자는 다른 사람들과 포도를 나누지 않고 천천히 다 먹었다. 그 가난한 남자는 매우 행복했고 그의 친구들은 놀랐다.
>
> ⇩
>
> 왕자는 보통 모든 것을 다른 사람과 나누고 함께 먹었다. 하지만, 그가 가난한 남자로부터 포도 한 송이를 받았을 때 그는 그것을 모두 혼자 먹어 버렸다. 그의 친구가 그에게 왜 그가 포도를 나누지 않았냐고 물었을 때, 왕자는 웃으며 포도가 너무 시었다고 말했다.
>
> ⇩
>
> 왕자는 만약 그들이 포도를 먹는다면 그들은 가난한 남자를 놀리며 가난한 남자의 감정을 상하게 할 것이라는 사실을 알았다. 그래서, 왕자는 모든 포도를 혼자 다 먹은 것이다. 그의 친절함에 모두가 감명을 받았다.

· ~ because he was **too** poor **to** buy anything else.
「too ~ to ....」는 '너무 ~해서 …할 수 없다'라는 의미를 나타낸다.

· So I thought it would be better if I ate all the grapes happily by myself to **please him**.
please는 '기쁘게 하다'라는 의미로 목적어 him이 동사 please의 대상이 된다.

· Slowly the prince finished the whole bunch of grapes **by himself**.
by 뒤에 재귀대명사가 오면 '혼자'라는 의미이다.

· The poor man **was** very pleased **and left**.
동사 was와 left가 and에 의해 병렬 연결되었다. pleased는 '기쁘게 하다'라는 동사 please에서 파생된 형용사로 '기쁜'이라는 의미이다.

모범 답안

단락 요약 (가급적 6하 원칙을 준수할 것)

(A) 어느 날 가난한 한 남자가 왕자에게 포도 한 송이를 선물로 주었다.

(B) 왕자가 그들에게 포도를 주면 그들은 우스꽝스러운 표정을 지으면서 별로라고 말할 것이다.

(C) 왕자는 천천히 혼자서 포도 한 송이를 다 먹었다.

(D) 왕자는 포도가 너무 시어서 혼자 다 먹었다고 말했다.

· He (S) would share (V) / with them / whatever he was given.
그는 나누었다 / 그들과 / 그가 받은 무엇이든

Unit 01 주제 파악하기

READING 01
Workbook p. 2

1 ④ 2 ② 3 ③ 4 is a thick layer of body fat
5 hair, skin

해설

1 주어진 문장은 북극곰의 검은 피부를 언급하고 있고, It soaks up the sunlight, ~.의 It이 검은 피부를 지칭하므로 ④에 들어가는 것이 가장 적절하다.

2 ② keep은 뒤에 형용사가 보어 역할을 하여 keep warm은 '따뜻하게 유지하다'라는 의미이다. 나머지는 모두 목적어를 취하는 타동사이다.

3 (A) '~처럼'이라는 의미의 전치사 like가 들어가야 적절하다.
(B) be filled with는 '~로 가득 차다'라는 의미이므로 전치사 with가 들어가야 적절하다.
(C) stop A from B는 'A를 B하지 못하게 하다'라는 의미이므로 전치사 from이 들어가야 적절하다.

4 부사구 underneath the black skin이 문장 앞으로 와서 주어(a thick layer of body fat)와 동사(is)가 도치된 문장 구조이다.

5 추운 북극에서 북극곰이 생존할 수 있는 비결은 특별한 털과 검은 피부라고 했다.
해석 북극곰은 그들의 특별한 털과 검은 피부 덕분에 영하의 북극 기온에서 살아남을 수 있다.

READING 02
Workbook p. 3

1 ⑤ 2 ④ 3 ② 4 It's → They're
5 remember to bring, or

해설

1 ⑤ 열대 우림 주변, 폭포 아래, 심지어 폭포 위에서도 하이킹을 할 수 있다고 했다.

2 (A) 앞에 the가 쓰인 것으로 보아 최상급 표현임을 알 수 있다.
(B) go -ing는 '~하러 가다'라는 의미이다.

3 밑줄 친 ⓑeven은 '~조차도, ~까지도'라는 의미로 쓰인 부사이므로 ②의 even과 그 의미가 같다. ①: 균등한, 동일한 ③: 짝수의

④, ⑤: (비교급을 강조하여) 훨씬
① 점수는 동점이다.
② 어린 아이조차도 그것을 할 수 있다.
③ 4는 짝수라고 불린다.
④ 어제보다 훨씬 더 춥다.
⑤ 그의 책은 우리가 기대했던 것보다 훨씬 더 좋다.

4 밑줄 친 문장 ⓐ의 주어는 the Iguazú Falls를 가리키며 이는 복수명사이므로 They're로 고쳐야 알맞다.

5 「remember+to부정사」는 미래에 '~할 것을 기억하다'라는 뜻이며, 명령문 뒤에 쓰인 or는 '그렇지 않으면'이라는 의미이다.

READING 03
Workbook p. 4

1 ① 2 ④ 3 ③ 4 Nothing makes sense to you.
5 looking

해설

1 세상을 다르게 보는 즐거움에 대해 말하고 있으므로 ① annoys를 pleases로 고쳐야 글의 흐름에 알맞다.

2 글의 주제에 대한 예를 드는 문장이므로 빈칸에는 For example (예를 들어)이 들어가야 적절하다.

3 세 사람을 그리지 않았고, 처음 볼 때는 알아차리지 못할 수도 있다고 했으므로 ③ '추상적인 형태'를 사용했음을 알 수 있다.
① 실제 물건　　　　② 선명한 색채
④ 특이한 재료　　　　⑤ 음악가들의 사진

4 make sense는 '이해가 되다, 타당하다, 말이 되다'라는 의미로, 부정어 nothing을 주어로 하여 배열해야 한다.

5 keep -ing는 '계속 ~하다'라는 의미이다.

Unit 02 제목 파악하기

READING 04
Workbook p. 5

1 ④ 2 ④ 3 ② 4 honor
5 (A) ancient Egyptians (B) the cats (C) the owners

1　④ '사람이 고양이를 죽였을 때, 그 사람 또한 죽임을 당했다'는 의미가 되어야 하므로 ⓓ의 killed를 수동태인 was killed로 고쳐야 한다.

2　주어진 문장은 '고대 이집트인들은 심지어 법으로 고양이를 보호했다.'는 내용이므로 뒤에 고양이를 죽였을 때 받는 처벌에 대한 언급이 나오는 ④에 들어가는 것이 가장 적절하다.

3　고양이를 반려동물로 처음 키운 것은 고대 이집트인들이었고, 고양이에 대한 그들의 지극한 사랑을 보여 주는 여러 예를 살펴보면 고양이는 이집트인들에게 단순한 반려동물 이상이었음을 알 수 있다.
　① 장난감　③ 먹잇감　④ 가족　⑤ 수호자

4　'(누군가를) 존경하고 감탄하며 대하다'라는 뜻이므로 '예우하다, 공경하다'는 의미의 honor가 알맞다.

5　(A)는 앞 문장의 고대 이집트인들을 가리킨다.
　(B) 부유한 가족들이 '그들에게' 보석을 걸어 주었다고 했으므로 them은 고양이들을 가리킨다.
　(C) 고양이들이 죽었을 때, 주인들이 자신의 눈썹을 밀어 슬픔을 드러냈다는 내용이므로 they는 주인들을 가리킨다.

READING **05**　　　　　　　　　　　　● Workbook p. 6

1 ④　　2 ②　　3 ②　　4 (우주에 갈 때) 충분한 음식을 가지고 가는 것　　5 (A) is → are (B) warmly → warm (C) health → healthy

---

1　④ 우주선에서 보통의 소금은 공중을 떠다닐 것이라서 소금은 액체로 나온다고 했다.

2　빈칸에는 '~처럼, ~와 같은'이라는 뜻의 전치사 Like(like)가 공통으로 들어가야 알맞다.

3　② 명사 store의 뜻(가게, 상점)을 설명하고 있다. 본문의 ②는 '저장하다'는 뜻의 동사 store이다.
　① 우주선을 타고 우주로 여행하는 사람
　② 물건을 파는 건물이나 공간
　③ 물건을 차갑게 유지하는 데 사용되는 장치
　④ 작고 얇은 포장
　⑤ 물처럼 자유롭게 흐를 수 있는 물질

4　캠핑을 갈 때 반드시 충분한 음식을 가지고 가는 것처럼 우주비행사들이 우주에 갈 때도 '같은 일을 한다'고 했다.

5　(A) 주어가 many different foods이므로 복수동사 are를 써야 한다.
　(B) 음식이 따뜻한 상태로 유지되는 것이므로 목적어 food의 목적격보어로는 부사 warmly가 아닌 형용사 warm을 써야 한다.
　(C) stay는 '~한 상태를 유지하다'의 뜻으로 뒤에 형용사가 온다. stay healthy는 '건강(한 상태)을 유지하다'라는 의미이다.

READING **06**　　　　　　　　　　　　● Workbook p. 7

1 ②　　2 ⑤　　3 ④　　4 two-thirds
5 we think of him as a champion, not as a failure

1　(A) 글의 주제에 대한 예를 드는 문장이므로 빈칸에는 for example(예를 들어)이 적절하다.
　(B) 앞 문장을 다른 말로 다시 설명하고 있으므로 빈칸에는 In other words(다시 말해서)가 적절하다.

2　'~보다 더 많은'을 뜻하는 비교 표현 more than이 사용된 문장이다. 형용사 many의 비교급 형태인 more가 들어가는 것이 가장 적절하다.

3　(C) Losing a game과 not passing a test가 or로 연결되어 주어가 되어야 하므로 병렬 관계의 동명사 passing이 알맞다.
　(D) 「try+to부정사」는 '~하려고 노력하다'는 의미이다.

4　영어로 분수를 나타낼 때는 먼저 분자를 기수(one, two, three…)로, 분모를 서수(third, fifth…)로 쓴다. 이때 분자가 2 이상이면 분모를 나타내는 서수를 복수로 만들어 주어야 한다.

5　think of A as B는 'A를 B라고 생각하다'는 의미이다.

Unit 03 목적·주장 파악하기

READING **07**　　　　　　　　　　　　● Workbook p. 8

1 ②　　2 ④　　3 ③　　4 학생들이 동물원에 쓰레기를 버리지 않도록 지도하는 것　　5 그들(동물들)은 이 쓰레기를 먹이로 착각할 수 있다

1 ② Danna Smith는 쓰레기를 먹고 동물들이 병이 날까 봐 우려하고 있으므로 내용과 일치한다.
① 선생님으로 일하고 있는 사람은 Mr. Kang이다.
③ 동물원에서 안내사로 일하고 있는 사람은 Danna Smith이다.
④ Danna Smith가 Mr. Kang에게 협조를 요청했다.
⑤ Mr. Kang과 학생들은 Fun&Joy 동물원으로 현장 학습을 갈 예정이다.

2 (A) 전치사의 목적어로 동사가 올 때는 동명사 형태로 쓴다.
(B) advise의 목적격보어는 to부정사가 적절하다.
(C) 조동사 should 다음에는 동사원형이 온다.

3 앞에서 동물들에게 해롭다고 언급된 단어가 들어가야 하므로 ③ '쓰레기'가 가장 적절하다.

4 바로 다음 문장에 a favor의 내용이 제시되어 있다.

5 조동사 may는 '~일 수도 있다'는 약한 추측의 뜻을 나타내며, mistake A for B는 'A를 B로 착각(오해)하다'라는 뜻이다.

READING **08** ● Workbook p. 9

1 ② **2** ① **3** ④ **4** mistakes
5 (to) read your writing carefully

1 (A) 보내기 버튼을 누르기 전까지는 어떤 일도 발생하지 않을 거라는 의미이므로 before가 적절하다.
(B) 이메일을 보내고 난 후에 실수를 발견하면 큰 문제가 될 수 있다는 의미이므로 after가 적절하다.
(C) 보내기 버튼을 누르기 전에 글을 주의 깊게 읽는 것을 잊지 말라는 의미이므로 before가 적절하다.

2 '보내기 버튼을 누르지 않는다면 문제가 되지 않는다'라는 의미이므로 빈칸에는 '만약 ~하다면'이라는 조건의 뜻을 나타내는 접속사 if가 적절하다.

3 '학교 과제나 업무로 보내는 이메일도 마찬가지이다'라는 것은 학교 과제나 업무로 보내는 이메일도 보내기 전에 주의 깊게 읽고 실수를 고칠 시간을 가지라는 의미이다.

4 주어진 문장은 '여러분이 쓴 이메일에는 잘못 쓴 철자나 사실의 오류와 같은 실수들이 있을 수 있다.'의 의미이다. There can be misspellings or errors of fact in your writing.의 문장에서 이유를 찾을 수 있으며, misspellings와 errors of fact는 mistakes에 해당한다.

5 이 글에서 '다시 보는 것'이라는 의미는 '글을 주의 깊게 읽는 것'과 같은 의미이다.

Unit 04 요지 파악하기

READING **09** ● Workbook p. 10

1 ② **2** ② **3** ⑤ **4** ③ → much
5 ended → started

1 친구를 가르치는 프로젝트에 참여하면서 깨달은 바를 말하고 있으므로, 빈칸에는 ② '다른 사람들 가르치기'가 가장 적절하다.
① 자신 가르치기
③ 나의 선생님 돕기
④ 서로 가르치기
⑤ 다른 사람들에게 도움 얻기

2 ② I volunteered as a student teacher.로 보아 'I'는 새로운 과학 프로젝트에 선발된 것이 아니라 자원했음을 알 수 있다.

3 thanks to는 '~ 덕분에, ~ 때문에'라는 뜻으로 because of와 바꿔 쓸 수 있다.

4 time은 셀 수 없는 명사이므로, ③의 many를 much로 고쳐 써야 한다. too much time은 '너무 많은 시간'이라는 의미이다.

5 tutor-tutee는 지난달에 새로 시작한 과학 프로젝트라고 했으므로 ended를 started로 고쳐 써야 적절하다.

READING **10** ● Workbook p. 11

1 ⑤ **2** ③ **3** ② **4** more comfortable
5 observing nature

1 (A) 글의 주제에 대한 예를 드는 문장이므로 빈칸에는 For example(예를 들면)이 적절하다.
(B) 앞 문장과 대조되는 내용을 말하는 문장이므로 빈칸에는 However(그러나)가 적절하다.

2 못처럼 생긴 것은 연잎의 표면에 있는 작은 돌기들이므로 연잎이
③ '작은 못처럼 생겼다.'는 일치하지 않는다.
① 항상 깨끗해 보인다.
② 표면이 거칠다.
④ 진흙 연못에서 볼 수 있다.
⑤ 특수 페인트의 원천이다.

3 주어진 문장의 this가 가리키는 것은 연꽃이 진흙 연못에 사는데
도 잎이 항상 깨끗해 보이는 것을 말하므로, 주어진 문장은 ②에
들어가는 것이 자연스럽다.

4 접속사 and는 문장 성분이 같은 것을 대등하게 연결하므로 앞에
있는 비교급 easier에 맞춰 comfortable도 비교급인 more
comfortable로 쓴다.

5 두 번째 문장에 요약문의 내용이 들어 있다. 전치사 by에 이어지므
로 동사는 목적어가 될 수 있는 동명사 형태로 써서 observing
nature가 적절하다.
사람들은 자연을 관찰함으로써 더 나은 삶을 살 수 있다.

Unit 05 요약하기

1 ③　　**2** ②　　**3** ⑤
4 모든 손동작이 모든 문화에서 같은 의미를 갖는 것은 아니다!
5 Same, Different

해설

1 엄지척 제스처가 태국과 한국에서 의미하는 바가 달라서 오해를
일으킬 소지가 있기 때문이므로, 빈칸에는 ③이 가장 적절하다.
Q: 왜 한국인들은 태국에서 엄지척 제스처를 사용할 때 주의해야
하는가?
A: ＿＿＿＿＿＿＿＿＿ 때문이다.
① 그것은 한국에서만 사용되기
② 그것이 태국에서는 안 알려져 있기
③ 그것은 오해를 불러일으킬 수 있기
④ 그것은 특별하게 좋은 의미를 가지고 있기
⑤ 그것은 태국에서 '무례하다'를 의미하기

2 빈칸의 앞과 뒤의 문장이 대조되는 내용이므로, 빈칸에는 역접의
연결어 However(그러나)가 들어가야 적절하다.

3 ⑤ 일본과 한국에서 엄지척 제스처는 동의를 나타내는 긍정의 의
미로 쓰인다고 했다.

4 not all ~은 '모두가 ~한 것은 아니다'라는 의미로, 전체가 아닌
부분만 부정하는 표현이다.

5 같은 손동작이라도 나라마다 의미하는 바가 다르다는 글이므로,
빈칸에는 Same과 Different가 들어가야 적절하다. 그러므로,
'나라마다 다른 의미를 가진 동일한 손동작'이 되어야 한다.

1 ①　　**2** ③　　**3** ④
4 ⑤, making(to make) a to-do list
5 할 일 목록 만들기, 시간 절약 서비스 이용하기

해설

1 글의 전반부에서는 시간 기근 현상에 대해 설명하고, 후반부에서
는 시간 기근 현상을 극복할 수 있는 방법을 제시하고 있으므로,
글의 주제로 ①이 가장 적절하다.

2 시간을 아꼈을 때 느낄 수 있는 감정을 말하는 문장이므로, 빈칸에
는 relaxed, calm 등이 들어갈 수 있다.

3 이 글에서 시간을 아끼는 방법으로 제시된 두 가지 방법은 할 일
목록을 만드는 것과 시간 절약 서비스를 이용하는 것이므로, 이에
해당하는 예는 ④ '오늘 할 일 쓰기'이다.
① 낮잠 자기　　　　　　② 늦게까지 깨어 있기
③ 내가 직접 저녁 만들기　⑤ 자기 전에 알람 맞추기

4 ①~④는 모두 time famine을 가리키고, ⑤는 바로 앞 문장에
나온 make a to-do list를 가리킨다.

5 To save time, make a to-do list., Also, use time-
saving services.의 문장에서 time famine을 이겨낼 수 있
는 방법을 알 수 있다.

1 ①　　**2** ④　　**3** ②
4 모두가 함께 사용해야 하는 화장실 휴지를 몇몇 사람이 자신의 몫보
다 많이 가져간 것　　**5** (A) another　(B) the other

1 ① Rhonda는 셰어 하우스에 살고 있었다고 했으므로, 글의 내용과 일치한다.
   ② 셰어 하우스 화장실 화장지는 청소부들이 주말마다 두고 갔다.
   ③ Rhonda는 공유 물품을 가져가는 사람들에게 화가 났다.
   ④ Rhonda는 한 화장실에 메모를 붙여 두었다.
   ⑤ 메모를 붙여 두지 않은 나머지 화장실에는 아무런 변화가 일어나지 않았다.

2 Rhonda가 메모를 붙여 두고 나서 화장실 화장지가 돌아오는 것이 변화된 내용(a surprising change)이므로 ④에 들어가는 것이 가장 적절하다.

3 share는 동사로 '공유하다, 함께 쓰다, 나누다, (감정 등을) 공유하다' 등의 의미로, 명사로 '몫, 주식' 등의 의미로 쓰인다. 밑줄 친 부분은 '몫'의 의미로 쓰였으므로, ②가 같은 의미로 쓰인 문장이다.
   ① 그들은 피자를 나눠 먹었다.
   ② 이것은 네 몫의 피자이다.
   ③ 그는 다른 두 명의 학생들과 집을 공유한다.
   ④ 너의 문제를 선생님과 공유해라.
   ⑤ Go Bank 주식 가격(주가)이 어제 9% 하락했다.

4 the matter는 앞 문장의 some took more than their fair share(누군가가 공평하게 공유할 부분보다 더 많이 가져갔다)의 내용을 의미한다.

5 (A)는 화장실 화장지의 one roll이 돌아오고 one more를 의미하는 '다른 하나'이므로 another, (B)는 두 개의 화장실 중 '나머지 하나'이므로 the other가 들어가야 적절하다.

Unit 06 안내문·도표 파악하기

READING 14   Workbook p. 15

1 ②   2 ②   3 ④   4 (s)ave
5 switch off the lights just for an hour / switch the lights off just for an hour

1 행사를 누가 주최하는지는 언급되지 않았다.
   ① 무엇을 위한 행사인가? – Earth Hour를 기념하기
   ② 누가 행사를 주최하는가? – 알 수 없음
   ③ 우리는 어떤 행동을 하는가? – 불을 (한 시간 동안) 끄기
   ④ 행사는 얼마나 자주 하는가? – 일 년에 한 번
   ⑤ 행사는 매년 얼마 동안 지속되는가? – 한 시간 동안

2 '저녁 8시 30분부터 9시 30분까지'라는 의미이므로 ②의 at을 from으로 고쳐야 한다.

3 (A) '기념하기 위해서'의 뜻으로 목적을 나타내는 to celebrate가 적절하다.
   (B) '~하자'의 뜻으로 제안을 나타내는 let's 뒤에는 동사원형이 와야 한다.

4 '(누군가 또는 무엇인가를) 안전하게 유지하다, (누군가 또는 무엇인가가) 죽거나 다치거나, 손상되거나, 잃어버리는 것을 막다'에 해당하는 단어는 save이다.

5 전 세계적 소등 행사를 설명하는 내용으로 '한 시간 동안만 불을 끈다'는 문장이다.

READING 15   Workbook p. 16

1 ③   2 ⑤   3 ⑤   4 submit
5 (1) study cafe (2) two months (3) December 7

1 심사 위원이 누구인지는 언급되지 않았다.

2 (A) 이어지는 문장과 내용상 연결되는 '창의성, 창의력'이 적절하다.
   (B) '참여하다, 참가하다'를 뜻하는 단어가 적절하다.
   (C) '제출하다'를 뜻하는 단어가 적절하다.

3 ⑤ 앞에 나온 a name의 소유격이어야 하므로 their를 단수인 its로 고쳐야 한다.

4 '문서, 제안서 등이 고려되거나 승인될 수 있도록 누군가에게 그것을 주다'에 해당하는 단어는 submit이다.

5 스터디 카페 네이밍(이름, 명칭) 공모전은 두 달 동안 개최된다. 수상자는 12월 7일에 발표될 것이다.

READING 16   Workbook p. 17

1 ②   2 ④   3 ④   4 the UK → Türkiye
5 Is there a big difference between the countries?

1 스위스는 GDP의 12.2%를 의료비로 지출하여 16.9%를 지출하는 미국보다 더 적게 지출하고, 튀르키예는 5% 미만을 지출하므로 빈칸에 공통으로 less가 들어가야 한다.

2 (A) 미국은 7개 국가들 중에서 가장 높은 비율로 지출했으므로 최상급이 적절하다.
(B) 프랑스가 벨기에보다 더 높은 비율로 지출했으므로 비교급이 적절하다.

3 영국은 그리스보다 의료비에 GDP의 2퍼센트 더 많이 지출했으므로 ④의 one은 two로 고쳐야 한다.

4 미국은 GDP의 16.9%를 의료비로 지출했다. 이는 튀르키예보다 약 4배 많은 수치다.

5 Is there ~? 의문문을 사용한다. between the countries 로 '그 나라들 사이에'라는 의미를 나타낼 수 있다.

Unit 07 내용 일치 파악하기

READING **17** • Workbook p. 18

1 ④   **2** ②   **3** ②   **4** author
5 When he was 12 years old

1 Benjamin Franklin은 18세기 미국 역사의 <u>중요한</u> 사람이었고 16세에 <u>글을 쓰기</u> 시작했다.
미국 역사상 가장 중요한 사람 중 한 명인 Benjamin Franklin은 16세에 Mrs. Silence Dogood이라는 필명을 사용하여 자신의 글을 쓰기 시작했다.

2 1706년 보스턴에서 태어났다는 의미이므로 ②의 born은 수동태 was born이 되어야 한다.

3 (A) 반대 의미를 나타내는 접속사 but이 있으므로 self-taught와 의미상 반대인 formal이 적절하다.
(B) 본명을 사용하는 '대신에' 필명을 사용했으므로 Instead of 가 적절하다.
(C) 사람들은 Mrs. Silence Dogood이라는 필명을 통해 저자가 결혼한 여자일 거라고 생각했고, 16세의 소년이라고는 결코 생각하지 못했다는 의미가 되어야 자연스러우므로 never 가 적절하다.

4 '직업이 책을 쓰는 사람; 작가'에 해당하는 단어는 author이다.

5 at the age of는 '~세의 나이에'라는 의미로 「when+주어+be동사+나이」로 바꿔 쓸 수 있다. 시제가 과거이므로 be동사는 과거형 was를 사용한다.

READING **18** • Workbook p. 19

1 ④   **2** ③   **3** ④
4 ⓐ → far(still / even / much / a lot) ⓓ → easier(easy)
5 It helps sharks to hide from threats.

1 ④ 강하고 날카로운 이빨을 가지고 있다고 했지만 얼마나 많은 이빨을 가지고 있는지는 언급되지 않았다.
① 상어는 어디에 사는가? – 바다의 모든 지역에
② 상어는 얼마나 오래 사는가? – 대부분 20에서 30년
③ 상어는 먹이를 잡기 위해 무엇을 사용하는가? – 이빨
④ 상어는 몇 개의 날카로운 이빨이 있는가? – 언급되지 않음
⑤ 상어는 무엇을 먹는가? – 물고기나 물개 같은 동물, 다른 먹이

2 주어진 문장이 For example(예를 들어)로 시작하는 것으로 보아 상어가 무엇을 먹는지 언급한 문장 뒤인 ③에 들어가는 것이 가장 적절하다.

3 밑줄 친 ⓑ와 ④의 like는 '~와 같은'의 뜻으로 such as와 같은 의미이다. ① ~처럼 ②, ③, ⑤ 좋아하다
① 그는 항상 나의 선생님<u>처럼</u> 행동한다.
② 그들은 생선회를 <u>좋아하지</u> 않는다.
③ 그냥 당신이 <u>좋아하는</u> 것을 먹고 쉬세요.
④ 나는 빙벽 등반<u>과 같은</u> 익스트림 스포츠를 즐긴다.
⑤ 그들은 매일 공원에서 산책하는 것을 <u>좋아한다</u>.

4 ⓐ 비교급을 강조하는 부사는 far, still, even, much, a lot 이다.
ⓓ 문장의 목적격보어이므로 부사인 easily를 형용사 easy로 고쳐야 한다. 글에서는 비교급인 easier가 쓰였다.

5 동사 help는 목적격보어로 to부정사 또는 동사원형을 쓰는데, 제시된 to부정사 to hide를 활용해서 「help+목적어+to부정사」 형태로 쓴다. '~로부터 숨다'의 의미가 되도록 전치사 from을 추가한다.

1 ④   2 ②   3 ④   4 because of → because
5 became one of the first three students to earn

해설

1 Elizabeth Catlett의 출생부터 죽음까지, 예술가로서의 삶에
대해 이야기하고 있으므로, 제목으로 가장 적절한 것은 ④이다.
① 멕시코의 많은 흑인 예술가들
② Elizabeth Catlett의 조부모
③ 미국에서의 노예 생활
④ Elizabeth Catlett의 예술가로서의 삶
⑤ Elizabeth Catlett의 유명 예술 작품들

2 '할머니로부터 노예에 관한 이야기를 들었다'라는 의미이므로 전
치사 from을 써야 한다.
hear A from B: B로부터 A를 듣다

3 (A) or 뒤의 unfairness와 의미상 연결되어야 하므로 '불평등,
부당함'을 뜻하는 injustice가 적절하다.
(B) 사회의 불공평함으로 인해 '고통을 받은 사람들'이라는 의미가
되어야 하므로 suffered가 적절하다.
(C) 멕시코에서 인정받고 60년 이상을 보냈다는 내용으로 보아
'시민'을 뜻하는 citizen이 적절하다.

4 because of 뒤에는 구가 오고, because 뒤에는 절이 온다.
뒤에 she was black이라는 절이 나오므로 because of를
because로 고쳐야 한다.

5 동사 뒤 「one of the (서수)(기수) 복수명사」의 어순에 주의하여
문장을 완성한다. to earn은 뒤에서 복수명사 students를 수
식한다.

Unit 08 분위기·심경 파악하기

1 ⑤   2 ①   3 ③
4 (A) opens → open (B) newly → new
5 It makes me keep smiling.

해설

1 ⑤는 동사의 목적어로 사용되었고, 나머지는 be동사 뒤에 사용
되어 '~하는, ~하는 중인'을 나타낸다. ④의 while cleaning은

while I am cleaning으로 바꿔 쓸 수 있다.

2 (C) 문맥상 봄이 되어 '막 꽃이 피려고 한다'는 의미가 되어야 하므
로 bloom이 적절하다.
(D) didn't like to clean before, '불평이 많은, 투덜거리는'
이라는 뜻의 Grouchy로 보아 complains가 적절하다.

3 '바람, 의도, 욕구'를 의미하는 wish와 바꿔 쓸 수 있는 것은
desire이다.

4 (A) make는 목적격보어로 동사원형이 오므로 opens를 open
으로 고쳐야 한다.
(B) '~하게 느껴지다', '~하게 보이다'를 뜻하는 feel과 seem 뒤
에는 보어로 형용사가 오므로 newly를 new로 고쳐야 한다.

5 make는 '~을 …하게 만들다'라는 뜻의 5형식 문장으로 쓰는데,
목적격보어로 동사원형이 온다. keep은 '계속해서 ~하다'의 의미
로 쓰일 때 뒤에 동명사(동사원형 -ing) 형태가 온다.

1 ③   2 ②   3 ④   4 nothing → something
5 gathered wood to build a fire

해설

1 (A) 먹을 것이 '거의 없어서' 배가 많이 고팠다는 의미이므로 little
이 적절하다.
(B) 힘들게 사냥에 성공한 뒤라 문맥상 '최고의 날'이 되어야 하므
로 best가 적절하다.

2 3일 동안 굶은 후 다람쥐를 잡아 먹을 준비를 하며 기쁨(joy)을 감
출 수 없음을 알 수 있다.

3 밑줄 친 ⓓ와 ④의 last는 '지속되다, 오래가다'라는 의미의 동사
로 쓰였다.
①, ②는 형용사로 '지난, 마지막의'라는 뜻으로 쓰였다.
③, ⑤는 부사로 '마지막으로'라는 뜻으로 쓰였다.
① 서둘러! 그것이 마지막 열차야.
② 나는 지난밤에 영어 소설을 읽었다.
③ 그녀는 마라톤에서 마지막으로 들어왔다.
④ 그 인기는 몇 년 동안 지속될 것이다.
⑤ 그는 내가 그를 마지막으로 본 이후로 많이 변했다.

4 '다행히도'를 뜻하는 luckily가 있고 문맥상 먹을 '무언가'를 찾았
다는 의미가 적절하므로, nothing을 something으로 고쳐야
한다.

5 to build가 '~하기 위해서'의 뜻으로 사용된다.

1 ④　　2 ④　　3 ①　　4 a book to me
5 imagining playing games with my friends

해설

1 밑줄 친 ⓐ와 ④의 present는 '선물'의 의미로 쓰였다.
　① 참석한 (형용사)　② 제출하다 (동사)
　③ 현재의 (형용사)　⑤ 주다, 제공하다 (동사)
　① 너는 회의에 참석해야 한다.
　② 그는 오늘 자신의 보고서를 제출할 것이다.
　③ 나는 현재의 내 상황에 만족한다.
　④ 우리는 Alice에게서 뜻밖의 선물을 받았다.
　⑤ 그 캠프는 특별한 경험을 제공할 것이다.

2 평소 갖고 싶었던 휴대폰을 선물로 받으면 친구들과 그것으로 소통할 수 있을 거라고 기대하는 상황이므로 '흥분한, 신이 난'을 뜻하는 thrilled가 적절하다.

3 (A) 새 휴대폰을 받고 앱과 게임을 '내려받고' 싶었다는 것이 자연스러우므로 download가 적절하다.
　(B) 문맥상 반전을 나타내는 연결어 However가 적절하다.
　(C) 새 휴대폰을 책 안에 '숨겼을'지도 모른다고 생각하고 있으므로 hidden이 적절하다.

4 「수여동사+간접목적어+직접목적어」의 4형식 문장을 「수여동사+목적어」의 3형식으로 바꿀 때 동사 hand는 전치사 to를 사용한다.

5 과거진행형 문장이므로 be동사 was 뒤에 imagining을 쓴다. '게임을 하다'라는 의미의 play games는 목적어가 되어야 하므로 -ing 형태의 playing을 쓰고, '~와 함께'를 나타내는 전치사 with를 추가하여 문장을 완성한다.

Unit 09 글의 순서 파악하기

1 ③, ④　　2 ①　　3 ④　　4 (b)enefits
5 is a great way to reduce stress levels

해설

1 독서는 심장 박동 수를 낮출 수 있다고 했다.
　스트레스를 줄이는 데는 차를 마시는 것이 산책보다 효과적이다.

2 ① 주어가 one이므로 동사는 단수형 is가 되어야 한다.

3 혈압이 낮아지고 심장 박동 수를 낮추어 '편안한' 상태가 된다는 의미이므로 relaxed가 적절하다.

4 '좋거나 도움이 되는 결과 또는 효과; 무엇인가로부터 얻은 이점이나 이익'에 해당하는 단어는 benefit이다. 앞에 many가 있으므로 복수형 benefits가 들어가야 한다.

5 to reduce가 명사구 a great way를 뒤에서 수식하는 형태로 문장을 완성한다.

1 ②　　2 ⑤　　3 ②
4 Come here once a week and I will help
5 (1) her brother (2) the doctor (3) Cut the legs of the bed

해설

1 ② 의사가 여자를 어떻게 도울 예정이었는지는 알 수 없다.
　① 여자의 문제는 무엇인가?
　③ 몇 번 더 여자는 의사를 방문해야 했나?
　④ 결국 누가 여자의 문제를 도왔나?
　⑤ 여자는 문제를 없애는 데 얼마를 지불했나?

2 '문제가 사라졌다', 즉 '문제가 해결되었다'는 의미이므로 was solved로 바꿔 쓸 수 있다.

3 ⓑ 의사가 '깜짝 놀란, 충격을 받은' 것이므로 과거분사 형태의 shocked가 적절하다.
　ⓒ 뒤에 than이 있으므로 비교급 형태인 cheaper가 적절하다.

4 '~해라, 그러면 ~할 것이다'를 나타내는 「명령문 ~ and」 구문을 사용한다.

5 여자의 문제는 의사가 아니라 남동생이 해결했는데, 그는 "침대 다리를 잘라"라고 말했다.

1 ②　　2 ①　　3 ③　　4 (1) size (2) weight (3) proper
5 (C) too bouncy (D) not bounce

해설

1 주어진 문장이 '구기 종목에는 사용되는 공에 대한 몇 가지 규칙이

있다'는 내용이므로, 그 규칙이 크기나 무게와 같은 공의 특성에 대한 규칙이라고 구체적으로 언급하는 문장 앞인 ②에 들어가는 것이 가장 적절하다.

2　'~와 같은'의 의미를 나타내는 것은 such as이다.

3　강철로 만들어지면 너무 단단할 것이고, 가벼운 발포 고무로 만들어지면 너무 부드러울 것이다.

4　공을 가지고 하는 스포츠 활동에는 공에 대한 몇 가지 규칙이 있는데, 그것은 정확한 크기, 적절한 무게, 특정 정도의 단단함, 그리고 적절한 반동력(튕김)이다.

5　고무공은 대부분의 스포츠에서 '너무 탱탱하게 잘 튈' 것이고, 점토공은 '전혀 튀지 않을' 것이다. be 다음에는 형용사가, would 다음에는 동사원형이 오는 것에 유의하여 완성한다.

Unit 10　주어진 문장 넣기

READING **26** ●　Workbook p. 27

1 ③　　2 ②　　3 ②　　4 ⓑ → themselves
5 그러나 그렇게 걱정할 필요는 없다.

해설

1　알파카가 무엇을 먹는지는 언급되지 않았으므로, 글을 읽고 답할 수 없는 질문은 ③이다.
　① 알파카는 어디에 사는가? – 칠레와 페루 같은 남아메리카 나라들에
　② 알파카는 무엇으로 유명한가? – 부드러운 털, 큰 몸과 귀여운 얼굴
　③ 알파카는 보통 무엇을 먹는가? – 언급되지 않음
　④ 우리는 왜 알파카에게 친절해야 하는가? – 안전하다고 느낄 때 평화로운 동물이어서
　⑤ 알파카는 안전하지 않다고 느낄 때 어떻게 하는가? – 침을 뱉을 수 있음

2　반대 내용을 언급할 때 사용하는 접속사 But에 유의하여 글의 흐름을 파악한다. 주어진 문장은 '그러나 이 동물을 만날 때는 항상 조심해야 한다'는 내용이므로 '큰 몸에 귀여운 얼굴로 유명하다'는 문장 뒤에, 그리고 왜 조심해야 하는지 이유가 언급되는 문장 앞인 ②에 들어가는 것이 가장 적절하다.

3　알파카가 침을 뱉는 이유를 설명하며 내용을 추가하고 있으므로 (A)에는 '게다가'를 뜻하는 In addition이 들어가야 한다. 그리고 알파카는 평화로운 동물이라는 내용 뒤에 친절하게 대해야 한

다는 말이 이어지므로 (B)에는 '그러므로, 따라서'를 뜻하는 So가 들어가야 한다.

4　ⓑ 목적어의 대상이 주어와 동일하므로 them을 재귀대명사 themselves로 고쳐야 한다.

5　'~해야 한다'를 뜻하는 have to의 부정형 don't have to는 '~할 필요가 없다'라는 의미다.

READING **27** ●　Workbook p. 28

1 ④　　2 ②　　3 ⑤　　4 (s)urvive
5 keep these tips in mind(keep in mind these tips), you will be safer

해설

1　무인도에서 가장 먼저 할 일로 물을 찾는 것을 추천했고, 이어서 깨끗하고 신선한 물을 찾는 몇 가지 조언을 제시하고 있으므로, 제목으로 ④가 적절하다.
　① 빗물을 깨끗한 물로 바꾸는 요령
　② 위험한 사막에서 안전하게 지내는 방법
　③ SOS 신호 만들기: 가장 먼저 해야 할 일
　④ 무인도에서 물을 찾는 방법
　⑤ 식량: 무인도에서 가장 필요한 것

2　② 내용상 '마실 물'을 찾는 것이므로 뒤에서 water를 수식하도록 drink를 to부정사 형태(to drink)로 고쳐야 한다.

3　(A) 몸에 물이 얼마나 중요한지 말한 후 뒤 문장에서 안전한 물을 찾아야 한다고 했으므로 '이런 이유로'라는 의미인 For this reason이 적절하다.
　(B) 내용상 '빗물은 마실 수 있기 때문에'라는 의미이므로 이유를 나타내는 because가 적절하다.

4　'살아 있다, 계속 살다'에 해당하는 단어는 '생존하다'라는 뜻의 survive이다.

5　If가 속한 종속절은 현재시제를, 주절은 미래시제를 사용한다. keep ~ in mind는 '~을 명심하다'라는 의미를 나타낸다.

READING **28** ●　Workbook p. 29

1 ⑤　　2 ②　　3 ①　　4 ⓑ (to) change ⓓ feel
5 they will get a snack if they show any negative emotions

1 밑줄 친 to calm은 앞의 명사 way를 수식해 '진정시키는 방법'
이라는 의미를 나타낸다. ⑤의 to drink는 앞의 명사 water를
수식해 '마실 물'이라는 의미를 나타낸다.
① 그녀의 꿈은 바이올리니스트가 되는 것이다.
② 아이들은 초콜릿을 먹는 것을 좋아한다.
③ 나는 Lisa를 만나기 위해 프랑스에 갔다.
④ 그는 너무 아파서 학교에 갈 수 없었다.
⑤ 우리는 마실 물이 필요했다.

2 ① way를 수식하는 형용사이므로 quick으로 고쳐야 한다.
③ 지각동사 feel은 보어로 형용사가 오므로 happier로 고쳐야
한다.
④ 동사가 단수 is이므로 주어 역할을 하는 동명사 using으로 고
쳐야 한다.
⑤ 아이들이 지루한 감정을 느끼는 것이므로 '지루해하는'의 의미
인 bored로 고쳐야 한다.

3 (A) 아이들은 음식을 먹으며 무엇에 화가 났는지 잊을 수 있으므로
forget이 적절하다. (B) 단기적으로는 음식을 이용하는 것이 효
과적이므로 effective가 적절하다. (C) 장기적으로는 음식을 이
용하는 것이 해로울 수 있으므로 harmful이 적절하다.

4 ⓑ 동사 help는 목적격보어로 동사원형 또는 to부정사를 쓴다.
ⓓ 동사 make는 목적격보어로 동사원형을 취한다.

5 If가 속한 조건절은 현재시제를 사용하여 '~하면'이라고 해석하고,
주절은 미래시제를 사용하여 '~할 것이다'로 해석한다.

Unit 11 무관한 문장 찾기

READING **29** • Workbook p. 30

1 ④ 2 ① 3 ③ 4 (s)ecret
5 wants people to enjoy shopping without thinking

1 요약문은 '백화점은 창문이나 시계가 사람들의 쇼핑을 방해한다고
생각하기 때문에 창문이나 시계가 없다.'라는 의미가 자연스러우
므로 빈칸에 '방해하다'를 뜻하는 interfere with가 적절하다.

2 동사 make가 '~가 …하게 만들다'의 뜻으로 쓰일 때는 목적어 뒤
에 목적격보어로 동사원형이 온다.

3 백화점들은 벽에 장식을 하거나 광고를 걸어놓는데 시계나 창문이
있으면 벽을 '사용하기가 어렵다'는 내용이 적절하다.

4 '다른 사람들로부터 숨겨져 있는 사실이나 정보'에 해당하는 단어
는 secret이다.

5 동사 want 뒤에는 목적어와 목적격보어(to부정사)가 오고,
enjoy는 목적어로 동명사 형태를 취하며, 전치사 without 뒤에
는 동명사(V-ing) 형태가 온다.

READING **30** • Workbook p. 31

1 ① 2 ④ 3 ① 4 can → cannot
5 ⓒ using(to use) caffeine ⓓ not having enough sleep

1 (A) 동사 help는 '~가 …하도록 돕다'의 의미로 쓰일 때 목적어 뒤
의 목적격보어로 동사원형 또는 to부정사를 취한다.
(B) 동사 make는 '~가 …하게 만들다'의 의미로 쓰일 때 목적어
뒤의 목적격보어로 동사원형을 취한다.

2 밑줄 친 ⓑ는 '가능성'을 의미하므로 possibilities와 바꿔 쓸 수
있다.

3 (C) 카페인의 효과적인 측면에 대해 말하고 있으므로 effective
가 적절하다.
(D) '카페인을 섭취한 후에도 시험에서 더 높은 점수를 받지 못했
다'는 의미로, 앞에 부정의 not이 있으므로 higher가 적절
하다.

4 However로 보아 '카페인은 숙면을 대신할 수 없다'는 내용이 적
절하므로 can의 부정형 cannot이 들어가야 한다. take the
place of는 '~을 대신하다'라는 뜻이다.

5 ⓒ 문맥상 '카페인을 이용하는 것은 충분한 수면을 취하지 못하는
것을 완전히 보충해 줄 수 없다'가 적절하므로 주어는 동명사나
to부정사 형태를 사용하여 using(to use) caffeine으로
써야 한다.
ⓓ 문맥상 부정의 의미를 나타내는 not과 전치사 뒤이므로 동명
사 형태를 사용하여 not having enough sleep으로 써야
한다.

Unit 12 빈칸 완성하기 1 (단어)

READING **31**　　　● Workbook p. 32

1 ⑤　**2** ③　**3** ③　**4** upcycling　**5** waterproof

해설

1　⑤ each bag is made from many different types of cloth로 보아, 'Freitag의 가방은 각각 많은 다른 종류의 천으로 만들어졌다'는 것을 알 수 있다.

2　(A) '쓰레기를 버리면 지구에 해를 끼치는 것이라고 생각할 수 있지만 패션에 있어서는 그렇지 않다'라는 흐름이 자연스러우므로 harm이 적절하다.
　(B) '~ 덕분에, ~ 때문에'라는 의미의 thanks to가 적절하다.
　(C) 뒤 문장에서 '당연히 수천 톤의 쓰레기가 사용된다'고 했으므로 '많은 조각들'을 의미하는 many pieces of가 적절하다.

3　이유를 나타내는 because가 들어가야 한다.

4　'폐자재나 불필요한 제품을 더 나은 품질의 새로운 소재와 제품으로 바꾸는 과정'에 해당하는 단어는 upcycling이다.

5　prevents water(물을 막아준다)로 보아, 공통으로 들어갈 단어는 waterpoof(방수의)이다.
　• 이 재킷은 방수 기능이 있어서 물을 막아준다.
　• 우리의 자외선 차단제는 자외선을 걸러주고 방수도 된다.
　• 여벌의 옷, 방수 마스크, 그리고 구급상자를 챙기세요.

READING **32**　　　● Workbook p. 33

1 ②　**2** ④　**3** ②
4 to show that all the things we feel can be music
5 cannot hear any sounds, can feel the music

해설

1　② '~처럼 보이다'를 의미하는 seem 뒤에는 주격보어로 형용사가 온다. (strangely → strange)

2　(A) 오로지 침묵만이 있는 음악으로 '예술가 없이'도 음악을 느낄 수 있다고 생각했으므로 without이 적절하다.
　(B) 뒤 문장에 공연장 내에 실제 소음이 있었다는 언급이 있으므로 '소리를 제어할(control) 방법'이 없었다는 의미가 적절하다.

3　ⓐ himself와 ② 의 myself는 주어를 강조한다. 나머지는 모

두 주어와 목적어가 동일할 때 사용되는 재귀대명사다.

4　wanted의 목적어로 to show를 쓰고 show의 목적어로 that절을 쓴다. that절의 주어는 all the things we feel, 동사는 can be이다.

5　John Cage의 4′33″에서는 예술가로부터 어떤 소리도 들을 수 없지만, 극장의 실제 소음에서 음악을 느낄 수 있다.

Unit 13 빈칸 완성하기 2 (어구·문장)

READING **33**　　　● Workbook p. 34

1 ②　**2** ②　**3** ④　**4** (1) attention time (2) longer than　**5** students also have difficulty focusing on their classes

해설

1　(A) 사람들이 점점 짧은 영상에 '익숙해지고 있다'는 내용이므로 familiar가 들어가야 한다.
　(B) 쇼트폼 미디어가 10대들의 집중 시간을 감소시켜 10초 이상에서 8초로 '줄어들었다'는 내용이므로 decreased가 적절하다.

2　② Short-form media가 주어이므로 동사는 has가 되어야 한다.

3　밑줄 친 ⓐ와 ④의 like는 '~와 같은'의 의미이므로 such as로 바꿔 쓸 수 있으며 like 뒤에 like 앞 단어의 예시가 나온다.

4　that은 앞 문장의 attention time을 가리키고 '금붕어의 집중 시간은 8초보다 더 길다'는 의미가 되도록 문장을 완성한다.

5　have difficulty -ing를 사용하여 '~하는 데 어려움을 겪다'라는 의미를 나타낸다. -ing 자리에 '~에 집중하다'라는 의미를 위해 전치사 on을 추가하여 focusing on ~으로 쓴다.

READING **34**　　　● Workbook p. 35

1 ③　**2** ②　**3** ②
4 ⓐ → to understand(understanding)　ⓓ → to see
5 to her → her

1   주어진 문장은 4세 아이는 엄마가 안에 있는 연필을 보지 못했다는 것을 알고 있기 때문이라고 '껌'이라고 대답한 이유를 설명하는 내용이므로, '여전히 엄마가 껌이라고 대답할 것'이라는 문장 뒤에 오는 것이 알맞다.

2   앞 문장이 원인, 뒤 문장이 결과를 나타내므로 빈칸에는 결과를 나타내는 접속사 so가 들어가야 한다.

3   밑줄 친 ⓔ와 ②의 as는 접속사로 '~대로'의 의미를 나타낸다. ① 부사 '~만큼', ③ 접속사 '~ 때문에', ④ 전치사 '~로서', ⑤ 접속사 '~할 때'

4   ⓐ 동사 start는 목적어로 to부정사와 -ing 둘 다 취한다. ⓓ 동사 need는 목적어로 to부정사를 취한다.

5   show는 간접목적어와 직접목적어를 갖는 4형식 동사이므로 간접목적어 her 앞의 전치사 to를 삭제해야 한다.

Unit 14 밑줄 친 부분 파악하기

READING **35**   • Workbook p. 36

1 ②, ③   2 ③   3 ③   4 (s)elective (m)emory
5 cannot remember all the things we did

1   Murphy's Law(머피의 법칙)은 '잘못될 수 있는 것은 무엇이든 잘못될 것이다'라는 의미로 머피의 법칙에 해당하지 않는 것은 ②, ③이다.

2   '~라고 불린다'라는 수동의 의미가 적절하므로 is called가 들어가야 한다.

3   (A) 앞에 제시한 내용에 반전되는 내용이 이어지므로 반대 의미를 나타내는 However가 적절하다.
  (B) '강한 기억만이 뇌에 남는다'는 의미가 자연스러우므로 remain이 적절하다.

4   '기억하고 싶은 것만 기억하는 경향'에 해당하는 말은 selective memory(선택적 기억)이다.

5   동사 remember의 목적어는 all the things이고 we did는 관계대명사절로 뒤에서 all the things를 수식한다.

READING **36**   • Workbook p. 37

1 ③   2 ⑤   3 ⑤
4 see someone with their arms crossed
5 Memorizing, social

1   몸짓 언어는 일련의 규칙이 아니다. 특정 신호를 암기하는 것은 몸짓 언어를 이해하는 데 충분하지 않다. 사회적 이해의 많은 측면을 고려해야 한다.

2   (A) 지각동사 see는 목적격보어로 동사원형이나 현재분사를 쓴다. 현재분사가 쓰일 때는 진행의 의미가 강하다.
  (B) 몸짓 언어가 '혼란시키는, 혼란스러운' 것이므로 -ing 형태의 형용사 confusing이 적절하다.

3   어떤 신호들을 '암기하는 것만으로는 더 큰 그림을 볼 수 없다. 즉, 그것보다 더 복잡하다'는 의미가 적절하므로 more complicated가 들어가야 한다.

4   '~한 채로'의 뜻으로 상태를 나타내는 전치사 with 뒤에 명사 their arms를 쓰고 명사가 '~되는 것'이므로 과거분사 crossed를 쓴다.

5   몸짓 언어 신호를 암기하는 것만으로는 충분하지 않다. 우리는 사회적 맥락 안에서 몸짓 언어를 이해하고 사용해야 한다.

Unit 15 장문 독해하기

READING **37**   • Workbook p. 38

1 ②   2 ①   3 ②, ⑤   4 role-plays
5 helpful, learning, effective

1   (A) 앞에 열거한 요소들이 모두 '관련이 있지만' 학습 스타일이 그 답을 제공한다는 문맥이 자연스러우므로 related가 적절하다.
  (B) 두 번째 유형은 듣고 말하는 것을 통해 배우므로 sounds가 적절하다.

2   학습 스타일은 효과적으로 학습할 수 있는 방법, 즉 '어떻게 가장 잘 배울 수 있는지'에 대한 답을 주는 것이다.
  ① 가장 잘 배울 수 있는 방법
  ② 얼마나 빨리 게임을 배울 수 있는지
  ③ 배우기 전에 해야 할 일

④ 학습 설명서를 읽어야 하는 이유
⑤ 충분한 공부 시간을 가질 수 있는 방법

3 ② what에 해당하는 동사 play의 목적어 a new board game이 뒤에 있으므로 '~하는 방법'을 의미하는 how to로 고쳐야 한다.
   ⑤ 동사 helps의 목적격보어로 사용되었으므로 (to) learn으로 고쳐야 한다.

4 '사람들이 특정한 상황에서 다른 사람인 척하면서 무언가를 하고 말하는 활동'에 해당하는 말은 '역할극(role-play)'이다.

5 효과적인 학습을 위해서는 학생들이 자신의 학습 스타일을 아는 것이 도움이 된다.

READING **38**   ● Workbook p. 39

1 ②   2 ③   3 ④
4 plays an important role in protecting
5 keeping → stealing

해설

1 주어진 문장의 big weak point와 ② 뒤 문장의 this problem이 연결되도록 ②에 들어가는 것이 적절하다.

2 밑줄 친 ⓐ와 ③의 to부정사는 '~하기 위해서'의 의미로 목적을 나타낸다.

3 (A) 해커들은 기술을 사용하여 '보안' 관련 문제를 찾으므로 security가 적절하다.
   (B) 화이트 햇 해커들은 법을 지키므로 '준수하다, 따르다'를 뜻하는 follow가 적절하다.
   (C) 문제를 해결하는 것을 도왔으므로 solve가 적절하다.

4 '~에서 역할을 하다'를 뜻하는 play a role in 뒤에 V-ing 형태를 사용한다.

5 화이트 햇 해커들은 블랙 햇 해커들이 인터넷에서 사람들의 정보를 지키는(→ 훔치는) 것을 막는 사람들이다.

Unit 16 복합 문단 독해하기

READING **39**   ● Workbook p. 40

1 ④   2 ④   3 ②   4 Keep quiet, or I will kill you.
5 pain, hurt, apologized

해설

1 ④ '~에 맞서, ~에 대응하여'라는 의미의 against가 적절하다.

2 be busy (in) V-ing ~하느라 바쁘다

3 (A) 개미는 '무서웠지만' 혼내 주려고 결심했다는 것이 의미상 적절하므로 scared가 들어가야 한다.
   (B) 코끼리는 개미를 떨쳐 내려 했지만 개미는 물기를 '계속했다'는 것이 의미상 적절하므로 continued가 들어가야 한다.

4 '~해라, 그렇지 않으면 …할 것이다'를 의미하는 「명령문, or …」 구문을 사용한다.

5 자신의 고통을 느낀 후, 코끼리는 자신이 얼마나 다른 작은 동물들을 아프게 했는지 깨닫고 사과했다.

READING **40**   ● Workbook p. 41

1 ②   2 ④   3 ④
4 ⓐ excited ⓑ surprised ⓒ impressed

해설

1 왕자가 신 포도를 모두 먹었다. 그것은 그 포도를 가져온 가난한 남자를 실망시키고 싶지 않아서였다.

2 ④ '혼자'를 뜻하는 by oneself가 적절하므로 yourself로 고쳐야 한다.

3 (A) 남자는 너무 '가난해서' 다른 것을 살 수 없었다는 내용이므로 poor가 적절하다.
   (B) 무엇이든 나누고 함께 먹었던 왕자가 이번에는 '달랐다'는 내용이므로 different가 적절하다.

4 ⓐ 왕자에게 선물을 가져가며 '신이 난, 흥분한' 상태이므로 excited가 적절하다.
   ⓑ 왕자가 평소와 다르게 행동하여 친구들은 '놀란' 상태이므로 surprised가 적절하다.
   ⓒ 왕자의 말을 듣고 그의 배려심에 친구들은 '감동받은' 상태이므로 impressed가 적절하다.

Unit 01 주제 파악하기

READING 01　Workbook p. 42

1 They keep warm / in the Arctic / thanks to their special hair and black skin.
그들은 따뜻하게 지낸다 / 북극에서 / 그들의 특별한 털과 검은 피부 덕분에

2 The hair is filled with / air, / and it traps / the sun's heat.
털은 채워져 있다 / 공기로 / 그리고 그것은 가둔다 / 태양열을

3 When they shake their body after swimming, / the water comes off / their body / right away.
그들이 수영 후에 그들의 몸을 흔들면 / 물이 떨어진다 / 그들의 몸에서 / 바로

4 It soaks up / the sunlight, / so / they / don't easily get cold.
그것은 흡수한다 / 햇빛을 / 그래서 / 그들은 / 쉽게 추워지지 않는다

5 Moreover, / underneath the black skin / is / a thick layer of body fat.
게다가 / 검은 피부 아래에 / ~이 있다 / 두꺼운 체지방 층이

READING 02　Workbook p. 42

1 You can enjoy / many types of activities / there.
여러분은 즐길 수 있다 / 다양한 종류의 활동들을 / 그곳에서

2 They're / the world's biggest waterfalls / with about 275 different waterfalls.
그것들은 ~이다 / 세계 최대의 폭포들 / 약 275개의 다른 폭포들로 이루어진

3 You can experience / the highest point, / the Devil's Throat, / by taking a boat tour, / helicopter ride, / or just by walking / on the trails.
여러분은 경험할 수 있다 / 가장 높은 지점인 / 악마의 목구멍을 / 보트 투어를 통해 / 헬리콥터 타기 / 또는 단지 걸음으로써 / 산책로를

4 You can hike / around the rainforest, / below the falls, / and even / on top of the falls.
여러분은 하이킹을 할 수 있다 / 열대 우림 주변 / 폭포 아래 / 그리고 심지어 / 폭포 위에서

5 Just / remember / to bring / your raincoat, / or you / may get wet.
단지 / 기억해라 / 가져가는 것을 / 여러분의 비옷을 / 그렇지 않으면 여러분은 / 젖을 수 있다

READING 03　Workbook p. 43

1 Sometimes / a different view / pleases / us.
때때로 / 다른 관점은 / 즐겁게 한다 / 우리를

2 For example, / Pablo Picasso, / a famous artist, / tried to see / the world / differently.
예를 들어 / 파블로 피카소는 / 유명한 예술가인 / 보려고 노력했다 / 세상을 / 다르게

3 When you first see his work, / you may not notice / the players.
여러분이 그의 작품을 처음 볼 때 / 여러분은 알아차리지 못할 수도 있다 / 그 연주자들을

4 But / when you keep looking at the painting, / you can see / them / in it!
하지만 / 여러분이 계속해서 그 그림을 볼 때 / 여러분은 볼 수 있다 / 그들을 / 그 안에서

5 His work used / shapes, objects, and colors / so differently / from the real world.
그의 작품은 사용했다 / 형태, 사물, 그리고 색깔을 / 매우 다르게 / 실제 세상과

Unit 02 제목 파악하기

READING 04　Workbook p. 43

1 For ancient Egyptians, / cats were / the most special animal.
고대 이집트인들에게 / 고양이는 ~이었다 / 가장 특별한 동물

2 To honor the cats, / rich families put jewelry / on them.
고양이들에게 경의를 표하기 위해 / 부유한 가정은 보석을 걸어 주었다 / 그들에게

3 When cats died, / their owners would shave / their eyebrows.
고양이들이 죽었을 때 / 그들의 주인들은 밀곤 했다 / 그들의 눈썹을

4 The ancient Egyptians / protected cats / even by law.
고대 이집트인들은 / 고양이들을 보호했다 / 심지어 법으로

5 Cats were clearly more than / just pets / to them.
고양이들은 분명히 ~ 이상이었다 / 단지 반려동물 / 그들에게

READING 05
Workbook p. 44

1 When you go camping, / you make sure to bring / enough food.
캠핑을 갈 때 / 여러분은 반드시 가지고 가야 한다 / 충분한 음식을

2 Like on Earth, / astronauts eat / three meals / a day.
지구에서와 마찬가지로 / 우주비행사들은 먹는다 / 세 끼를 / 하루에

3 There is / also an oven / in a spacecraft / and it can make / food / warm.
~이 있다 / 오븐도 / 우주선 안에 / 그리고 그것은 / 만들 수 있다 / 음식을 / 따뜻하게

4 So / all the food / comes in packets / for easy storage.
그래서 / 모든 음식은 / 포장되어 있다 / 쉬운 보관을 위해

5 Sauces / like ketchup, mustard, and mayonnaise / are also available / in tubes.
소스들은 / 케첩, 머스타드, 마요네즈 같은 / 또한 이용할 수 있다 / 튜브에 넣어져서

READING 06
Workbook p. 44

1 Or / can you think of / anyone / in sports history / with a record of only wins?
아니면 / 여러분은 생각할 수 있나요 / 누군가를 / 스포츠 역사상 / 우승 기록만 있는

2 Roger Federer, / for example, / is the world's greatest tennis player / with twenty Grand Slam titles.

Roger Federer는 / 예를 들어 / 세계 최고의 테니스 선수이다 / 20개의 그랜드 슬램 타이틀을 보유한

3 In other words, / he lost / in more than / two-thirds of the tournaments.
다시 말해서 / 그는 패했다 / 이상에서 / 토너먼트의 3분의 2

4 Still, / we think of / him / as a champion, / not as a failure.
여전히 / 우리는 ~로 생각한다 / 그를 / 챔피언으로 / 실패자가 아닌

5 Try to accept / your failure / and move on / from it.
받아들이도록 노력해라 / 여러분의 실패를 / 그리고 나아가도록 / 그것으로부터

Unit 03 목적·주장 파악하기

READING 07
Workbook p. 45

1 Thank you / for visiting / our zoo / for your field trip!
당신에게 감사하다 / 방문하는 것에 대해 / 우리 동물원을 / 여러분의 현장 학습으로

2 Before your visit, / please advise / your students / not to throw / waste / in the zoo.
여러분의 방문 전에 / 지도해 달라 / 학생들을 / 버리지 않도록 / 쓰레기를 / 동물원에

3 Plastic bags and other trash / can be very harmful / to our animals.
비닐봉지들 그리고 기타 쓰레기들은 / 매우 해로울 수 있다 / 우리 동물들에게

4 Like small children, / animals love / to test things / with their mouths.
어린아이들처럼 / 동물들은 아주 좋아한다 / 사물을 시험하는 것을 / 그들의 입으로

5 They may mistake / this trash / for food / and swallow it.
그들은 착각할 수 있다 / 이 쓰레기를 / 음식으로 / 그래서 그것을 삼킬 수 있다

1 Don't click / the Send button / right away / when you send emails.
누르지 마라 / 보내기 버튼을 / 바로 / 이메일을 보낼 때

2 However, / it doesn't matter / if you don't click the Send button.
그러나 / 그것은 상관없다 / 여러분이 보내기 버튼을 누르지 않으면

3 Looking again and fixing / should come first; sending / should come later.
다시 보고 수정하는 것이 / 우선 와야 한다 / 보내는 것은 / 나중에 와야 한다

4 So, / don't forget / to read your writing carefully / before you click the Send button.
따라서 / 잊지 말아라 / 여러분의 글을 주의 깊게 읽는 것을 / 여러분이 보내기 버튼을 누르기 전에

5 The same goes for / sending school assignments / or business letters / by email.
마찬가지이다 / 학교 과제를 보내는 것 / 또는 업무 서신(을 보내는 것) / 이메일로

Unit 04 요지 파악하기

1 We started / a new tutor-tutee project / in science class / last month.
우리는 시작했다 / 새로운 tutor-tutee 프로젝트를 / 과학 수업 시간에 / 지난달

2 I was good at science, / so I volunteered / as a student teacher.
나는 과학을 잘했다 / 그래서 나는 자원했다 / 학생 교사로

3 At first, / I thought / I was spending / too much time / with the tutee.
처음에 / 나는 생각했다 / 내가 보내고 있다(고) / 너무 많은 시간을 / 배우는 사람과

4 As a tutor, / I began to understand / the material / better and more clearly.
가르치는 사람으로서 / 나는 이해하기 시작했다 / 자료를 / 더 잘 그리고 더 명확하게

5 I also got / a better grade / on the final exam / thanks to the project.
나는 또한 받았다 / 더 좋은 점수를 / 기말시험에서 / 그 프로젝트 덕분에

1 Observing nature can make / human life / better.
자연을 관찰하는 것은 만들 수 있다 / 인간의 삶을 / 더 낫게

2 After using this paint, / you can wash / the outside / of your house / less often.
이 페인트를 쓰고 난 후에 / 여러분은 청소할 수 있다 / 외부를 / 여러분의 집의 / 덜 자주

3 This discovery came / from looking at / lotus leaves.
이 발견은 왔다 / ~을 관찰하는 것에서 / 연잎을

4 They look like / small nails / and make / the surface / rough.
그것들은 ~처럼 보인다 / 작은 못들 / 그리고 만든다 / 표면을 / 거칠게

5 Always / try to observe / nature / closely!
항상 / 관찰하도록 애쓰라 / 자연을 / 면밀히

Unit 05 요약하기

1 We communicate / with others / through language.
우리는 소통한다 / 다른 사람들과 / 언어를 통해

2 Therefore, / we should be careful / about when and how we use them.
그러므로 / 우리는 주의해야 한다 / 언제 그리고 어떻게 우리가 그것들을 사용할지에 대해

3 It usually means / agreement or "okay" / in many countries / like Korea and Japan.
그것은 일반적으로 의미한다 / 동의 또는 '좋다'를 / 많은 국가에서 / 한국 그리고 일본과 같은

4 Gestures / such as a thumbs up / have different meanings / in many cultures or countries.
제스처는 / 엄지척과 같은 / 다른 의미를 지닌다 / 많은 문화나 국가에서

5 So, / to avoid misunderstandings, / be careful / how you use them!
그러니 / 오해를 피하기 위해서 / 주의해라 / 여러분이 그것들을 어떻게 사용할지

READING 12
Workbook p. 47

1 It is the feeling / of having too much to do / when you do not have enough time.
그것은 감정이다 / 할 일이 너무 많다고 느끼는 / 여러분이 충분한 시간을 가지지 않을 때

2 It makes / you / feel nervous.
그것은 만든다 / 여러분을 / 긴장하도록

3 One study shows that / time famine / can make students / feel more stressed / than when they get a low score.
한 연구는 ~을 보여 준다 / 시간 기근은 / 학생들을 만들 수 있다 / 더 많은 스트레스를 느끼도록 / 그들이 낮은 점수를 받았을 때보다

4 There is a way / to overcome this.
방법이 있다 / 이를 극복하기 위한

5 For instance, / you can use / a food delivery service / instead of / eating out or cooking meals.
예를 들어 / 여러분은 이용할 수 있다 / 음식 배달 서비스를 / ~ 대신에 / 외식이나 요리하는 것

READING 13
Workbook p. 48

1 When the cleaners came on weekends, / they left / some toilet paper / in the two bathrooms.
청소부들이 주말마다 왔을 때 / 그들은 남겨 두었다 / 약간의 화장지를 / 두 곳의 화장실에

2 However, / all the toilet paper / was gone / by Monday.
그러나 / 모든 화장지가 / 사라졌다 / 월요일쯤

3 So, / she decided / to put a note / in one of the bathrooms.

그래서 / 그녀는 결심했다 / 메모를 붙여 놓기로 / 화장실 중 한 곳에

4 She was glad / to see / that one roll came back / in a few hours / and another the next day.
그녀는 기뻤다 / 보고 / 화장지 한 통이 돌아온 것을 / 몇 시간 후에 / 그리고 다른 한 통은 다음 날에

5 However, / in the other bathroom / with no note, / no toilet paper came back / until the cleaners brought more.
하지만 / 다른 화장실에는 / 메모가 없는 / 화장지가 돌아오지 않았다 / 청소부들이 더 가져올 때까지

Unit 06 안내문·도표 파악하기

READING 14
Workbook p. 48

1 Your small actions / can save / our Earth!
여러분의 작은 행동들이 / 구할 수 있다 / 우리 지구를

2 Switch off / and give an hour / for Earth!
불을 꺼라 / 그리고 한 시간을 투자해라 / 지구를 위해

3 But / it is so much more / than that.
그러나 / 그것은 훨씬 이상이다 / 그것보다

4 Let's show / the power / of collective action / for our future and planet!
보여 주자 / 힘을 / 집단행동의 / 우리의 미래와 지구를 위한

5 If we are together, / we can do / more!
우리가 함께라면 / 우리는 할 수 있다 / 더 많은 것을

READING 15
Workbook p. 49

1 The name is / for the study cafe / of our school.
그 이름은 ~이다 / 스터디 카페를 위한 / 우리 학교의

2 This new space / will open / next year.
이 새로운 공간은 / 문을 열 것이다 / 내년에

3 Any student / in our school / can take part / in this contest.
어떤 학생이든 / 우리 학교의 / 참가할 수 있다 / 이 대회에

4 We hope / many of you / will participate.

우리는 바란다 / 여러분 중 많은 수가 / 참여하기를

5 How: / Post a name / with its meaning / through a QR code.

방법: / 이름을 게시하라 / 그것의 의미와 함께 / QR 코드를 통해

1 The graph above / shows / the percentage of GDP / spent on health care / in 2018.

위 그래프는 / 보여 준다 / GDP 비율을 / 의료비에 지출된 / 2018년에

2 Which country spent / the least / among the countries shown?

어느 나라가 지출했는가 / 가장 적게 / 표시된 국가들 중에서

3 The US spent / the highest percentage of GDP / on health care / among the countries shown.

미국은 지출했다 / GDP 대비 가장 높은 비율을 / 의료비에 / 표시된 국가들 중에서

4 The UK and Greece / spent / the same percentage of their GDP / on health care.

영국과 그리스는 / 지출했다 / 그들의 GDP의 같은 비율을 / 의료비에

5 They also each / spent / more than 5 percent / of their GDP / on health care.

그들은 또한 각각 / 지출했다 / 5퍼센트 이상을 / 그들의 GDP의 / 의료비에

Unit 07 내용 일치 파악하기

1 Benjamin Franklin is / one of the most important people / in American history.

Benjamin Franklin은 ~이다 / 가장 중요한 인물 중 한 명 / 미국 역사상

2 He got / some formal education / but he was mostly self-taught.

그는 받았다 / 약간의 학교 교육을 / 하지만 그는 대부분 스스로 공부했다

3 After he worked for four years, / he began to write / his own stories.

그가 4년 동안 일한 후 / 그는 쓰기 시작했다 / 그 자신의 이야기를

4 Instead of his real name, / he wrote / under a pen name, / Mrs. Silence Dogood.

그의 진짜 이름 대신 / 그는 썼다 / 필명으로 / Mrs. Silence Dogood이라는

5 People never thought / that she was a 16-year-old boy!

사람들은 결코 생각하지 않았다 / 그녀가 16세 소년이라고

1 We can see / them / in shallow water / to the deep sea.

우리는 볼 수 있다 / 그들을 / 얕은 물에서 / 깊은 바다까지

2 Most sharks live / 20 to 30 years, / but some species / can live / far longer.

대부분의 상어는 산다 / 20에서 30년을 / 하지만 일부 종은 / 살 수 있다 / 훨씬 더 오래

3 While humans use their teeth to bite and chew food, / sharks use their teeth / to grab food / and swallow it / all at once.

인간은 치아를 사용하여 음식을 물고 씹는 반면에, / 상어는 그들의 이빨을 사용한다 / 먹이를 잡기 위해 / 그리고 그것을 삼키기 위해 / 한 번에

4 The bodies of sharks / have / dark skin / on top / and light skin / on the bottom.

상어의 몸은 / 가지고 있다 / 어두운 피부색을 / 윗부분에 / 그리고 밝은 피부색을 / 아랫부분에

5 It helps sharks / to hide / from threats.

그것은 상어들을 돕는다 / 숨도록 / 위협으로부터

1 So / she often heard / the stories of slaves / from her grandmother.

그래서 / 그녀는 자주 들었다 / 노예 이야기들을 / 그녀의 할머니에게서

2 A mostly white college / turned Catlett down / just because she was black.
대부분이 백인 학생들인 한 대학은 / Catlett을 거부했다 / 단지 그녀가 흑인이라는 이유만으로

3 She became / one of the first three students / to earn an MFA / at the university.
그녀는 되었다 / 최초의 세 명의 학생들 중 한 명이 / 미술 석사 학위를 취득한 / 그 대학교에서

4 In her art, / she showed / the injustice or unfairness / of society.
예술에서 / 그녀는 보여 주었다 / 부당함이나 불공평을 / 사회의

5 She also showed / the people / who suffered from it.
그녀는 또한 보여 주었다 / 사람들을 / 그것으로 인해 고통받는

Unit 08 분위기·심경 파악하기

READING 20
Workbook p. 51

1 Their singing makes me / open the window.
그들의 노래는 나를 만든다 / 창문을 열도록

2 Flower buds are about to bloom / outside the window.
꽃봉오리가 피려고 한다 / 창밖에

3 Suddenly, / I feel a strong wish / to clean my own room / and put a new blanket / on the bed!
갑자기 / 나는 강한 욕구를 느낀다 / 내 방을 청소하는 / 그리고 새 이불을 까는 / 침대 위에

4 Surprisingly, / I see myself / humming and dancing / while cleaning!
놀랍게도 / 나는 내 모습을 본다 / 흥얼거리고 춤추는 / 청소를 하면서

5 You see, / Grouchy always complains, / but not me now!
여러분도 알다시피 / Grouchy는 항상 불평한다 / 하지만 지금 나는 아니다

READING 21
Workbook p. 52

1 They were very hungry / for a month / because there was little food / to eat.
그들은 매우 배가 고팠다 / 한 달 동안 / 음식이 거의 없었기 때문에 / 먹을

2 However, / after starving for three days, / Salva and the boys / luckily got / something to eat.
하지만 / 3일 동안 굶은 끝에 / Salva와 소년들은 / 운좋게 얻었다 / 먹을 것을

3 While hunting, / one of them caught a squirrel.
사냥하는 동안 / 그들 중 한 명이 / 다람쥐를 잡았다

4 It won't last / long enough / — we need / more wood.
그것은 지속되지 않을 것이다 / 충분히 오래 / — 우리는 필요로 한다 / 더 많은 나무를

5 The air was filled / with a delicious smell.
공기는 가득 찼다 / 맛있는 냄새로

READING 22
Workbook p. 52

1 I was waiting / for my mom / to come back / from the mall / with a special present for me.
나는 기다리고 있었다 / 나의 엄마가 / 돌아오기를 / 쇼핑몰에서 / 나를 위한 특별한 선물을 가지고

2 I was thrilled/ because I would soon have / a new cell phone / to communicate with!
나는 매우 신이 났다 / 내가 곧 가질 수 있어서 / 새 핸드폰을 / 소통할 수 있는

3 I was daydreaming about / using / all of the apps.
나는 ~에 대한 꿈을 꾸고 있었다 / 사용하는 / 모든 앱을

4 I thought / that maybe she had hidden / my new phone / inside the book.
나는 생각했다 / 아마 그녀가 숨겼다고 / 내 새 핸드폰을 / 그 책 안에

5 But / I slowly realized / that my present was not / a new cell phone, / just a little book.
하지만 / 나는 천천히 깨달았다 / 내 선물이 아니라는 것을 / 새 휴대폰이 / 그저 작은 책 한 권

1 Some studies found / that reading is a great way / to reduce stress levels, / lowering them / by 68%.
몇몇 연구들은 알아냈다 / 독서가 좋은 방법이라는 것을 / 스트레스 수준을 줄이는 / 그것들을 낮추다 / 68퍼센트까지

2 And it is far more effective / than playing video games (21%).
그리고 그것은 훨씬 더 효과적이다 / 비디오 게임을 하는 것보다 (21퍼센트)

3 Another study showed / that just 30 minutes of reading / can lower / blood pressure.
또 다른 연구는 보여 주었다 / 30분의 독서만으로 ~라는 것을 / 낮출 수 있다 / 혈압을

4 Then / worries or tensions / may go away.
그러면 / 걱정이나 긴장이 / 사라질 수 있다

5 Why not / open the pages / of a book / instead?
~하는 게 어떤가? / 페이지들을 펼치다 / 책의 / 대신에

1 When I get into bed, / I think / that there is somebody / under it.
내가 침대에 들어갈 때, / 나는 생각한다 / 누군가가 있다고 / 그 밑에

2 I look / under the bed, / then I think / there is somebody / on top of it.
나는 본다 / 침대 밑을 / 그러면 나는 생각한다 / 누군가가 있다고 / 그것의 위에

3 It costs / fifty dollars / for a visit.
비용이 든다 / 50달러 / 한 번 방문하는 데

4 My brother helped me / with the problem / for just ten dollars.
내 동생이 나를 도와줬다 / 그 문제를 / 단돈 10달러로

5 He told me / to cut the legs / of the bed.
그는 내게 말했다 / 다리를 자르라고 / 침대의

1 Ball sports / have some rules / about the balls / used.
구기 종목에는 / 몇 가지 규칙이 있다 / 공에 대한 / 사용되는

2 They are rules / about the characteristics / of the balls, / such as size or weight.
그것들은 규칙이다 / 특성에 관한 / 공의 / 크기나 무게와 같은

3 However, / if it is made of steel, / it will be too stiff.
그러나 / 그것이 강철로 만들어지면 / 그것은 너무 단단할 것이다

4 Similarly, / along with stiffness, / a ball needs / a proper amount / of bounce.
마찬가지로 / 단단함과 함께 / 공은 필요로 한다 / 적절한 양을 / 튕김의

5 And / a solid clay ball / would not bounce / at all.
그리고 / 점토 공은 / 튀지 않을 것이다 / 전혀

1 Alpacas live / in South American countries / like Chile or Peru.
알파카는 산다 / 남아메리카 나라들에 / 칠레나 페루와 같은

2 They have / bad habits, / so they may spit / at you.
그들은 가지고 있다 / 나쁜 습관을 / 그래서 그들은 침을 뱉을 수도 있다 / 여러분에게

3 First, / they want to show / that they feel / angry or upset.
첫째, / 그들은 보여 주고 싶어 한다 / 그들이 느끼는 것을 / 화가 났거나 기분이 좋지 않은

4 In addition, / their spit has / a very bad smell / because it includes / the food they recently ate.
게다가 / 그들의 침은 가지고 있다 / 매우 고약한 냄새를 / 그것이 포함하기 때문에 / 그들이 최근에 먹은 음식을

5 So, / when you see some alpacas, / you need to be kind / to them.
그래서 / 여러분이 알파카를 보면 / 여러분은 친절하게 해야 한다 / 그들에게

READING **27**
Workbook p. 55

1 Imagine / that you have to stay alone / on a desert island.

상상해 보라 / 여러분이 혼자 머물러야 한다고 / 무인도에

2 For this reason, / you must find water / that is safe / to drink.

이러한 이유 때문에 / 여러분은 물을 찾아야 한다 / 안전한 / 마시기에

3 Here are / some tips / to help you / find clean drinking water.

여기에 있다 / 몇 가지 조언들이 / 여러분을 도울 / 깨끗한 마실 물을 찾는 것을

4 But / you should remember / that it may still have / some diseases / in it.

그러나 / 여러분은 기억해야 한다 / 그것도 역시 가지고 있을 수 있다는 것을 / 질병들을 / 그 안에

5 If you keep these tips in mind, / you will be safer / on a desert island.

여러분이 이러한 조언을 명심한다면 / 여러분은 더욱 안전해질 것이다 / 무인도에서

READING **28**
Workbook p. 55

1 When children are upset, / what is a good way / to calm them down?

아이들이 화가 났을 때, / 무엇이 좋은 방법일까 / 그들을 진정시키는

2 This helps them / change their focus / from being upset / to something else.

이것은 그들을 돕는다 / 그들의 초점을 바꾸도록 / 화난 것에서 / 다른 것으로

3 If you give them snacks, / such as candy or chocolate, / children will feel happier.

그들에게 간식을 준다면 / 사탕이나 초콜릿과 같은 / 아이들은 더 행복할 것이다

4 In the short term, / using food in this way / is effective.

단기적으로는 / 이렇게 음식을 이용하는 것이 / 효과적이다

5 Then, / when they feel bad, upset, or even bored, / they will want / some food / to make themselves / feel better.

그러면 / 기분이 나쁘거나, 화나거나, 심지어 지루할 때 / 그들은 원할 것이다 / 음식을 / 그들을 만들기 위해 / 기분이 더 좋아지도록

Unit **11** 무관한 문장 찾기

READING **29**
Workbook p. 56

1 Can you see / any window or clock / in a department store?

여러분은 볼 수 있는가 / 창문이나 시계를 / 백화점에서

2 Windows and clocks / make you think / about the time.

창문과 시계는 / 여러분을 생각하도록 만든다 / 시간에 대해

3 Also, / department stores / decorate or hang advertisements / on their walls.

또한 / 백화점들은 / 장식하거나 광고들을 건다 / 벽에

4 If there are some clocks or windows on the walls, / it is hard / to use the walls.

벽에 시계나 창문이 있으면 / 어렵다 / 벽을 사용하기가

5 So, / the next time / you visit a department store, / look around carefully.

그러니 / 다음번에 / 여러분이 백화점을 방문하면, / 주변을 잘 둘러보라

READING **30**
Workbook p. 56

1 And even just 60mg of caffeine / can make you / react faster.

그리고 심지어 60mg의 카페인도 / 여러분을 만들 수 있다 / 더 빠르게 반응하도록

2 Caffeine is also effective / for relieving headaches / when it is used together with medicine.

카페인은 또한 효과적이다 / 두통을 완화하는 데 / 그것이 약과 함께 사용되면

3 One study showed / that caffeine can increase / the chances of people / with little sleep / making mistakes.

한 연구는 보여 준다 / 카페인이 증가시킬 수 있다는 것을 / 사람들의 가능성을 / 수면을 거의 취하지 않은 / 실수할

4 Also, / they did not get / higher scores on tests, / even after having caffeine, / than a group / with enough sleep.
또한, / 그 사람들은 받지 못했다 / 시험에서 더 높은 점수를 / 카페인을 섭취한 후에도 / 그룹보다 / 수면을 충분히 취한

5 Therefore, / using caffeine / cannot fully make up for / not having enough sleep.
따라서 / 카페인을 이용하는 것은 / 완전히 보충할 수 없다 / 충분한 수면을 취하지 못한 것을

Unit 12 빈칸 완성하기 1 (단어)

READING **31**　　　　　　　　　● Workbook p. 57

1 Where / does the trash go / after you throw it away?
어디로 / 쓰레기가 갈까 / 여러분이 그것을 버린 후에

2 But, in the fashion field, / trash can become / new, fancy products / thanks to creative thinking.
그러나 패션 분야에서 / 쓰레기는 될 수 있다 / 새롭고 멋진 제품이 / 창의적인 사고 덕분에

3 They need / many pieces of cloth and belts / to make their bags.
그들은 필요하다 / 많은 천과 벨트가 / 그들의 가방을 만들기 위해서

4 Also, all their bags in the world / are different / because each bag is made / from many different types of cloth.
또한, 세상의 모든 그들의 가방은 / 다르다 / 각각의 가방이 만들어지기 때문에 / 많은 다른 종류의 천으로

5 This trend in the fashion field / is not only unique, / but also good / for the environment.
패션 분야의 이러한 경향은 / 독특할 뿐만 아니라 / 또한 좋다 / 환경에

READING **32**　　　　　　　　　● Workbook p. 57

1 One late evening / in August of 1952, / a man

opened and closed / the piano cover / three times / in a theater.
어느 늦은 저녁에 / 1952년 8월 / 한 남자가 열었다가 닫았다 / 피아노 덮개를 / 세 번 / 극장에서

2 Cage thought / people could feel the music / without the artist, / so he removed the artist / from the music.
Cage는 생각했다 / 사람들이 음악을 느낄 수 있다고 / 연주자 없이 / 그래서 그는 연주자를 제거했다 / 음악에서

3 Even Cage himself / had no way / to control the sounds / in the theater.
심지어 Cage 자신조차도 / 방법이 없었다 / 소리를 제어할 / 극장에서

4 There was still real-life noise / and people also had / some feelings and thoughts.
여전히 실생활 소음이 있었다 / 그리고 사람들도 가졌다 / 느낌과 생각을

5 He wanted to show / that all the things we feel / can be music.
그는 보여 주고 싶었다 / 우리가 느끼는 모든 것이 / 음악이 될 수 있다(는 것을)

Unit 13 빈칸 완성하기 2 (어구·문장)

READING **33**　　　　　　　　　● Workbook p. 58

1 Short-form media has content / which is under 10 minutes / or under 1,000 words.
쇼트폼 미디어는 콘텐츠를 가진다 / 10분 미만인 / 또는 1,000단어 미만인

2 With the rise of short-form media, / people are turning away / from long-form media / like books and movies.
쇼트폼 미디어의 등장으로 / 사람들은 외면하고 있다 / 롱폼 미디어를 / 책과 영화와 같은

3 They lose their focus quickly / and don't want to know / the full content.
그들은 집중력을 빠르게 잃는다 / 그리고 알고 싶어 하지 않는다 / 전체적인 내용을

4 A study by Microsoft / shows / that short-form media decreased / the attention time / of teenagers.
Microsoft의 연구는 / 보여 준다 / 쇼트폼 미디어가 감소시켰다는 것을 / 집중 시간을 / 십 대들의

5 They provide quick information / but also decrease / students' attention time.
그것들은 빠른 정보를 제공한다 / 하지만 또한 감소시킨다 / 학생들의 집중 시간을

<hr>

◁ READING **34** ●──────── Workbook p. 58

1 When children become four years old, / they start to understand / other people's thinking.
아이들이 4세가 되었을 때 / 그들은 이해하기 시작한다 / 다른 사람들의 생각을

2 You open the package / and show her / what's inside.
당신은 껌 통을 연다 / 그리고 그녀에게 보여 준다 / 안에 무엇이 있는지

3 Her mom is waiting / outside the room, / so she cannot see / what's inside.
그녀의 엄마는 기다리고 있다 / 방 밖에서 / 그래서 그녀는 볼 수 없다 / 안에 무엇이 들어 있는지

4 They do not know / someone needs to see inside / to know / what is in there.
그들은 모른다 / 누군가가 내부를 볼 필요가 있다는 것을 / 알기 위해 / 무엇이 거기 있는지

5 So, they think / everyone thinks / the same way / as they do.
그래서 그들은 생각한다 / 모두가 생각한다고 / 같은 방식으로 / 그들이 하듯이

Unit 14 밑줄 친 부분 파악하기

◁ READING **35** ●──────── Workbook p. 59

1 But all the traffic lights / you meet / are red.
그러나 모든 신호등이 / 여러분이 만나는 / 적색이다

2 They say / that the reason for the way we think / is selective memory.
그들은 말한다 / 우리가 생각하는 방식의 이유가 ~라고 / 선택적 기억이다

3 Only strong memories / remain in the brain, / so we remember / a failure or bad things / much more / than positive things.
오직 강렬한 기억들만이 / 뇌에 남는다 / 그래서 우리는 기억한다 / 실패나 안 좋은 일들을 / 훨씬 많이 / 긍정적인 것들보다

4 This small difference / makes us think / we meet more red lights / than green lights.
이런 작은 차이가 / 우리를 생각하게 만든다 / 우리가 더 많은 적색 신호를 만난다고 / 녹색 신호보다

5 If this thinking is repeated often, / we mostly remember / the bad things / and finally think / that we always fail.
만약 이런 생각들이 자주 반복되면 / 우리는 대부분 기억한다 / 안 좋은 것들을 / 그리고 결론적으로 생각한다 / 우리가 항상 실패한다고

<hr>

◁ READING **36** ●──────── Workbook p. 59

1 When we talk to people, / we also use / our body language.
우리가 사람들에게 이야기를 할 때 / 우리는 또한 사용한다 / 우리의 몸짓 언어를

2 With this dictionary approach, / they cannot find / the many sides / of social understanding.
이러한 사전적인 접근으로 / 그들은 찾을 수 없다 / 많은 측면을 / 사회적 이해의

3 But when people communicate / by just memorizing certain signals, / they cannot see / the bigger picture.
그러나 사람들이 소통한다면 / 단순히 어떤 신호들을 암기하는 것만으로 / 그들은 볼 수 없다 / 더 큰 그림을

4 Trying to use body language / by reading a body language dictionary / is like trying to speak French / by reading a French dictionary.
몸짓 언어를 사용하려고 하는 것은 / 몸짓 언어 사전을 읽어서 / 프랑스어를 말하려고 하는 것과 같다 / 프랑스어 사전을 읽어서

5 Our body language / might be thought of / as robotic and confusing / if we don't use it naturally.
우리의 몸짓 언어는 / 생각될 수 있다 / 로봇 같고 혼란스럽다고 / 우리가 그것을 자연스럽게 사용하지 않으면

Unit 15 장문 독해하기

READING **37**

Workbook p. 60

1 To find / your own learning style, / there is a simple question.
찾기 위한 / 여러분 자신의 학습 스타일을 / 간단한 질문이 있다

2 Third, / you can watch / others play / and try it yourself.
셋째 / 여러분은 볼 수 있다 / 다른 사람들이 놀이하는 것을 / 그리고 여러분 스스로 그것을 시도할 수 있다

3 For them, / drawing a diagram or pictures / is helpful / for learning.
그들에게 / 도표나 그림을 그리는 것이 / 도움이 된다 / 학습에

4 So, / reading the text aloud / can be a good way / for them / to learn something.
따라서 / 글을 큰 소리로 읽는 것이 / 좋은 방법이 될 수 있다 / 그들에게 / 무언가를 학습하기 위한

5 Knowing one's own learning style / helps the student / learn more effectively.
자신의 학습 스타일을 아는 것은 / 학생을 돕는다 / 더 효과적으로 배우도록

READING **38**

Workbook p. 60

1 The name "white hat" hacker / is from old American movies / about the country's "Wild West" days.
'하얀 모자' 해커의 이름은 / 오래된 미국 영화에서 따왔다 / 미국 "거친 서부"시대에 대한

2 Heroes in those movies / wore white hats, / and the bad guys / wore black hats.
영웅들은 이런 영화에서 / 흰 모자를 썼고 / 나쁜 사람들은 / 검은 모자를 썼다

3 Because of this problem, / black hat hackers / could get into the software / and steal its data.
이 문제 때문에 / 블랙 햇 해커들이 / 그 소프트웨어에 침입할 수 있었다 / 그리고 그것의 데이터를 훔칠 수 있었다

4 He made / a new program / to protect the software.
그는 만들었다 / 새로운 프로그램을 / 소프트웨어를 보호할 수 있는

5 Since we use the Internet a lot, / a white hat hacker / like Maiffret / plays an important role / in protecting our personal information.
우리는 인터넷을 많이 사용하기 때문에 / 화이트 햇 해커는 / Maiffret과 같은 / 중요한 역할을 한다 / 우리의 개인 정보를 보호하는 데

Unit 16 복합 문단 독해하기

READING **39**

Workbook p. 61

1 He was proud of / his strength / and wanted to show it off.
그는 자랑스러워했다 / 그의 힘을 / 그리고 그것을 과시하고 싶어 했다

2 One day, / when the ant family was going to work, / the elephant sprayed / a lot of water / on them.
어느 날 / 개미 가족이 일하러 갈 때 / 코끼리가 뿌렸다 / 많은 물을 / 그들 위로

3 The ant slowly crawled / into the elephant's body / and started biting him.
개미는 천천히 기어갔다 / 코끼리의 몸으로 / 그리고 그를 물기 시작했다

4 The elephant was a big animal, / but he couldn't do anything / against the tiny ant.
코끼리는 큰 동물이었다 / 하지만 그는 아무것도 할 수 없었다 / 작은 개미에 대항해서

5 From that day on, / he didn't hurt / other small animals / anymore.
그날부터 / 그는 해치지 않았다 / 다른 작은 동물들을 / 더 이상

1 One day / a poor man / gave a bunch of grapes / to a prince / as a gift.
어느 날 / 가난한 한 남자가 / 포도 한 송이를 주었다 / 왕자에게 / 선물로

2 Slowly / the prince finished / the whole bunch of grapes / by himself.
천천히 / 왕자는 다 먹었다 / 포도 한 송이 전체를 / 혼자서

3 One of the friends asked, / "Prince! / Why did you eat / all the grapes / by yourself / and not share them / with us?"
친구들 중 한 명이 물었다 / "왕자님! / 왜 드셨나요 / 모든 포도를 / 혼자서 / 그리고 그것들을 나누지 않고 / 우리와 함께"

4 The prince said, / "I thought that / if I shared the grapes with you, / you would make funny faces / and say / the grapes were bad."
왕자는 말했다 / "나는 생각했다 / 만약 내가 여러분들과 포도를 나눠 먹었다면 / 여러분은 우스꽝스러운 표정을 지었을 것이다 / 그리고 말했을 것이다 / 포도가 별로라고"

5 So I thought / it would be better / if I ate all the grapes happily / by myself / to please him.
그래서 나는 생각했다 / 그것이 더 낫겠다고 / 내가 포도 전부를 행복하게 먹는다면 / 나 혼자서 / 그를 기쁘게 해 주기 위해